T0207604

Spirituality, Religion, and Education

Series Editors
Jing Lin
University of Maryland
College Park, MD, USA

Rebecca Oxford
Huntsville, AL, USA

Sachi Edwards
University of Hawaii at Manoa
Honolulu, HI, USA

Edward J. Brantmeier
James Madison University
Harrisonburg, VA, USA

This series publishes books that examine fundamental questions of life, touching on the meaning, purpose, and mission of education from a variety of spiritual and religious perspectives. The series provides a forum for scholars to explore how to engage learners spiritually and holistically. It studies how spirituality, religion, and education intertwine with the learning of wisdom, peacebuilding, cultural and interfaith dialogues, and the integration of learners' body, mind, emotions, and spirit. Commonalities and differences among spiritual and religious traditions are explored alongside new developments from science that bridge the spirit and the mind. The series especially pays attention to the educational initiatives, outcomes, and programs that simultaneously engage the cognitive, affective, and spiritual dimensions of both students and educators. The world we live in focuses mostly on education for the intellect, thus restricting our ability to explore and understand deeply the nature of the cosmos and the meaning of our life. Although education is accessible to more people than ever before in human history, the dominant paradigm focuses solely on knowledge, skill, and material acquisition that neglects the meaning and purpose of life. This creates a huge void in learners and produces a huge number of people who are unhappy, unfulfilled, restless, lost, or desperate. An education that distills and recovers wisdom from spiritual and religious traditions can fill the void and help cultivate citizens who have love, compassion, knowledge, and the capacities for enlightened action. Books in the series address these age-old pursuits of inquiry, meaning, purpose, growth, transformation, and change. To submit proposals to the series for consideration please contact Jing Lin at jinglin@umd.edu.

Jwalin Patel

Learning to Live Together Harmoniously

Spiritual Perspectives from Indian Classrooms

Jwalin Patel
Together In Development and Education Foundation
Ahmedabad, Gujarat, India

Faculty of Education
University of Cambridge
Cambridge, UK

ISSN 2629-365X   ISSN 2629-3668   (electronic)
Spirituality, Religion, and Education
ISBN 978-3-031-23541-2   ISBN 978-3-031-23539-9   (eBook)
https://doi.org/10.1007/978-3-031-23539-9

This Palgrave Macmillan imprint is published by the registered company Springer Nature Switzerland AG.
The registered company address is: Gewerbestrasse 11, 6330 Cham, Switzerland

FOREWORD

We live in a time of division, fragmentation, and conflict. The political divisions are so strong in the United States that politicians of one party demonise members of the opposing party. Conspiracy theories are developed to feed people's anger. Anger and hatred are fuelled by social media, talk shows, and cable networks that appeal to a specific audience. There seems little effort to bring people together and to help us live more harmoniously. I believe that the education systems in many countries with their limited focus on developing skills so one competes in the global economy have contributed to these divisions. There has been little emphasis on education of the heart or nourishing student well-being which would help us to live together more equitably and harmoniously.

In this climate Jwalin Patel's book *Learning to Live Together Harmoniously* deserves our attention. In the west, we can look at how India has given the world some of the most inspiring educational visionaries—Tagore, Gandhi, Krishnamurti, Sri Aurobindo, and most recently the Dalai Lama. Patel's research focuses on schools connected to these visionaries and the teachers in these schools. One of the main strengths of the book is how Patel lets us hear how teachers in these schools work to create learning environments that are truly holistic and are helping students live together.

Teachers in these schools use dialogue and group work to help students work together. They also employ meditative activities such as birdwatching, nature appreciation, writing reflective poems, and breathing practices. Silence is valued and supported, not as a classroom management technique, but to slow down and listen more deeply. Silence also supports the appreciation of beauty which was emphasised by several teachers. Patel comments, "This appreciation of beauty around us leads to a very different way of living and being; I believe it moves students from an anthropocentric, extractive ways, to more humane, sustainable ways of living and being." Awareness of beauty and its importance is not part of schooling in most countries and needs to become more central in teaching and learning since it can nourish students' well-being.

The teachers' comments in the book moved me. Here is one:

> "The day I am close to my inner being there comes a different tone in the class. Finding and connecting with your own psychic being is the most important thing you can do as a class teacher." In my work in teacher education, I ask students to do meditation so that they can connect to their "inner being" and teach from that place.

Here is what one student wrote reflecting on her meditation practice:

> Through meditation I feel that I am being gently invited to observe the nature of my own humanity. Personally, I had been strongly moved and transformed through the beautiful nature of this spiritual practice. I had heard my voice and soul with amusement. I had slowly let my inner judge go away and be more in touch with the unspoken, the unseen, and the sacred part of myself. I had achieved a larger vision of myself and my reality, a vision that tenderly dilutes my fears, preconceptions, judgments and need for control. Because of meditation I had been able to transform my fear, anger, and resistance into joy, forgiveness, acceptance, and love. (Miller, 2014, p. 154)

Another quote from a teacher in Patel's book:

> The overall goal is to be kind, it's my prayer that I will be kind in class, just help me to be kind.

What beautiful words and aspirations. The Dalai Lama talks about a religion of kindness and this teacher aspires to make kindness central to her teaching.

Teachers emphasised the importance of living their lives more harmoniously. They felt that more important than any teaching technique was living harmoniously as a way of life. Patel writes, "There was a constant sentiment that learning to live together harmoniously requires one to work consciously on oneself and all teachers shared an inner conviction to change themselves. In order to do so, teachers were frequently engaged in dialogues, sessions where they read spiritual texts, meditation, and regular and constant introspection/reflection." The teachers saw their work as an ongoing process of awakening and being compassionate. As much as possible they were actualising holistic learning and an education of the heart. Reading the comments from these teachers, I would want my children in their classrooms.

A final strength of the books is that Patel presents his ideas and research in an open manner that encourages the reader to examine their own beliefs and explore their own ideas. In this way Patel asks the reader to participate in a conversation with the ideas presented in the text. I encourage the reader to engage the inspiring material in this book and participate in that conversation.

Toronto, ON, Canada   John Miller

Foreword

All human beings are essentially social creatures and their survival, progress, well-being, and happiness are entirely dependent upon others. An individual human being, unlike other creatures, cannot thrive, unless the person is loved and cared for by parents and family members, especially the mother. Basic requirements for life such as water, food, clothing, and shelter cannot be produced and provided without collective efforts of many people. This is a clear fact and doesn't need any arguments to establish it. To live together harmoniously, therefore, is a key to well-being and progress of the entire humanity. If we look back at the entire history of the human race, whatever progress and achievements we see at present are all due to cooperation and collective efforts. On the other hand, entire miseries of sentient beings are due to negative relationships and conflicts among the individuals, groups, communities, and nations. In particular, the present-day post-modern civilisation has created a mindset that considers the self to be more important than the others and individual rights to be more important than the collective rights. Thereby we have lost the culture of living together and caring for the well-being of every individual.

Among the ancient Indian traditions, the Buddhist concept of education is a threefold process, called *Trishiksha* in traditional language. This includes morality (*Sheel*), stability of mind (*Samadhi*), and awakening of wisdom (*Pragya*). The real aim of education is not a to impart knowledge from external information, but to stimulate and awaken the inner wisdom of an individual. For this, the individual must have a stable and unconditioned mind that can only be achieved with moral discipline and right livelihood.

For imparting this threefold education, the process too is threefold. First, to acquire the necessary knowledge through hearing and reading. This is called *Shrutimaya gyan*, a knowledge acquired from information. This is a borrowed and unprocessed knowledge. Thereafter, the learner shall have to analyse this knowledge through one's own logic, reasoning, and analytical examination and ascertain the reality of things acquired from information. Thereafter, the logical conclusion and finding of the fact shall be put as an object of meditation and thereby one gets the direct perception of things that is an authentic understanding of the subject. Through this threefold process one achieves the threefold education as mentioned before. Missing out on any one point of the threefold education is not real education and lacking on any one point of the threefold process will fail to achieve the real education. For this kind of education, Jiddu Krishnamurti used to say, "[T]he purpose of education is to awaken the inner intelligence so that the person may flower in goodness".

The majority of the ancient Indian traditions never consider the purpose of education is the livelihood of the individuals. The root cause of all human miseries is ignorance. Therefore, to dispel ignorance by wisdom is the only way to achieve human happiness and well-being. Thus, the awakening of wisdom is the sole purpose of education and this objective cannot be achieved by imparting mere information or acquiring some skills.

The fundamental challenges that face humanity in the twenty-first century are a degradation of ethics and morality, conflict and violence, disparity, degradation of environment and ecosystem threatening the survival of living beings on planet earth. The fact that modern science and technology as well as the socio-political economic system of the present day have failed to find any effective remedy to these challenges clearly indicates that the present education system is inadequate to educate the mind and heart of the coming generations.

I am delighted to find an intelligent young person, raised in the modern education system, who realised the necessity and importance of 'learning to live together harmoniously' in our present education system. This effort is very encouraging and offers a ray of hope to the coming generations. A system of imparting unprocessed information to the mind of a growing child does not help to awaken the inner wisdom of the young person. On the contrary, it becomes a kind of indoctrination for conditioning the young mind in such a manner that the person forgets the nature of interdependence, the basis of human relationship. As a result, conflict and structural violence are becoming ever more menacing in society.

The author of this book has thoroughly surveyed the inadequacies of the present education system, has proposed possible alternatives, and the different alternatives suggested by ancient traditions, as well as many great thinkers of the recent time. I am sure these will draw the attention of educationists, teachers, students, and parents and initiate a serious consideration and positive action for evolving an education system that can inculcate a compassionate heart in the coming generations. Only then can the total destruction of planet earth and all its living beings be averted. I appreciate the efforts of the author.

May all sentient beings be happy.

Dharamshala, Himachal Pradesh, India   Samdhong Rinpoche

ACKNOWLEDGEMENTS

I am grateful to the various alternative schools that allowed me to visit and spend extensive time on their campuses. I am extremely grateful to all the teachers who participated in multiple research studies and who I have now come to regard as friends and colleagues. I would also like to thank my spiritual mentor, family, fellow spiritual colleagues and aspirants, colleagues at the TIDE (Together In Development and Education) Foundation, and friends for their love, and support over the years, informing key themes of the book and transforming my ways of living.

I would like to thank my academic mentors—Professor Hilary Cremin, Professor Nidhi Singal, and Dr Benjamin Alcott—for their feedback and helping to inform the development of the book. I am deeply appreciative of the authors of the two forewords and the afterword: Professor John Miller, Venerable Professor Samdhong Rinponche, and Brahma Kumari Shivani. I would also like to thank Mrs Layla Patel and Mr Nishith Patel for helping reading through and providing critical feedback, to Dr Siddharth Pandey and Mrs Layla Patel for sharing photos as potential book covers, and to Mrs Darshini Sundar for helping design one of the graphics in the monograph. I am also grateful to the Cambridge Trust, SMUTS memorial fund, Education Faculty Fieldwork Grant, Mary Euphrasia Mosley, Sir Bartle Frere's Memorial & Worts Travelling Scholars Fund, and Robinson College for supporting the fieldwork and its analyses as well as the Economic and Social Research Council (ESRC) UK for their support in writing the monograph.

Finally, I am grateful (to the universe) for the opportunity to explore alternative education systems and to write this book. It has transformed my own ways of living and being. This monograph is written in loving memory of Dr Ami Meghani, who despite her terminal illness, supported various social action initiatives and simultaneously completed her Doctorate in Education and Psychology.

CONTENTS

Abbreviations

EI   Emotional Intelligence
GCE   Global Citizenship Education
GRL   Generated Resource Learning
LTLT   Learning To Live Together
LTLTH   Learning To Live Together Harmoniously
MBK   Mirambika (school in Delhi)
MGIS   Mahatma Gandhi International School (school in Ahmedabad, Gujarat)
NCERT   National Council of Educational Research and Training
NCF   National Curricular Framework
NEP   National Education Policy
PB   Patha Bhavan (school in Shantiniketan, West Bengal)
PGCE   Post-Graduate Certificate of Education
RVS   Rishi Valley School (school in Madanapalle, Andhra Pradesh)
SDG   Sustainable Development Goal
SEC   Social Emotional Competency
SEE   Social Emotional and Ethical curricula
SEL   Social Emotional Learning
SES   Socio Economic Status
SF   Shreyas Foundation (school in Ahmedabad, Gujarat)
TIDE   Together In Development & Education
TSR   Teacher Student Relations

LIST OF FIGURES

LIST OF TABLES

CHAPTER 1

Introduction

This book proposes an alternative vision and practices for education for togetherness and harmony through the discovery of oneself, others, and the larger society along with a transition to harmonious ways of living and being. The current, mass educational system and its practices were born in the light of the industrial revolution, capitalism, and modernity. Meanwhile, in today's world a vastly different educational system is required; a system that propels students to learn to live and work together to deal with the many 21st century issues. In an interconnected and interdependent world, it is essential to move away from tolerating diversity to appreciating it, from stereotyping to empathetic understanding and from civic duties to intrinsic responsibility taking.

Several international development reports and educational thinkers have called for alternative forms of education, emphasising holistic education, learning to live together, character education, social emotional learning, and global citizenship education. Similarly, various Indian philosophers and spiritual leaders—like Mahatma Gandhi, the Dalai Lama, Aurobindo Ghose, Rabindranath Tagore, and Jiddu Krishnamurti—have foregrounded various local equivalents like education of the heart, education of the spirit, education for inner flowering, and education for a wholesome human being. They founded schools that have experimented to bring about this kind of education, some of which have existed for more than a century. The book leverages ideologies and practices of teachers within

© The Author(s), under exclusive license to Springer Nature Switzerland AG 2023
J. Patel, *Learning to Live Together Harmoniously*, Spirituality, Religion, and Education,
https://doi.org/10.1007/978-3-031-23539-9_1

these alternative schools to build a contextualised conceptualisation of Learning To Live Together Harmoniously (LTLTH) and to outline practices that can aid in bringing about such an education. The book showcases teacher voice, whilst bringing to the fore lesser heard and discussed philosophies, voices, and practices from the global south about an alternative vision for education, which integrates spirituality within the teaching learning processes through shared lived experiences of togetherness, harmony, and spiritual exploration.

The book draws upon southern knowledge and primary data collected from various Indian schools that have been founded/inspired by the aforementioned Indian thinkers. Learning To Live Together (LTLT) is reconceptualised to LTLTH, with a novel conceptual framework being developed for the latter. Specifically, three domains for discovery of the self, other, and society are intersected with the six dimensions of 'awareness', 'empathetic and caring relations', 'sense of purpose', 'change in perspective', 'compassion(ate action)', and 'meaningful engagement'. The book also explores how LTLTH can be translated into practice and shares meaningful practices that teachers adopt. This book calls for creating a continuum of lived experiences through pedagogy, systems, and processes for autonomy, autonomous behaviour regulation, Teacher Student Relations (TSR), school-wide ethos, and teachers' ways of living and being.

The book makes a case for **adaption** rather than the **adoption** of frameworks as per the local micro-contexts. It guides the reader through a practical alternative educational system that brings about togetherness and harmony through a lived experience-based pedagogy and an ethos of harmonious living. It calls for the reader to explore and define what ideas and practices for education for harmony could look like in their respective contexts. The book's propositions and frameworks are extremely relevant to practitioners (including parents, teachers, and school leaders), academics, masters and undergraduate students from both education and development studies, and to PGCE (teacher training) students.

My Positionality and Purpose of the Book

I have been exploring and questioning the purpose of modern education for several years; while by many modern standards I can be regarded as being well educated, I have frequently questioned whether that is really the case. I have come to realise that I have developed as a fragmented individual with different parts of myself in imbalance with each other. I have always been conflicted about the emphasis on one's ownself and the complete disregard for others or, even more still, of the larger living world beyond human beings. Over the past several years I have been trying to unlearn things I picked from mainstream education system, including anthropocentrism, competitiveness, and self-centrism, result-/goal-oriented approaches, as well as a fragmented hierarchical view of the living world. Instead, I have been consciously trying to work on myself as an integrated whole (where there are no components like head, heart, hands, and spirit and rather, they come together), looking beyond the narrow needs of oneself and the human society, moving beyond to a postcritical approach to life, and developing a more interconnected understanding of the world.

I completed my schooling in India, where I studied at progressive schools that aimed to bring about education of all components of a person, but these can broadly still be seen as more traditional in their vision for education and approach to holistic education. Luckily, I got the opportunity to spend a lot of time within alternative spaces that did not comply with modernist approaches to life. My parents took me on several short- and long-term visits to spiritual *ashrams* (spiritual community living spaces) and this led to an inherent recognition and appreciation of a different way of living and being. I finished my schooling and pursued higher education in the UK. At some point, I decided to return to India to work on quality of life in slums and villages. This led me to working on educational reforms, as a cofounder of two charities in India and consultant to several others around the world. Over the past few years, I have found myself questioning the purpose of education and the grassroots level work we have been doing through one of the charities (Together In Development & Education [TIDE] Foundation). At TIDE Foundation, we had been predominantly remained focused on improving access to education; however, quality was narrowly defined as education of the head and interventions focused on progressive pedagogy. I have come to believe that education needs to go beyond narrow modernist vision for functional literacy and numeracy, instrumental vision of education and academic learning to other more holistic visions of education including focusing on intrinsic value of education and bringing about an integral education. I found myself seeking the integration of learning experiences from my stays in spiritual spaces; the development of a non-anthropocentric, ecological, and interconnected epistemology; and ways of living and being. I then embarked on a journey to explore more integral and holistic approaches to education that were called for by several Indian thinkers and have been adopted and are being practiced by several alternative schools in India. The book draws upon several research studies in many such schools and deep immersion at a few of them.

We are at a pivotal moment and educational visions need to be reconsidered and rethought. Through this book, I envision a different kind of education that relies on integral and holistic education, with the aim of bringing about an education for harmony (and togetherness) within oneself, in the surroundings around oneself, and in the larger world (including human and non-human, living and non-living). I want to encourage debate, dialogue, and reflection around what is the purpose of education. Should it be instrumental and help fulfil the needs of the society (or an individual) or hold an intrinsic value and be pursued for its own sake? Rather than pushing for a single vision or a prescriptive vision, my aim is to encourage discussion and introspection around the importance of education for harmony. I strongly appreciate and believe that there cannot be one universal theory; it is up to individual students, parents, teachers, schools, and communities to engage in a reflective process to contextualise and define their own vision for education. There are no specific dos or do nots and instead good educators can leverage any tool or strategy in different contexts. Through this book, I introduce some theories and practices that I collected through case studies of alternative schools in India across multiple years. These case studies and my interpretation of the findings can hopefully prompt readers to reflect on their visions for education. It is important also to recognise that, while I draw upon my own experiences in the spiritual spaces and the lived experiences (students, teachers, and mine) within the alternative schools, these are not representative of all schools in India. Furthermore, the key findings revolve around a different way of living and being. However, despite my best efforts to articulate them, these descriptions come nowhere close to the real lived experiences.

TOGETHERNESS AND HARMONY

Both terms are broad terms and while the book explores what they could mean and develops a framework, these terms need to be contextualised and defined by each of us. As we begin the exploration of what they could mean within educational settings, I leave you with a prompt and personal reflection to begin exploring what these terms mean to you, within your respective contexts. The prompt:

I have frequently questioned do we not already live together? Well, there have been constant struggles and wars at the macro level, but leaving those aside one could argue that we do live together most of the time, even if it's merely coexisting. However, I wonder how much of this togetherness is actually harmonious. Do we live together grudgingly, tolerate each other, or merely coexist? What could living together in harmony within the larger natural world (including human and non-human, living and non-living beings), with each other, and with oneself mean?

I write this introduction after most of the book has been written and have been struggling with what could serve as being appropriate to set the scene. I find myself seated on one of the benches on the boardwalk along the beaches of Puducherry (Pondicherry) initially awaiting and then seeing the sunrise. I am currently visiting the city to interact with a few more teachers in my continued exploration of education for togetherness and harmony, and over the past few days I have constantly been asked how I understand harmony. I have used different descriptions, including of those of balance, inner peace, active forms of harmony (discussed in Chap. 4), and from the framework later described in Chap. 5 (notably, harmony within oneself, with immediate surroundings, and within the wider world that one is not directly connected with).

As I sit by the beach, I find myself surrounded by all kinds of people. At 5am the ocean is peppered with fishermen's boats, some rowing while others are cutting across with their loaded motor driven boats. The beach is filled with people going about their daily business; including morning walkers and joggers, tourists taking a leisurely stroll, a few people practising morning yoga and pranayama, and people learning tai chi and other martial arts. Many are going down to the beach to play in the waves, whilst others are sitting and awaiting the sunrise. While crows fly around, other birds are chirping and insects are hovering around the streetlights. There is a cacophony of noises as the waves crash against the rocks, crows caw, people chat away, and all kinds of music ranging from prayers to Bollywood songs playing from phones. Yet, still people continue undisturbed, adapting and making space for others—notably the practitioners of tai chi continue their practice and learn from their instructors as people stared at them amused. People start taking photographs of the sun as it peaks out from behind the clouds, while many others continue walking around those that decided to stop and take pictures. As the sun rises the tai chi practitioners turn around to face the sun, admire it, and bow to it as they continued their practice.

On another day, I would have found it very difficult to work and write in such busy and loud environment; the sound of dragging feet alone would have been disturbing enough let alone all the other sounds. I would perhaps have actively sought a quiet space to sit and listen to the waves, to meditate, and to work. Yet still I found myself enveloped in a calm silence; connected to myself, to the ocean, and to others around; frequently, appreciating all the activities happening around me and being grateful for the place, the people, and the various activities.

In hindsight, I have reflected upon whether this was the case because I was relatively free. However, I did have quite a few emails to reply to, needed to prepare for data collection, had yet to write down reflections from the previous day, an overdue grant application to write, as well as needing to work on the book. This incident reminded me of other reflections, where I had found peace in loud and busy environments, including the sense of sacred silence that I felt at some of the schools, the deep appreciation for a busy train ride from Kolkata to Shantiniketan, and during a collective meditation session within a building adjoining an extremely busy street. I invite you to reflect on what harmony, togetherness, and living together in harmony means to you. I would like to invite you to reflect specifically upon experiences of these as you explore and develop your own understanding of these terms.

BOOK OUTLINE

The book is divided into two parts. Part I, containing five chapters, explores theory and visions for education for togetherness and harmony. Part II, containing four chapters, explores praxis for these visions of education. Each of the parts begins with a reflective poem that draws on direct quotes from my various interactions and interviews with practitioners, thinkers, and experts. Each of the chapters ends with a couple of reflective prompts for you to contextualise the propositions of the chapter and to explore their relevance within your respective settings. I would love to hear your thoughts and hope to compile varied responses to the prompts and various possibilities of an alternative vision for education on www. empowereducators.in.

Chapter 2 explores the limitations of the modern and mass education systems and the consequent calls for alternative purposes of education. The modern education system is marred by reductionism, objectification, fragmentation, materialism, segregation, self-centrism, and anthropocentrism. These inevitably lead to the reproduction and propagation of inequality, arbitrary separations of me and them, fragmented societies, loss of reverence, awe and wonder for the world, and a limited understanding of an interconnected world. Instead, I explore alternative visions of education that prioritise an ecological and spiritual perspective regarding integral and holistic education that will eventually lead to harmony within oneself and wider society. I draw on my own personal reflections and experiences, some data from practitioners in alternative schools in India, as well as the works of various Indian and international thinkers.

Chapter 3 involves a deeper investigation into the work of various Indian educationists and thinkers, exploring their visions, recommendations, and direct and indirect impact on practice and policy. Notably, they call for an education for both an inner renewal and social change, both, through the process of education and as a result of it. This brings about an education that is intrinsically harmonious and also leads to an education for harmony. The chapter also introduces some of the alternative schools that the book draws upon, not only providing context to the schools, but also striving to create an immersive experience for the reader.

Chapter 4 explores various calls for alternative visions for education, especially those calling more specifically for equivalents of education of the heart and/or for harmony (both within oneself and in the larger community). While education of the heart has been one of the primary goals within various educational systems, especially within the global south, there have been several synergetic concepts like learning to live together, social emotional learning, global citizenship education, emotional intelligence, and peace education that have emerged across the world. These fundamentally call for a more holistic and integral education, where a child is educated as a whole (within a larger community/world) as opposed to an academic education for future careers. Drawing on practitioners' vision, the chapter emphasises the role of education for harmony (within oneself and in the wider world) for building a commitment to the wellbeing of oneself, others, and the world at large, with the hope that this will inevitably shape an intrinsically and naturally just, peaceful, and harmonious society.

Conceptualising terms like learning to live together and education of the heart have several challenges and this, in turn, has led them to being treated as broad and vague umbrella terms, thus making it difficult to translate them into practice. Chapter 5 unpacks the nuances and limitations of developing a conceptual framework and then proposes an interconnected framework with three domains (discovery of the self, other, and world) and six dimensions (awareness, empathetic and caring relations, sense of purpose, change in perspective, compassionate action, and meaningful engagement). The framework embodies a non-anthropocentric perspective, with the domains including other living and non-living things beyond human society. The domains are related through one's responsibility and commitment to each other and their wellbeing, whilst similarly, the dimensions are interconnected, as the development of one leads to the development of others.

Chapter 6 explores various nuances of the framework and moves beyond a simplistic 2D model to a deeply interconnected framework of education for harmony that needs to be pursued as a way of living and being. The framework is suggested as being intrinsically linked and an indivisible whole. Education for harmony relies on the integration of education of the head, heart, hands, and the spirit; these cannot be developed directly through piecemeal efforts, but rather must be developed holistically. Teachers advocated a pluralistic approach to pursue education for harmony as a purpose of education, rather than a predetermined goal following a singular path. They frequently believed that education for harmony was a nonlinear journey wherein different students took different paths to developing their own ways of living in harmony. Notably, education for harmony is seen as a way of living, being, knowing, and seeing the world around one, rather than a mere acquisition of knowledge, skills, and/or habits.

Chapter 7 explores classroom practices for education for harmony. It emphasises the role of pedagogy (how to teach) over curricula (what to teach). It explores a range of pedagogical practices, including dialogic teaching, peer- and project-based learning, meditation, reflection, and social action. Thereafter, the chapter highlights the importance of a lived experience-based pedagogy as a means of bringing about an intrinsic form of education for harmony. Such pedagogy relies on embodied education, recognition that everything and everyone is a potential educator, as well as awareness that education is a continuous process that extends beyond textbooks, curricula, and schools' four walls.

Chapter 8 problematises notions of pedagogy as being limited to teaching learning practices within the classroom and explores what pedagogy could be like when education goes beyond transfer of content knowledge or development of skills and competencies. The chapter emphasises that education for harmony is brought about by a continuum of shared lived experiences and that these are not just engendered through classroom practices, but also by the culture and people within the school. It emphasises the importance of classroom and school-wide ethos, Teacher Student Relations (TSR), and autonomous behaviour regulation as underpinning the continuum of lived experiences.

Chapter 9 emphasises the importance of teachers consciously trying to live together harmoniously for themselves as opposed to merely modelling behaviours. It highlights the teachers' intrinsic commitment to pursuing LTLTH both for themselves and for their students. It encourages questioning if schools need to be just learning centres for children or if they can be restructured as learning spaces for everyone, spaces for community living, and spaces for experimenting with different ways of living and being. It exemplifies some of these alternatives and finds that the schools had several supportive systems for teachers: including those for autonomy, dialogue, collaboration, reflection, meditation, action on issues of social justice, and ethos of harmony. These helped teachers question educational purpose, find their own purpose of life, and pursue LTLTH for themselves.

Chapter 10 concludes the book by summarising the key findings and epistemological underpinnings for education for harmony. The chapter is primarily a call to action that encourages the reader to **adapt**, rather than **adopt**, the conceptual frameworks, classroom teaching learning practices, and school-wide processes and systems as per the local micro-contexts. It also invites the reader to share their own understandings, reflections, and experiments with other readers and practitioners.

PART I

An Alternative Vision for Education For Togetherness and Harmony

1.1 EDUCATION, 12 (+2) LONG YEARS AT SCHOOL

Education, 12 (+2) long years at school

That we want to put everyone through.
Why do we even care? What is the purpose?

A child "does not know anything" and a school will educate him,
To make money, prepare him for the future;
To make an economic contribution, create good citizens.

But is education just that, an instrument for future success?
Do we even know what the future will be like?
Did we know about the financial crisis, Brexit, or the pandemic?
In an ever-changing world, change is the only constant.

And what about the inherent value of education?
The intrinsic value of the process of learning;
The value of developing multifaceted perspectives;
The intrinsic value in appreciating beauty around us;
The value in understanding one's ownself.

Perhaps, an education that frees one,
Opens the head, heart and hands;
To appreciate and celebrate rather than just accept diversity;
To find beauty in understanding "others" rather than just tolerate "others";
To develop values of unity, kindness, empathy, gratitude, and compassion;
Might make the 12 long years value-able.

~Jwalin Patel 2020

The modern, mass educational system and its practices were borne in the light of the industrial revolution and designed to create technicians. It is based on materialistic, reductionist, and anthropocentric epistemologies and has led to homogenisation of diverse cultures and ways of knowing, a narrow emphasis on what can be measured, frequently lead to reproduction and propagation of social inequity, and fragmented ways of living and being. These epistemologies have led to several crises including those of wellbeing, equity, justice, knowledge, democracy, and climate change (Cremin, 2022; Illich, 1971a, 1971b; Mignolo & Walsh, 2018; Santos, 2018).

While the modern education system, much like modernity, has its own benefits, I believe that a very different system is required as of today: a system focused on quality rather than access, a system that contributes to building harmony—both through inner renewal and through social transformation—, and a system that propels to not just tolerate others but to also deeply respect others. This part explores what an alternative, more holistic, and more integral vision for education could look like. It draws upon various philosophies and visions of several Indian thinkers and holistic educators to propose the need for education for harmony, to explore what education for harmony could mean, and to extend it beyond a prescriptive definition to a nuanced, interconnected, deeply contextualised way of living and being.

This part explores the limitations of the current educational vision and processes, explores calls for a more holistic vision for education, and proposes education for harmony as an alternative vision for education. I draw upon my own experiences, various international and Indian theorists, and practitioners from alternative schools in India.

CHAPTER 2

Calls for Alternative Purposes of Education

Modern education and its practices have commonly propagated education as narrowly focusing on academic education, following a factory-based model to train people to conform and prepare them to contribute to industries, treating education instrumentally as a means of nation-building, and, finally, promoting anthropocentric, self-centric, and consumerist ways of living and being that have directly led to many social and ecological issues around the world. Similarly, mass education and international development have predominantly remained focused on access to education and functional literacy and numeracy due to several systemic conditions, including an emphasis on competitive testing, curricular completion, rote memorisation, and top-down implementation of developmental agenda. These have been criticised by many as being a very reductive vision of education. In this chapter, I draw upon my own personal reflections and writings of various Indian and international thinkers to explore alternative visions of education that weave in the importance of education for harmony and harmonious living. Furthermore, I explore active forms of peace, togetherness, and harmony, as well as how harmony/peace is not the absence of violence or chaos, but rather the presence of justice.

© The Author(s), under exclusive license to Springer Nature
Switzerland AG 2023
J. Patel, *Learning to Live Together Harmoniously*, Spirituality,
Religion, and Education,
https://doi.org/10.1007/978-3-031-23539-9_2

LIMITED SCOPE OF THE MODERN EDUCATION SYSTEMS

Personal Reflections

I have always questioned the purpose of the current system of education through my various roles and positionalities: as a student, as a teacher, as a social changemaker, as an adult, and as a scholar.

As a student, I questioned the role of rote memorisation, some of the content that I learnt, and the various exams. I appreciated learning and being exposed to new ideas and concepts, the degree of care and support that I received from teachers, and opportunities for engaging in various non-academic interests. However, more recently through discussions with my classmates and peers, I have come to realise how non-inclusive the schools were, and that I had potentially been afforded preferential treatment. Reflecting upon my own schooling experience, I question the relevance and applicability of much of the content that I learnt. I do not remember much of the academic content that I learnt, which says something. I would have preferred to learn how to file my taxes, how to farm, about the interconnectedness in the world, and about issues of social justice developing. Yes, I did develop some transferable skills at school, like team working and leadership skills. However, I developed many others at home, including various socioemotional skills, entrepreneurial skills, and, importantly, learning to learn. In hindsight, I would have preferred going to schools that focused on living in the present moment, learning to be happy, learning to live together, and helped develop values like kindness, empathy, compassion, and gratitude. I notably recall one of my reflections that I had noted down while organising a Model United Nations (MUN) conference at school.

> While as delegates we debated solutions to international issues, including poverty, we conveniently overlooked the children in tattered clothes we passed by on our way to the conference. We positioned ourselves as experts, while not recognising, let alone understanding, the issues around us and the opportunities and privilege that we took for granted.

Furthermore, while my educational journey included a degree of spiritual, emotional, and social education, which was brought about by my family and extended stays in ashrams, I always saw school and schooling to have little to do with the same.

As an educator, I questioned the applicability and relevance of some of the curricula, the arbitrary separation of subjects, streaming of students, and the limited scope for personalisation. I strongly appreciated (and still do) some of the other educators who leveraged varied student interests, aspirations, and experiences. Learning from them I experimented with various strategies, including a learn-at-your-own-pace course, integration of various subjects, as well as education through and within public spaces. However, with hindsight, much of what we did was limited in scope and it rarely touched upon deeper understanding of one's ownself, interconnectedness in the society, and the relevance of the content to their lives. Additionally, I saw the impact that the education and perhaps the wider society had on students; it appeared to make them very self-centred seeking arbitrary materialistic social norms, with limited connection to themselves, others around them, and nature. While I take heart in the fact that, over the years, I have now seen many of my students 'find success' professionally, I have also seen some of them struggle with various personal issues. This has led me to realise how education systems can fail to prepare students for various emotional and personal struggles that people are bound to face.

As a 'social changemaker' (I have now come to dislike the word), I started my journey perceiving education as the silver/magic bullet that could uplift under-resourced and marginalised communities. While there are several success stories from the work that other organisations and we at TIDE Foundation have done and more broadly from the various communities themselves, I found myself questioning the narrow purpose and vision of education as academic learning. Notably, a school leader of a public school that TIDE Foundation worked with pointed out that, at times, educational goals are dissociated from students' own interests and even from the wider society. She gave an example of a student that the typical education system would have considered to be a failure, but who understood how the school functioned, including its electricity, plumbing, and construction design. Additionally, I found under-resourced community members face severe unemployment, where postgraduates from marginalised communities sought underpaid jobs, like home-helps and office peons. Furthermore, I came to realise that the mass educational system has had a very narrow focus on things that we can measure. But "what about skills and attitudes that cannot be measured such as, kindness, compassion, gratitude, courage, justice, leadership, contentment, discernment, and community living? While many of these may still be describable, what about other aspects of education that cannot be put in words, for example, deeper spiritual understanding?" While I recognised education's potential, its need as a human right, and valued some of the processes more holistic education could involve, I questioned my initial stance of education as the silver bullet to all social issues. Furthermore, I was struck by the decontextualised and colonial nature of the curricula and pedagogy, and its impact-where in students in villages and marginalised communities were taught content that was designed for and by a very different population, which in turn led to a certain degree of estrangement and looking down upon one's own and their family's professions, cultures, and ways of living and being.

As a changemaker, I have been involved in a journey of questioning the role, purpose, and philosophies of changemaking. Over the years, my own reasoning for being involved in social changemaking has evolved: as a child I started with ideas of "I want to help others". During my teenage years, these quickly evolved to "I am here because I feel good about myself (I feel satisfied and get a good night's sleep)", and as I engaged more in the processes by working full time on changemaking, as an adult, these evolved to "am I actually helping them or harming them through my own violent approaches to changemaking? I came to recognise that imposing my own ways of living and being and the modern, colonial education system as being extremely violent." Over time, my vision for changemaking has evolved to the notion of "the communities I work with actually help me rather than the other way around", then to "I am not the doer, I am just the medium (for the 'universe/existence' or communities to find their interests)", and finally, to "perhaps our journeys through time and life is not about changing anyone, but rather, about building meaningful relations". When there are meaningful relations the notion of help disappears and dissolves- a parent does not help the child; they love the child. As I write this book, I have become extremely wary of words like changemaker, change agent, and agent of change. I am still unsure of an alternative; a medium for change is better, but with its own issues, as it is still based on the premise of a change being required and that change is brought about by someone external to the group. Instead, I identify more strongly with ideas of building relations, being/recognising oneself as being connected with the group, and having meaningful engagement with each other. While this paragraph might be a tangential discussion, I believe the same applies to educators. I believe that we need to move away from perceptions of helping the child to those of educators and children engaging with each other through a series of shared, meaningful lived experiences.

As an adult, I have wondered how distant we have become from others that are different from us, the nature, and our deeper selves. I wonder if the education system is creating fragmented individuals (Krishnamurti, 2013); individuals with arbitrary separations between aspects of life: arts and sciences, work and life, personal and public rights, self and the other, as well as by various labels and stereotypes. Perhaps our society—which is divided by class, caste, religion, and race—and our education system—which has various arbitrary divisions based on age, subjects, and times-pans—are replicating and propagating further fragmentation. Furthermore, within education, the ideas of multiple intelligences, and labelling students based on their ability, needs, and speed of learning, further fragment them arbitrarily, rather than treating them as a composite whole with varying sets of needs. We not only train students to perceive themselves, but also others and the world, as fragmented with limited interconnections. It is a very divisive process that can lead to isolation where in one can keep dividing society and people based on gender, race, geography, politics, caste, class, interests, so on, and so forth, till each person is left isolated as an individual. Unfortunately, many education systems have been designed in ways that have led us to see things through narrow, anthropocentric, fragmentary, self-centric perspectives. Perhaps we need an integrated education that enables students to perceive various divides and labels as arbitrary and reductive, and appreciate the interconnectedness between individuals, within the human society, within nature, and within the larger world (Thapan, 2001). This could allow for William Blake's suggested possibility of seeing reality in a more interconnected manner: "[I]f the doors of perception were cleansed, everything would appear to [one][1] as it is, infinite".

As a scholar, I started exploring whether education, with its narrow visions, constituted a form of violence. The argument for modern education has been based on promises of social mobility, and while this does happen in a few instances, more frequently it can act in a means to maintain status quo. Many sociologists have highlighted the sociocultural violence that is embedded in terms of who gets access, whose voice is heard, the hidden curricula at school, and how various educational systems and processes not just replicate, but also propagate social inequity and fragmented sociocultural societies. I wonder if educational systems and processes in and of themselves are violent. There is a degree of violence in

[1] The original quote used the word 'man' instead.

limiting education to that within four walls, promoting the development of a fragmented purview of life, and enforcing a predefined curriculum and standardised exams with little scope for contextualisation let alone being informed by student interest. Additionally, students are frequently looked down upon and ridiculed, the student autonomy and freedom are replaced by top-down teacher-enforced restrictions on their natural tendencies, and they are subject to being treated as machines that need to serve the future society. I question whether the modern system with its reductionist view aims to shape all children into identical people: consumers, global citizens, and/or workers. Modernisation has frequently done this in other aspects of human life by promoting a monoculture across all industries, for example, agriculture,[2] clothing, architecture, design, and so on. This, in my opinion, is perhaps the biggest form of violence: getting diverse children to discard their own identities and selves to fit into an arbitrary mould. As a social changemaker I have come across and experimented with various forms of autonomous learning systems, including adapting prescribed curricula to student interests, learn at your own pace courses, self- and peer-directed learning initiatives, the teachers and students co-defining curricula, and discovery education. These were extremely meaningful to students, allowing for building student onus and setting the foundations for lifelong learning. Furthermore, I questioned why education must be thought as being delimited to schools and universities. Much of education has always happened beyond school spaces and through lived experiences. This can be observed in various Indigenous populations, where children join in with the community and learn by doing, partaking, and experiencing, thus leading to a more embodied education. Similarly, all of us are learning all the time- at school, workplace, home, and in the community. However, within the school confines education is restricted to

---

[2] This pressure for the most efficient monocultures is best demonstrated by some simple statistics on the variety of rice seeds in India. A couple of centuries ago there were nearly 110,000+ varieties, of which, now, only around 5000–6000 survive. Despite the 1000s of varieties still available I can only name a handful and through my life would have eaten probably no more than 20. This culture of monocultures while seemingly in pursuit of efficiency is known to be counter-productive and this has been exemplified by the potato blight, where a monoculture was wiped out by a single strain of virus. Moreover, the loss of diversity has meant that most people consume only one kind (rice in this instance), thus accessing only a limited set of nutrients (potentially limited in quantity as the variety of rice prioritised within the monocultures has been focused on other aspects, like quantity produced, rather than nutrition and the diversity of nutrients contained within).

an abstract predefined curriculum, which many a times is taught in a manner separated from children's lived experiences.

These questions led me to delve deeply into educational theories, philosophies, and research. Furthermore, given the strong impact of both colonial and modernist agendas along with their associated dangers, it is important also to consider various Indian thinkers and their educational propositions. Explorations beyond my own experiences lead to the realisation that the limitations of modern education have existed for a long time, having drawn criticism from both Indian and international thinkers.

Indian Thinkers

My social changemaker journey led me to meeting several educationists and government officials in Gujarat, India. The opinions of the various educationists that I met resonated with my personal reflections on the limitations of the current education systems. They highlighted the narrow emphasis on English (and not Gujarati, the mother tongue of many children) and mathematics, limited contextual relevance of much of what was taught, how education had become a tool to replicate social inequity (with the access to types of schools and, finally, finding a job depending on students' backgrounds), and the strong disconnect from spiritual ideas of holistic development. Up until a few years ago, most of the government officials that I met spoke out against the modernist approach to international aid and development, criticising it for replacing more holistic approaches of education to a narrow focus on literacy and numeracy. However, unfortunately, it appears as if we have come back in a full circle now, with several modernist agendas finding a strong footing, including those of literacy and numeracy (driven by a coalition of iNGOs), privatisation of education (Anjela Taneja, 2021; RTE Forum, 2021), and the development of an Ofsted-inspired school rating model that in its current, albeit very early phase, fails to account for the massive sociocultural differences across communities.

Many of the local educationists have frequently called for a different educational system, referring to Indian educational thinkers from the twentieth century. These discussions led me to read and explore philosophies, visions, and practices proposed by various Indian educational thinkers, like Mohandas Gandhi, the Dalai Lama, Jiddu Krishnamurti, Aurobindo Ghose, Gijju Badheka, Rabindranath Tagore, and Radhakrishnan (I elaborate upon their backgrounds in the next chapter).

They provided stark criticism of education of the colonial and modern education systems for several reasons. First, they condemned it for sacrificing of a holistic approach of education by focusing only on literacy (Gandhi, 1968a, 1968b; Krishnamurti, 2000; Tagore, 1929). For example, Gandhi (1968b) suggested "literacy is not the end of education nor even the beginning. It is only one of the means whereby [people]³ can be educated. Literacy in itself is no education." Second, they rued the absence of an emancipatory nature, whereby modern education practices do not strive to overcome the divides of class, caste, religion, and socioeconomics (Gharse & Sharma, n.d.; Tagore, 1929). Moreover, they fail to free one from one's own conditioning and oppressive societal structures (Gandhi, 1968b; Krishnamurti, 2000; Tagore, 1929). Third, they lamented the failure to stimulate critical engagement (Gandhi, 1968a; O'Connell, 2003), with there being a limited applicability and relevance of what is learnt/taught. Fourth, they highlighted the failure to cultivate sympathy, empathy, and compassion (O'Connell, 2003; Tagore, 1929). Fifth, they criticised the top-down implementation of colonial/developmental agenda with very limited contextualisation and say for local stakeholders (Freire, 2005). Sixth, they contended that the current arrangements have led to the development of a fragmented mind and person, who also learns to see the world as fragmented and recreates various divisions and hierarchies (Jinan, 2021; Krishnamurti, 2000). For example, Tagore criticising the modern education system suggested:

> The young mind should be saturated with the idea that it has been born in a human world which is in harmony with the world around it. And this is what our regular type of school ignores with an air of superior wisdom, severe and disdainful. It forcibly snatches away children from a world full of the mystery of God's own handiwork, full of the suggestiveness of personality. It is a mere method of discipline which refuses to take into account the individual. It is a manufactory specially designed for grinding out uniform results. ... According to the school, life is perfect when it allows itself to be treated as dead, to be cut into symmetrical conveniences. ... We may become powerful by knowledge, but we attain fullness by sympathy. The highest education is that which does not merely give us information but makes our life in harmony with all existence. But we find that this education of sympathy is not only systematically ignored in schools, but it is severely repressed. (Tagore, 1917, pp. 116–117)

---

³ The original quote used the phrase "men and women" instead.

All these criticisms hold true even today. Vandana Shiva (in Black, 2010) notes that, modern education is removed from the pursuit of wisdom, and even that of knowledge, and is reduced to a mere transmission of information that too partial information. While Jinan (2021) provides a stark criticism of the modern education system and notes that such systems have distanced one from connecting with, observing, understanding and learning, from the real world in favour of learning from the written word. In a more recent conversation with an ex-head of nation he noted the modern education system has driven modern societies into consumerism—promoting competition and comparison over cooperation, prioritising self-interest over the wellbeing of others and the world, driving people to *bhog* (consuming/using things out of greed or for pleasure) rather than *upyog* (using things in a considerate and uplifting manner), and inevitably driving conflict and issues of social and environmental justice.

International Thinkers

While there are several contradictory and partial accounts of the purpose and impact of the rise of mass education, many commonly argue that it aimed to prepare individuals to serve the economy (Robinson & Aronica, 2015), build a degree of conformity, differentiate people based on social divides, and maintain the status quo (Bowles & Gintis, 2011). A few have challenged this perspective, arguing for mass education as a means of building reasoning and cultural values like social cohesion and citizenship (Durkheim, 2013). While this is a different discussion in its own stead, there is a general condemnation of it for its factory/prison-like model: cells and bells, division and hierarchy of subjects, and systemic killing of creativity (Robinson & Aronica, 2015). Furthermore, Freire (2005) strongly advocated against the colonial nature of education, the culture of silence that it propagated as a means of maintaining the status quo, and the narrow vision of the banking model of education, whereby students are reduced to receiving objects, thus controlling their thinking and actions, and stifling creative thinking.

Mass education has predominantly remained focused on functional literacy, numeracy, and measurable outcomes (Global Education Monitoring Report, 2012). Similarly, education for international development research and interventions has primarily engaged with increasing access to education, improving infrastructure, and measurable outcomes. Moreover, the **implementation** of Millennium Development Goals and Education For

All has been focused on access, despite their emphasis on quality (Global Education Monitoring Report, 2012; Skinner et al., 2013; United Nations, 2013). Several international reports and thinkers have called for broadening the focus of education from beyond measurable inputs and outcomes of the learning processes (Alexander, 2004; Delors et al., 1996; Global Education Monitoring Report, 2016; Nussbaum, 2010; Skinner et al., 2013). The United Nations (2013) has stated that "a failure to ensure that schooling actually leads to education … [has resulted in] a need to recapture the broad understanding of education and its purpose in future goals and frameworks". This has led to parallel discourses criticising the perceived purpose of education and emphasising the need to go beyond perceiving it as a means of bringing literary, numeracy, and economic development (Global Education Monitoring Report, 2012). Regarding which, Nussbaum (2010) noted that education for democratic citizenship is failing, if not completely absent, in favour of education for economic development due to (a) unawareness, (b) lack of acknowledgement of the role of education in building pluralism and social cohesion, and (c) shifting the focus to rote memorisation and competitive testing. Similarly, within international development, the 'western' instrumental view of international development and by extension developmental education has been challenged by scholars (Escobar, 1995; Sen, 1999), who instead call for an alternative conceptualisation of good life based on sociocultural development. Sen (1985, 2003) emphasised the role of capability, freedom of opportunities, and wellbeing over human capital.

Several holistic education scholars have criticised the current system for merely dispensing information. R. Miller (1991) derided the current educational systems for their materialistic, reductionist, and economic-centric epistemologies, worldviews, and approaches and argued that these have only led to divisions between people, a loss of reverence for life, the lack of ecological and spiritual perspectives, as well as failure to understand the interconnected nature of the world. Similarly, de Souza (2018) and Hart (2018) claimed that the simplistic focus on information acquisition, compartmentalisation, as well as the reliance on competitive and narrow measures dehumanises and devalues students. They contended that educational systems conveniently deem ideas of wonderment, imagination, liberation, and emancipation as impractical due to pressures to complete an arbitrary course that students frequently find irrelevant and/or only memorise its content for exams. Moore (2018) further criticises current education for its distancing from the soulful life within and around one.

Hart (2018a, 2018b) argues against the modernist ways of knowing. He suggests that the narrowing of our epistemologies to those based on objectification (separating oneself from the object, be it human or non-human), reductionism (reducing it to parts), dualism (everything can be neatly segregated into one or the other), and materialism (material interactions and value) have led to an education system that primarily relies on knowing by detachment, reduction, and possibly domination. This reductionist view of understanding, while powerful at times, cannot be used all the time, because while it allows for understanding of various parts of a given thing, it leaves out others and, even more importantly, the interconnectedness between the parts. Such reductionist and materialistic epistemologies and societies end up ravaging, dominating, and exploiting the natural world, other societies, and each other for selfish gains. For example, Leonardo Da Vinci (cited in Capra, 2007, p. 12) suggests that reductionist approaches lead one to "fall into the same error as one who strips the tree of its adornment of branches full of leaves, intermingled with fragrant flowers or fruit, in order to demonstrate that the tree is good for making planks".

CALLS FOR ALTERNATIVE PURPOSES OF EDUCATION

Personal Reflections on a Spiritual Education

The mass educational system and its practices were born in the light of the industrial, economic, and cultural revolution. I believe that this educational system is responsible for literate yet uneducated citizens, (re)creating a society fragmented by various divides and creating fragmented individuals that are, at best, technicians. I believe that a very different system is required as of today: a system that brings about holistic development of students and propels them to learn to live in harmony, respect, appreciating and celebrating diversity and to engage in social action to address twenty-first-century issues.

While my own vision for education developed over time, the first step was the previous reflection on the MUN conference. It stood in stark contrast to my lived experiences at a spiritual ashram at around the same time. The spiritual leader (Brahmavedantji), other *ashramites*, and visitors dedicated a part of their time to *shram* (physical service) on a daily basis, where they (a) desalinated farmland by developing an exquisite system for rainwater harvesting, diverting, and storing flood water and for the water to percolate into the aquifers; (b) engaged in reforestation; and (c) transformed an abandoned mine. They constructed a forest area and multiple lakes as well as creating public spaces and institutions (including a school, bakery, and a community kitchen). The desalination efforts have notably improved farm yields, increased ground water levels, and ultimately improved local livelihoods across several villages in the area. The forest and the reclaimed mine have become spaces for meditation and the local public, whilst the public spaces and institutions remain operational today, despite COVID-19 and the spiritual leader taking *samadhi* last year. This strongly contrasted with our efforts at MUN. There was no hue and cry about what the ashramites were doing. There were no extended planning meetings. It kept growing organically and everyone engaged in social changemaking processes as a form of *dharma* as opposed to holding long discussions. These initiatives were always viewed with the utmost humility, as if they were nothing special. Instead, they were considered a natural, nature-friendly, and obvious response to what needed to be done. This seemed like an ideal objective for education, where people come together with a commitment to resolving social issues that may or may not affect them and engage in social action through deep insight and understanding of interconnectedness within and across the human and the natural world, while at the same time remaining extremely humble.

A second major transition in my vision for education was based on reflections on the way of living and being of Brahmavedantji, who had had limited "schooling" and yet was one of the most educated people that I have met in my life. While he exhibited typical educated people's qualities, including critical thinking, he also had a spiritual connection with his soul, profound understanding of the world, a sense of wonder, deep empathy, and was the epitome of compassion. This form of deep understanding, relations, and connection with others should be one of the most natural/ obvious goals of education, where one learns to see things from another's point of view, learns to connect with others, learns to live with each other, not just by tolerating diversity, but rather by appreciating (and celebrating) diversity and each person as they are, as well as living compassionately by being considerate of and supporting other's welfare and wellbeing.

The third transformation was driven by the interactions with educationists that I met through the TIDE Foundation and visits to the various alternative schools and interactions with their students, teachers, and school leaders. Up until that point in time, I believed that education had nothing to do with deep understanding of oneself and the profound insights about the world, both of which are potentially interconnected. Given that modern education did not acknowledge this let alone emphasise this, I took the view that perhaps those discussions were meant for spaces beyond the school, for example, at home or within ashrams. However, through the various interactions with educationists, discussions of their educational experiments, and visiting alternative schools in India, I started exploring the role of spirituality in education and its potential for understanding the interconnected and integral nature of things (Mani, 2009, 2013), for developing a profound connection with nature, as well as for transforming one's ways of living and being.

Such an education would be very different from our current mass educational system and would lead to development of a deep understanding of oneself, others, nature, and the world as a whole. While these visions are valuable in and of themselves, we need to explore what they mean, and whether and how they can be practised. I intend to do so in Parts I and II of the book, respectively. I must emphasise that, instead of treating education for togetherness and harmony as an add-on example, through a class a day or week, it would need to be integrated into the various educational processes, systems, and ethos. Furthermore, my work with the two grassroots-level foundations, especially in the public education system and low fee charging schools, has made me starkly aware of the potential limitations and challenges to large-scale transformation and reforms.

Education as a Means of Inner Renewal and Social Change: A Vision from Contemporary Indian Thinkers

I decided to explore other visions and philosophies of education proposed by various Indian thinkers. Ancient India had a very different system of education, namely *gurukul* (literally translating to the teacher's home or family), where a *guru* worked with the *shishyas* (students) for years. The students developed deep bonds with each other and their *guru*, receiving a holistic education going beyond various subjects and spiritual/religious texts to a different way of living. However, this was systemically destroyed during colonisation, with very little documentation left on its visions, processes, and practices. So, instead, I decided to explore more contemporary Indian thinkers. I prioritised exploration of philosophical traditions that also have schools that currently pursue these visions because I hoped to explore if and how these visions and philosophies remain relevant to the twenty-first centuries. Unfortunately, there are very few gurukuls that can be studied. Some of these have been (re)established only recently and are still trying to develop their practices and/or have now become inextricably tied with religious bodies. I believe that these may merit a different study; however, for the scope of this book, I draw upon non-religious schools that were inspired by various Indian thinkers from the twentieth century.

Several Indian thinkers have called for a very different education system that brings about holistic development. A range of Indian philosophers (Dalai Lama et al., 2009; Gandhi, 1968b; Krishnamurti, 2000; Radhakrishnan, 1956; Tagore, 1929; The Mother, 1977a) concur in the role of education for freedom/emancipation, equality, peace, harmony, unity of life, and enlightenment (self-consciousness and self-realisation). Education in India has historically been emancipatory: "*sa vidhya ya vimuektye*" (*Vishnu Purana*, n.d.) and this was commonly emphasized by the philosophers. Regarding which, Radhakrishnan (1959) suggested that "education has to give us a second birth, to help us to realise what we have already in us. The meaning of education is to emancipate the individual and we need the education of the whole [human being]⁴—physical, vital, mental, intellectual, and spiritual." Similarly, Gandhi (1968b) emphasised, "education is that which liberates". These ideas of freedom were also resonated by Tagore, Krishnamurti, and Aurobindo, all of whom referred to freedom, not just from external oppression and/or conditioning but also from one's own self, including one's own emotions, mind, attachments, and fragmented identities (Krishnamurti, 2000; Tagore, 1929).

All of them called for a spiritual renewal, whereby children reconnect with their spiritual roots and move away from the modernistic ways of living and being to those that embody understandings of interconnectedness, interdependence, and coexistence with living beings and non-living things. Several Indian thinkers (Gandhi, 1968b; Tagore, 1929) have strongly emphasised engaging students in social changemaking processes, where the education is not delimited to the four walls of the classrooms and instead the students actively engage within the society to practice resolving issues of social justice. Similarly, the TIDE and ITSA Foundations, both charities that I cofounded, engage students in various changemaking processes by having them contribute to ongoing movements and design as well as developing their own social changemaking projects. Gandhi and Kumarappa (1953, p. 32) noted:

⁴ The original quote used the word "man" instead

Whilst Sir M. Vishweshwarayya has emphasized one grave defect of our present education which places exclusive emphasis on literary merit, I would add a graver defect in that students are made to think that whilst they are pursuing their literary studies, they may not do acts of service at the sacrifice of their studies, be it ever so small or temporary. They will lose nothing and gain much if they would suspend their education, literary or industrial, to do relief work, such as is being done by some of them in Gujarat. The end of all education should surely be service.

Education was generally considered as a means of inner renewal and social change (Gandhi, 1968b; Sharma, 2018; Thapan, 2001). These seemingly two separate goals, one focusing on the spiritual self and the other on society at large, were considered to be related to each through ideas of individual responsibility in maintaining social order (Thapan, 2001). Indian thinkers have commonly suggested that conflicts within oneself are usually reflected in the world around oneself and have called to "be the change that you want to see in the world" (Gandhi, 1968b; Krishnamurti, 2000). Additionally, there are underlying spiritual episte-mologies of collective consciousness, where the world is not separate from the individual. Hence, education and human existence should not be frag-mented into personal and public or inner and outer, but rather perceived more holistically as the relation between the individual, the community, natural environment, and human society (Thapan, 2001). Similarly, other thinkers also extended their understanding of the purpose of life and edu-cation to building connectedness with the wider community, encompass-ing the natural environment and all human beings (Dalai Lama, 2015; Tagore, 1962). Education for both these goals (inner renewal and social change) was proposed as being brought about through holistic education (also referred to as integral education): education of the heart or spirit, intellect, and physical body (or as The Mother, 1977a, conceptualised it, education of the psychic, vital, mental, and physical).

I explore the idea of the various Indian thinkers in depth in the next chapter. Similarly, there have been many international movements that have called for broader purposes of education.

International Calls for Broader Purposes of Education

In the past two decades, several international development reports such as Delors et al. (1996), Sustainable Development Goal (SDG) 4.7 (UN General Assembly Resolution, 2015), Delors et al., (1996) UNESCO,

(2014, 2018), and the Council of Europe (2017) have called for Learning To Live Together (LTLT). Delors et al. (1996, p. 92) conceptualised LTLT as an effort to alleviate, resolve, and prevent conflict by "developing respect for other people, their cultures and their spiritual values". There has also been a concurrent rise in interest and relevance of synergetic concepts like Global Citizenship Education (GCE), peace education, Social Emotional Learning (SEL), and Emotional Intelligence (EI), stemming from the international development, peace research, school improvement, and psychological educational subfields, respectively (these are further discussed Chap. 3). While GCE, SEL, and EI treat the broader goals as content to be transferred or skills to be developed, LTLT suggests a different vision by foregrounding processes of **discovery** of the self and others as well as **experiences** of shared purpose.

Some of the ideas proposed by the Indian thinkers, especially Gandhi, Tagore, and Krishnamurti, have been compared to those of citizenship of Dewey (Nussbaum, 2010) and Freirean emancipation (Ghosh, 2019). Freire (2005) calls for a critical and emancipatory education that allows the oppressed to regain their sense of humanity, take responsibility for their emancipation, and bring about social transformation, example, "reflection and action directed at the structures to be transformed" (Freire, 2005). Furthermore, Freire (2005) and Greene (1995) call for education for 'conscientization' and 'wideawakeness', respectively (resonating with John Dewey's 'extraordinary experiences'). Both refer to developing critical awareness of one's reality through reflection and action; mindfulness of oneself, others, and communities; understanding systems of oppression; and the societal construction of knowledge, awareness of power, and inequality. They believed that this would lead individuals to ask meaningful questions, make critical deliberate choices, and bring about a positive change in the world (Freire, 2005; Greene, 1995, 2005). Dewey (1916, 1944), resonating with Indian thinkers, notes that education is the foundation for democracy as a form of life. It must be perceived "not as acquisition of what others know but as development of capital to be invested in eager alertness in observing and judging the conditions under which one lives" (Dewey, 1944, p. 463) and it must equip children to use their skills for the greater social good. Dewey advocated against training students for a future workplace, essentially because we do not know what it will look like and instead suggested educating children for the present and the intrinsic value of education.

There have been several parallel discourses drawing attention to the broader purposes of education: Dowbor (Freire et al., 2016) emphasises the need for reflection upon one's values, while Noddings (2003) calls for the need of ethical caring. Dewey (1916) and Nussbaum (1997) highlight the need for an education that shapes people to be citizens of a complex interlocking world, whilst Freire (2005), Giroux (2010), and Kumar (2008) introduced emancipatory and participatory education aimed at bringing about a social change. Similarly, Bourn (2022), Sharma (2018), and Shor (1992) have called for an education for social change through which they hope that students engage in social changemaking process. There have been several calls for holistic education and these are further discussed below.

International Efforts for More Holistic Education

"What is the purpose of education?" has been a crucial question for many years. It has been philosophised as having a role in how people work together, shaping societies, development, and values since ancient Greece, with conceptualisations like Plato's *Paideia* (education for the ideal member of the state; Zovko, 2018) and Aristotle's *Eudaimonia* (living well, happiness, or living in a divine way; Kraut, 2008). There was a strong emphasis on living a good life, with this being understood as living in a divine way. It led to the rise of the liberal arts (arts for liberty). Whilst the education system then was limited to the elite and there were many systemic sociocultural divides and issues (for example, slavery), the liberal arts sought to bring about holistic education by tapping into full human potential for one's ownself and society as a whole. Liberal arts called for an education that cultivated virtues and liberated the mind by bringing freedom from ignorance, emotions such as greed, and prejudice. Hadot (2002) notably expanded the ambit of education to a different way of living and being by suggesting that the liberal arts were "a method for training people to live and look at the world in a new way. It is an attempt to transform humankind" (p. 107). Hadot (2002) and Jaeger (1944) described education as not just an intellectual exercise, but also as a spiritual pursuit of self-transformation, with the latter suggesting that "the purpose of all Socrates educational activity can be described as caring for the soul" (p. 304), which plays an important role in "reaching harmony with the nature of the universe … through complete mastery over [oneself][5] in accordance with the law [one][6] finds by searching [one's] own soul" (p. 44).

Many Indian thinkers have proposed ideas of integral and holistic education (e.g., Badheka, 1962; The Mother, 1977a). These are linked to and/or resonated by several international thinkers, for example, many of Socrates and Tolstoy's thoughts and writing informed Gandhi. Internationally, there has been a noted emphasis on aspects of holistic education over the past two centuries. While there is not enough space to explore the works of many of the thinkers in detail, I outline some of the ideas that have a strong resonance and links with Indian perspectives. Tolstoy believed that the purpose of education was learning how to live, which included exploring fundamental questions of 'who am I?' and 'what is the purpose of life?'. Rousseau, Froebel, and Tolstoy all believed in the intrinsic purpose of education, inherent goodness of children, and that children should be allowed to develop naturally and as a whole, with limited suppression and top-down teacher-driven imposition. They, Tolstoy in particular, believed that teachers' role is to help students explore (and not offer answers) as well as encourage them to build meaningful, caring, and loving relations. They consciously refrain from top-down impositions, work on their own moral and spiritual development, and prevent various indirect impositions from social conventions (Moulin, 2011). In more recent times, Maria Montessori, Rudolf Steiner, A. S. Neill, and Carl Rogers promoted alternative forms of education that aimed at teaching the whole child, advocated person-centred approaches and values, with an emphasis on self-initiated and self-directed learning. These have led to international movements and inspired chains of schools.[7] While these have their own limitations, they have pushed back against the mass education system and called for humanistic approaches. They, in resonance with many Indian thinkers like Aurobindo and Krishnamurti, believed that anything that could be taught was inconsequential and education that impacts on one's ways of living and being is self-discovered (see C. Rogers, 1961, 1979). However, Dale (1982) argued that such radical educational

---

[5] The original quote used the word "himself" instead.

[6] The original quote used the word "he" instead.

[7] Montessori has inspired several Montessori schools around the world, Rudolf Steiner has led to a movement of Steiner or Waldorf schools, and A. S. Neill's work at Summerhill prompted the free school movement.

experiments were tolerated and were a means of managing the tensions without radically changing the mass education systems.

It is important to note the work of Maria Montessori, who had a strong link with the alternative education thought and practices in India. She visited the country on several occasions, gave talks, and inspired several Indian schools and thinkers. She was the director of an alternative school in India, which continues to run (and is included in my own research). Montessori proposed alternative visions for education, developed practices, piloted them in at schools and/or centres, and has had a lasting impact on education, continuing to inspire schools around the world, including in India. Montessori believed in lifelong learning and highlighted the intrinsic value of education through ideas of joy of learning and intrinsic motivation to learn. She was of the view that the key goals of 'education' were to cultivate children's curiosity, motivation, and desire to learn. Montessori also forefronted ideas of respect, love, and autonomy of children, where they would follow their own learning trajectories within a caring community (including peers across multiple ages and the teacher). She (Montessori, 1949, p. 27) highlighted the role of education in peace-building "preventing conflicts is the work of politics; establishing peace is the work of education". She further emphasised the importance of developing ethically and socially conscious individuals: "The crux of the question of peace and war thus no longer lies in the need to give human beings[8] the material weapons to defend the geographical frontiers separating nation from nation, for the real first line of defence against war [are human beings themselves], and where [human beings are[9]] socially disorganised and devalued, the universal enemy will enter the breech" (Montessori, 1949, p. xv). Duckworth C. (2006), commenting on Montessori's work and classroom practices, highlights the role of social imagination in leading to empathy and action against issues of social justice. Gijjubhai Badheka, an Indian educationist, was inspired by Montessori's work and extended it to the rural Indian contexts. He led the Montessori movement in Western India, setting up schools, organising conferences, and extensively experimenting and writing about his experiments. Badheka (1962) emphasised freedom, self-directed learning, and intrinsic purposes of education (e.g., education for the sake of education in itself and the happi-

[8] The original word used the word "men" instead.
[9] The original quote used the phrase "the real first line of defence against war is man himself, and where man" instead.

ness/satisfaction derived from learning, rather than marks, rewards, or future jobs). He extended Montessori's methods to include several community-based activities, including storytelling, music, singing, dancing, and others, to bring about holistic development, improve student engagement, as well as tapping into and contributing to students' socio-cultural knowledge, with particular emphasis on harmony.

Furthermore, internationally, there is growing interest amongst researchers and practitioners in holistic education, with several networks, special interest groups, and conferences having been produced. Culham et al. (2018), Lin (2006), Lin et al. (2019), J. P. Miller (2010), and J. P. Miller et al. (2005, 2018) have called for a transformative holistic education that includes education for emancipation, love, compassion, wonderment, and awe, as well as spiritual consciousness. J. P. Miller et al. (2007) suggest that holistic education differs from wholistic education, the latter being propounded by Dewey and Noddings and while involving a broader view of education, does not include spiritual dimensions. In a similar vein, several holistic scholars are also critical of Freirean critical pedagogy believing it to be anthropocentric and lacking the spiritual dimension. Instead, holistic education calls for educating the person as a whole (soul, emotions, body, and mind) and not the parts, within an interconnected world (Cajete, 1999; Darroch-Lozowski, 2018; Four Arrows, 2018; Kessler, 2000; Miller, 2000). Various authors in the handbook of holistic education (Miller et al., 2018b) recommend a reflexive, decentralised, contextualised, and autonomous decision-making, leading to educational systems and processing become more meaningful to both teachers and students. They call for a shift from materialist and reductionist worldviews to co-constituted, interdependent, and integrated ones, with schooling shifting from categorical knowing to more embodied knowing that recognises wholes and connections. Furthermore, holistic education notably emphasises education for harmony, both within oneself and with the world (including the nature), thus focusing on interconnectedness and interdependence.

CONCLUSION

The chapter has demonstrated that the purpose of education has been questioned for a long time, with various holistic visions being proposed. These have led to some transformations to varying degrees (further discussed in this and the next chapter). Unfortunately, many of these have waned in light of the various colonial and/or modernist systems. However, these ideas have continued to exist and thrived in certain communities of thinkers and practitioners.

I invite the reader to explore their own vision for education and how it compares with the current educational systems' vision and practices. Additionally, I would also like to ask you to explore the question from various perspectives, including that of the child, teacher, parent, and government. I also invite you to consider the following questions: is education just a tool/instrument for future success (academic or financial success of the individual or the development of the nation)? How can education go beyond being a mere academic education, training children to conform, and reproducing and propagating social inequity? What can holistic education look like? I believe that a single vision and set of practices may not be the answer and instead individual readers have to find their own contextualised vision and supporting practices. But then, what is the point of me, with my limited set of experiences, writing this book and you reading this book? I hope to draw on my experiences, a few readings, and some data that I collected to articulate a form of holistic education, which may or may not resonate with visions of various stakeholders or those in different contexts. The book is best considered as a case study that prompts you to explore other visions and potentially contextualised purposes of education, by drawing on your experiences and educational thinkers local to your context.

CHAPTER 3

Alternative Visions from Indian Thinkers and Schools

The various shortcomings of the modern education systems prompted me to explore alternatives that are relevant to the twenty-first century. Various Indian thinkers strongly emphasised education of the heart (Gandhi and the Dalai Lama), education of the spirit (Aurobindo and Tagore), education of the psychic (Aurobindo), and flowering in inner goodness (Krishnamurti). I was driven to explore what these alternative visions are and how they are practised. While I value the original thinkers' visions, I was more interested in whether and how these ideologies are relevant to the twenty-first century and if so, how are they conceptualised and practised by educators. It led me to visit, deeply immerse myself in, and explore schools that were founded on these principles and claimed to actively pursue education for the aforementioned alternative visions for education. Before we go further, it is important to provide some more context to the various Indian thinkers and the schools that the findings are based on. In this chapter, I specifically explore the key ideas of some of the Indian thinkers and the lasting impact and relevance of their ideas within India and more globally. Finally, I provide some more context on some of the schools that the aforementioned thinkers set up/inspired. I collected primary data from these schools, which I later draw upon throughout the rest of the book.

© The Author(s), under exclusive license to Springer Nature Switzerland AG 2023
J. Patel, *Learning to Live Together Harmoniously*, Spirituality, Religion, and Education,
https://doi.org/10.1007/978-3-031-23539-9_3

INDIAN THINKERS

The book specifically focuses on educational thought and ideas from the twentieth and twenty-first centuries. While there have been various educational thinkers and each of them merit (and at times have) a book about their ideas, it is not possible to review their individual contributions in this work. For readers interested in Indian thinkers I would strongly advocate reading the works on Gijju Badheka, Nana Bhatt, Mohandas Gandhi, Aurobindo Ghose, Zakir Hussain, Jiddu Krishnamurti, Dalai Lama, Manu Pancholi, Sarvepalli Radhakrishnan, Rabindranath Tagore, and Har Trivedi. Herein, I explore key themes and ideas that come up across the various thinkers, including calls for education of inner renewal and social change, child-led education, and holistic education. Many of these thinkers were engaged in several other pursuits and did not only work on education. Despite this, they have had a profound impact on the Indian education system, practices, and, at times, policies (see the next section for more details).

Education as a Means of Inner Renewal and Social Change: A Vision from Contemporary Indian Thinkers

As previously described in Chap. 2, Indian educational thinkers (Dalai Lama et al., 2009; Gandhi, 1968b; Krishnamurti, 2000; Radhakrishnan, 1956; Tagore, 1929; The Mother, 1977a; Vivekananda, 1947) concur on the role of education for freedom/emancipation, equality, peace, harmony, universal brother/sisterhood, unity of life, and enlightenment (self-consciousness and self-realisation). They strongly emphasised education as a means of inner renewal and social change (Gandhi, 1968b; Sharma, 2018; Thapan, 2001). They envisioned an education that will immerse and engage students in emancipation from various social conditioning, build a sense of kinship and diversity-based oneness, as well as drive them to engage in social changemaking processes.

Calls for Spiritual Education (Education of the Heart and Its Equivalents)

Over the years, there has been a consistent call for inner renewal and spiritual education. This has been referred to by various names, including education of the heart, education of the spirit, psychic education, and education for flowering in inner goodness. Gandhi spoke about the education of the heart, referring to ideas of moral training, character development, and spiritual development, as being more important than intellectual development. He suggested education of the heart as referring to spiritual training and character education as a means of self-realisation, with individuals empathising with each other, building tolerance, living together, and enacting conflict resolution (Gandhi, 1968b). Similarly, the Dalai Lama speaks of education of the heart in terms of mindfulness, oneness of humanity (shared humanity, interconnectedness, and interdependence of everyone), better understanding of emotions, forgiveness, compassion, and tolerance (Dalai Lama, 2014, 2015; Dalai Lama et al., 2009). Moreover, Aurobindo Ghose asserted that the central aim of education is to bring about mental and spiritual transformation, leading to free and moral beings who show extreme love for all others (Mehra, 2011; The Mother, 1977a, 1977b). On a similar note, Radhakrishnan (1956) noted, "For a complete human being, we require the cultivation of the grace and joy of souls overflowing in love and devotion and free service of a regenerated humanity. If we wish to realise the reign of law and justice in this world, it is to enable the soul to gain inward peace. Physical efficiency and intellectual alertness are dangerous if spiritual illiteracy prevails." Krishnamurti (1981, 2000, 2013) asserted the role of education for the oneness of humanity, inner flowering (freedom, self-realisation, and consciousness), and building individual responsibility to create a better society. He referred to ideas of 'cultivation of total human being', awareness, awakening consciousness, inner peace, and harmony. Further advocating the cultivation of a human being who maintains the 'right relations' with people, society, and ideas. Whilst Rabindranath Tagore emphasised education of feelings (*Bodhersadhāna*), self-awareness, oneness with others and nature, self-realisation, love for humanity, freedom, and creativity (O'Connell, 2003; Tagore, 1929; Tirath, 2017).

Calls for Education for Peace (and Social Justice)
The calls for education for social change relied on emancipation of students from various forms of social conditioning that they may have developed over the years. There was a strong emphasis on engaging in various kinds of social changemaking processes, including short-term relief work and long-term changes to counter issues of social justice. The latter were embedded in ideas of breaking down systems of sociocultural and systemic violence and in notions of 'positive peace', which Galtung (1964) described as "there are two aspects of peace as conceived of here: negative peace which is the absence of violence, absence of war—and positive peace which

is the integration of human society". Similarly, Gandhi differentiated peace as containing a negative and a positive sense: "[E]limination of wars, absence of conflicts between classes, castes, religions and nations is a negative sense, and love, rest, mental equilibrium, harmony, co-operation, unity, happiness are the positive indices of peace" (Gharse & Sharma, n.d.). There is a strong resonance with Freirean (2005) emancipation and critical consciousness (or conscientisation, example, critical awareness of one's reality through reflection and action; Ghosh, 2019), while like Freire, the Indian thinkers envisioned students bringing about emancipation. They believed that the oppressed and oppressors were inherently interconnected, and education needed to engage both in creating a social change through ideas of universal brotherhood, kinship, and empathy. Some of the ideas proposed by Gandhi, Tagore, and Krishnamurti have been compared to those of active citizenship of Dewey (Nussbaum, 2010), whereby students engage in resolving issues of social justice.

Child-Led Education

Various Indian thinkers believed and proposed that education needs to be led by the child. There are two common subthemes: the first that teachers and other adults around the child should not interrupt the process and instead should merely just support them in the self-discovery. Regarding which, Swami Vivekananda (1947, p. 383) noted:

> Each of us is naturally growing and developing according to our own nature … what can you and I do? Do you think you can teach even a child? You cannot. The child teaches oneself.[1] Your duty is to afford opportunities and to remove obstacles. A plant grows. Do you make the plant grow? Your duty is to put a hedge round it and see that no animal eats up the plant and there your duty ends. The plant grows itself.

There is a strong resonance with various international thinkers, including Froebel and the ideas of educere-ing,[2] which emphasise letting children be

---

[1] The original quote used the word "himself" instead of "oneself".

[2] The etymology of education leads us to one of the two Greek words: *educare* and *educere*. *Educare* has been predominantly used as a form of training and moulding, while *educere* refers to leading or bringing out what is already there in a person.

and letting them develop naturally. This has been associated with ideas of bringing out what one possesses within and helping one excel within one's own talents within.

Second, while a few others emphasised consciously educating the child, they strongly advocated for it to be a child-centric approach, where the child's natural tendencies, interests, and pace are taken into account. There is a strong emphasis on a teacher not being a tutor, but rather a facilitator who creates an appropriate learning environment and supports students' learning based on their interests. All thinkers have emphasised that all children develop at different paces and take different paths, which educational approaches need to factor in. Such a child-centric approach and its associated experiential learning pedagogies are related to various ideas of Dewey and Montessori.

Both these ideas led to the various thinkers (Badheka, 1962; Chaube, 2005; Chaube & Chaube, 2016; Gandhi, 1968a; Krishnamurti, 2000; The Mother, 1977a; Tagore, 1929; Vivekananda, 1947) to call for education to be rooted in children's lived experience and led by children. Regarding which, Aurobindo and The Mother suggested three principles of education: (a) nothing can be taught, (b) the mind has to be consulted in its own growth, and (c) education is brought about by working from the near to the far. Similarly, Vivekananda, as seen in the previous quote, suggested that the child grows by him/herself according to his or her tendencies and Krishnamurti questioned education for facts and knowledge. Instead, he advocated for the holistic flowering of children through student autonomy, deep observation of oneself (thought patterns, habits, conditioning, and fears and desires), and the world around them as well as active (experiential) learning.

Holistic Education

The various Indian thinkers adopted a holistic epistemology, which underpinned all their philosophies and approaches to education. This is reflected in multiple aspects including (a) their approach to life and calls for non-anthropocentric epistemologies and ways of living and being; (b) calls for harmony both within oneself and in the world (and their understanding of the interconnectedness between oneself and the world); (c) approaches to educating the whole child, rather than education of separate parts of an individual (further discussed below); (d) emphasis on embodied and experiential learning, whereby students learn through interactions and experiences within the world around them; and (e) emphasis on school-wide systems that are applicable to everyone at the school (including administrative and supporting staff, teachers, and students).

Holistic education has been proposed as meaning educating the following: (a) the whole person (all 'parts of a person'); (b) a person as a whole (not educating an assimilation of parts); and (c) the person within a larger whole (including the human community, nature, and the universe; Tagore's vision is described by Forbes, 2000). In India, it is referred to as the latter two. Various Indian thinkers have proposed an education that learns from the whole movement of life, with many referring to ideas of 'life is the best educator' and education for life. There is a significant difference between educating the parts of a person individually and educating the whole person; it relates to the common maxim of the whole is greater than the sum of the parts. That is, a group of 100 ants can do a lot more than what 100 ants can do individually. In education, we have commonly trained individual parts of a person separately through special classes for training the body (like sports and physical education), the heart (sessions on value and moral education and social emotional learning), and the brain (through academic sessions). Instead, we need to educate the person as a whole through an integrated education. Such that all parts of the individual are engaged in the learning process. While some specialised training for each part might be important, the modern education in certain instances has become extremely reductionist (e.g., through excessive emphasis on academic education or training only certain aspects of the body or the mind, like training certain sets of muscles or an overemphasis on certain cognitive skills[3]).

There is a strong call for education of the whole person (including the physical, emotional, mental, and spiritual). This entailed, both, specific, targeted education of individual aspects/parts of oneself (with equal weightage being given to each), and an integrated education where education is considered for the whole person (all aspects are trained together). Physical education includes aspects of understanding breathing, various movements, building physical capacities, training the various senses, developing healthy bodies (and stronger immune systems), and using the hands creatively to make things. These are related to the development of aspects

---

[3] It is important to note that frequently modern education's narrow focus on literacy and numeracy goals or more progressive modern education's emphasis on specific cognitive skills may not contribute to the education of the mind and its various facets.

like awareness, self-control, and creativity. Emotional education is based on ideas of developing the right relations, empathy, compassion, self-governance, and control. These will lead to the development of other aspects, including that of kinship. Mental education far exceeds a mere transfer of information, for while such information is valued, mental education is seen to include ideas of independent thinking, critical thinking, and emancipation from various forms of conditioning. Spiritual education has focused on polishing the inside, reconnecting with one's soul, and linked to ideas of bringing about wider social justice. In a recent interaction with an Indian educationist, he emphasised the importance of education of the spirit, as it can help develop *vivek* (there is no exact translation though it roughly translates to discretion based on wisdom) and guide one's actions.

The Indian thinkers have strongly emphasised that such a holistic (or integral) education of the whole person needs to happen with an understanding of the larger whole. This means that students cannot be separated from the real world beyond the four walls of schools and their education needs to take place within the community, within the forests, and through deep immersion in the world around them. Internationally, there has been a strong increase in the numbers of forest schools and at times (some of) these schools are situated in urban environments, aiming to take students into the natural environment for a couple of hours a week. I believe that, while this is a step away from modern educational systems, we need to go further and have schools situated within nature, where students are in constant interaction with that around them. This is also tied to their emphasis on a non-anthropocentric epistemology, emphasis on contextual education (and ideas like education from near to far), as well as various pedagogical approaches that prioritise embodied and experiential learning.

Discussion and Limitations

It is also important to note the background of these educational philosophies. Many of these philosophers exhibited a spiritual background and were critical of religious structure. They were in communication with each other, with their works spanning pre- and post-Indian independence. All of them questioned the purpose of life and the role of society (despite some differences around social reforms and independence) before they turned to educational interventions. They held similar opinions on the purpose(s) of education, albeit they placed different emphasis on the various means to achieve the same ends, these views being partly informed by their positions on other questions about society and independence. For example, Tagore placed a strong emphasis on arts and poetry, while Gandhi's ideas of *swaraj*, *swadeshi*, and *satyagraha* led to his insistence on independent thinking, self-governance, and vocational training, and Krishnamurti called for critical thinking and continued awareness. Many of these philosophers are humanists by nature, and at times have been suggested as being idealists, lacking a formal background in education, and having educational thoughts, ideas, and opinions scattered across different works. Additionally, their writings in the spatio-temporal context of Indian independence have been critiqued for having contradictions across time as their ideas and practice evolved (Aronson, 1961; Ghosh, 2019; Parekh, 1989). Furthermore, some scholars have highlighted that, at times, some of the thinkers failed to embody some of the ideas they suggested. However, I believe that their visions are not necessarily eclipsed by these proposed limitations, because everyone, including researchers, can be subject to similar criticism especially regarding their ways of living and the contradictions within their written works over time. For instance, I started my journey with a strong emphasis on independent, critical, and creative thinking, before realising that education could help bring about something much more meaningful. I started off with ideas like learning to live together before transitioning to the notion of education for harmony. Additionally, I doubt if I will ever be able to make the claim that I embody all the aspects of education for harmony 24*7.

The visions and ideas of the various Indian thinkers have informed policy, inspired many schools, and informed teachers across India and the world (further discussed below). I must highlight again that the current book is aimed at exploring how teachers in schools inspired by such thinkers understand and practise these alternative visions of education.

THE RELEVANCE OF INDIAN EDUCATION THOUGHT IN THE TWENTY-FIRST CENTURY

The various educational thinkers' ideas are widely used and extremely relevant today, if not more so (Table 3.1) than previously. Gandhi's ideas started a national movement, where the government used his thought to start *buniyadi shalas* and tribal schools across the country. Moreover, there was the nation-wide implementation of the *nai taleem* curriculum and materials across government-run schools. The Dalai Lama's thought informs various schools run by the Central Tibetan Association in multiple

Table 3.1 Summary of impact of some of the key Indian educationists who emphasised LTLT

Thinker	Life span	Key educational ideas	Key texts	Impact
Rabindranath Tagore	May 1861– Aug 1941	Education of the spirit and education for the wholesome human being. Education of feelings (Bodhersadhāna). Oneness with others and nature. Freedom, creativity, questioning societal structures, and self-governance. Self-realisation and love for humanity.	Tagore (1929, 1962)	Informs national curricular framework. Set up Shantiniketan, Sriniketan, and Vishwabharati (university).
Mahatma Gandhi	Oct 1869– Jan 1948	Education of head, heart, and hands. Spiritual training and character education. Empathy, equality, tolerance, and self-governance.	Gandhi (1968a, 1968b, 1983)	Informs national curricular framework. Experimented at a few initial schools. Set up Gujarat vidyapeeth (university). *Nai Taleem* movement. *Buniyadi shalas.*
Aurobindo Ghose and Mirra Alfassa	Aug 1872– Dec 1950 Feb 1878– Nov 1973	Integral education. Education of the psychic. Mental and spiritual transformation. Free and moral beings that love all.	The Mother (1977b, 1977a)	Informs national curricular framework. Chain of schools across India. Large-scale in-service teacher training programme across multiple states.
Jiddu Krishnamurti	May 1895– Feb 1986	Flowering in inner goodness. Oneness of humanity. Deconditioning and questioning societal structures. Inner flowering (freedom, self-realisation, and consciousness).	Krishnamurti (1981, 2000, 2013)	Informs national curricular framework. Set up and inspired a chain of schools (including a school in the UK and another in the USA). Inspired activity-based learning movement.

(*continued*)

Table 3.1 (continued)

Thinker	Life span	Key educational ideas	Key texts	Impact
His Holiness Dalai Lama	Jul1935–	Education of the heart mindfulness. Oneness of humanity (shared humanity), interconnectedness, and interdependence. Understanding emotions. Kindness, compassion, forgiveness, and tolerance.	Dalai Lama (2015); Dalai Lama et al. (2009)	Informs central Tibetan administration run schools. Curricular development through social emotional ethics and Ayur Gyan Nyas.

Adapted from Patel (under review). Table is sorted by the birth year of the prominent thinkers

countries, while the Krishnamurti and Aurobindo foundations have chains of institutes. Additionally, school leaders and schools in many cities have tried to experiment with their ideas. However, these schools have remained a minority as 'centres of experimentation' in comparison to others. Several factors can explain this including lack of appropriate teacher education and training, absence of proactive school management committees that understand the philosophies, limited scalability, and a rapidly spreading mass education system (both private and government). Dale (1982) argued that such radical educational experiments are tolerated and are a means of managing the tensions without radically changing the mass education system. However, one can also perceive these schools as sites of excellence, experimentation, and noncompliance with modern education systems.

These thinkers have had a much wider impact than the organisations with which they were directly associated. Gandhi, Krishnamurti, Aurobindo, Vivekananda, and Tagore's thoughts on the role of education in building peace and harmony have been highlighted and have informed various policies, including the Sri Prakasa Committee (Committee on Religious and Moral Instruction, 1959), Chavan Committee (Chavan, 1999), and new National Educational Policy (NEP, 2020). The former two informed Indian National Curricular Framework 2005 (NCF) developed by the National Council of Educational Research and Training (NCERT, 2005; Rajesh, 2002) and a later position paper on peace education (NCERT, 2006). Krishna Kumar criticised NCF 2000 for its neglect of the work of Indian "teacher-philosophers", like Gandhi, Tagore,

Aurobindo, Krishnamurti, and Badheka (Pinar, 2015). Later, as a director of NCERT, he weaved their opinions more strongly into NCF 2005 (Kumar, 2017; NCERT, 2005). This led to development of various frameworks and guidance notes for teachers (Central Board of Secondary Education, 2012) and schools (NCERT, 2012). They also form a key component in teacher training programmes, with various authors authoring books compiling their educational thought (Chaube, 2005; Chaube & Chaube, 2016) as well as continuous professional development plans and proposed resources (Kumar, 2010; NCERT, 2010). In contemporary India, the NEP (2020) reaffirms its commitment to "develop[ing] good human beings capable of rational thought and action, possessing compassion and empathy". Furthermore, the Happiness Curriculum (Delhi State Council of Educational Research and Training, 2019), a noted SEL intervention, was inspired by another Indian thinker named A. K. Nagraj (Das et al., 2022) and was launched in 2018 by his holiness Dalai Lama. It and its adaptations are currently being implemented across tens of thousands of public schools across multiples states in India including Delhi, Uttarakhand, Jharkhand, and Tripura with ongoing efforts to scale it to other states. The programme involves daily sessions on social emotional wellbeing, mindfulness, and happiness. These sessions are facilitated by trained schoolteachers, with the help of a grade-specific teachers' handbook. The curriculum aims to promote lifelong learning, prosocial relations, emotion regulation, and goal setting in classrooms. Despite the widespread recognition of the ideas and ideologies and development of specific curricula, attempts for integration across school-wide systems and processes, within the core academic curricula, and within classroom pedagogy remain scarce, due to sustained emphasis on literacy and numeracy, lack of supporting school-based systems, and limited emphasis on practices for the implementation of these ideologies during teacher education and training.

Several ongoing large-scale national and international movements have been driven and inspired by these ideas and have successfully implemented parts of the aforementioned educational thinkers' visions: (a) the peace education movement in India was driven by Gandhi, Krishnamurti, and Tagore (Kumar, 2010; NCERT, 2006). This has led to incorporation of various closely related international ideas, like Learning To Live Together (Delors et al., 1996), into the National Curricular Framework 2005 (Kumar, 2010; NCERT, 2006). (b) The Dalai Lama organises educational deliberations on mind and life, which have engaged researchers like

Richard Davidson, Kimberly Schonert-Reichl, Adele Diamond, and Matthieu Ricard, with an emphasis on SEL. (c) The Dalai Lama has inspired and funded the development of an international curriculum for Social Emotional and Ethical (SEE) learning (Emory University & SEE Learning, 2019), which Daniel Goleman coined as SEL 2.0). (d) The activity-based learning and Multi-Grade Multi-Level approach, developed at Rishi Valley and inspired by Krishnamurti, was scaled up to many government schools in India from the early 2000s and is now being introduced to other countries, including Ethiopia, Bangladesh, France, Germany, and Nepal. Additionally, this is being supported by an online teaching enrichment programme and slowly being rolled out across teacher training colleges. (e) The happiness curricula, described above, draw on the ideas of A. K. Nagraj and were launched by the Dalai Lama.

Alternative Schools

Background to Alternative Schooling in India

India has many diverse types of schools, including government-run, government-aided, and private. Private schools are unaided by the government and typically charge a fee. There are several subtypes of private schools, including low-fees private schools, trust (charity) run schools, private (high-fees) schools, and international schools. The latter two try and maintain classroom sizes of 20–30 students. There is another means of classifying education in India: mainstream and alternative. There is a small set of alternative schools (both government-run/aided and private), which have been inspired by the various Indian thinkers and operate as centres of experimentation. They follow limited government mandates (related to teacher recruitment and curricula, except when close to the national assessment; e.g., grades 9–12 the last four years of schooling). "Alternative schooling" arose out of dissatisfaction with mainstream education systems, with schools adhering to a different vision for education and pedagogical philosophy. Their yardstick of success relies on different measures for the individual and the school. That is, they generally aim to be child-centric, inclusive, and have an explicit focus on a child's life-enriching needs, with many such schools also focusing on the development of spiritual values, identity, self-respect, and a sense of belonging (Vittachi et al., 2007).[4]

Please note that, as previously discussed, India had a rich tradition of the gurukul system; however, currently there are very few secular gurukuls, with many of these only being founded more recently. I decided to visit and explore 21 alternative schools founded/inspired by Indian thinkers from the 20th century, primarily looking at 5 such schools. I completed short visits at 17[5] of the schools, while I spent extended periods of time (and at times with multiple visits) at the other 5, thus allowing for deep immersion in them. I have also been running a community of holistic educator practitioners from alternative schools across India and draw on some of the interactions from there. The five schools where I spent extended time are Mahatma Gandhi International School (MGIS; private international school), Mirambika (MBK; trust-run school), Patha Bhavana (PB; government-aided school), Rishi Valley School (RVS; private school), and the Shreyas Foundation (SF; private school). The schools were founded by different thinkers and I discuss each of their contexts in the following section. Despite the alternative nature of these schools, many also do relatively well academically, with some of them being considered as the best school in the city (SF), the state (MGIS and PB), and the country (MBK and RVS). Furthermore, their students, upon graduation, seek admission to a large host of institutions and their alumni (including a Nobel laureate at PB) subsequently do well in their respective fields of choice.

The schools are influenced by spiritual leaders and philosophers who spoke out against gender, socioeconomic, religious, and caste divides. All schools sought to be diverse and inclusive, especially embracing students from under-resourced backgrounds. MBK and PB charge no fees, while SF has relatively affordable ones. Whilst RVS and MGIS charge higher

---

[4] See Patel (2020, 2021), Sibia et al. (2006), Thapan (2018, 2006), and Vittachi et al. (2007) for studies on various alternative schools in India. They have researched these schools in India, including some of those covered in this book.

[5] These schools have been inspired by a wide range of thinkers, including Aurobindo, Dalai Lama, Gandhi, Krishnamurti, Mr M, Sri Sri Ravi Shankar, and Tagore. The schools visited were Sri Aurobindo International Centre of Education, Deepanam, Tong-Len Trust, Mewoen Tsuglag Petoen School, Tibetan Children's Village—Upper Dharamshala, Vishwagram, Sahyadri School, Rishi Valley Rural Education Centre, Satsang Vidyalaya, Peepal Grove School, Ramakrishna Mission Vidyalaya—Narendrapur, Sri Sri Academy—Kolkata, Ananda Vidyalaya, Shikha Shastra, Shishu Tirtha, and Marudam Farm School.

fees, at RVS this covers boarding and lodging facilities and at MGIS various international board affiliation costs are met. The majority of children who attend PB are from local and rural areas and SF provides girls' scholarships and free education to children within an on-campus orphanage that they run. MGIS and RVS run scholarship programmes, with the former being studied as a model school for the development of the Indian Right To Education Act, which seeks to integrate children from various backgrounds into schools, with those unable to afford the fees being cross-funded by other students. All the schools seek to be inclusive and do not consider religious or caste backgrounds in their admission decisions. However, given the intersectionality of caste, religion, and class this can possibly lead to replication of societal inequalities. The schools also make proactive effort to be inclusive and secular by appreciating different traditions, supporting diverse children's unique needs, and celebrating varied Indian festivals.

The philosophers and the schools are generally well reputed in the local area (as well as nationally), with many parents believing in the school's philosophy and thus choosing to send their children there. However, ethnographic observations and informal interactions with teachers, parents, students, and alumni suggest that the admission to all the schools sampled was not limited to parents' belief in the philosophers' ideologies. That is, they applied for admission to the school for other reasons, including their infrastructure, academic rigour, location, the integration with nature, and teaching pedagogies. This has led to engaged/reflective parents being involved in the schools, who hold and express various expectations (academic, extracurricular, and the associated philosopher's ideology). The schools' philosophy, reputation, and parental bodies also lead to very well-educated, proactive, and reflective teachers being recruited.

Context to Some of the Alternative Schools

As aforementioned, I spent extended periods of time at some of the schools and I share a bit more context on them here, including their background, philosophy, educational practices, and school-wide systems. I also include a notable highlight from each of the schools. While the schools share many characteristics and there were multiple highlights, I only share a few, with the hope that the subsections help build a sense of what some of these alternative schools are like.

Shreyas Foundation, Ahmedabad, Gujarat

SF is in Western India and was cofounded in 1947 by the educationist Leena Sarabhai, with its first president being Maria Montessori. The school follows the ideologies of Gandhi, Tagore, and Montessori. Various Montessori-based activities are integrated through the pre-primary and primary school, the high school being affiliated with the Gujarat Secondary and Higher Secondary Education Board. The school aims to bring about holistic education and many of the teachers, during my visit to the school, had studied under, lived with, and were trained directly by Leena Sarabhai. Post Leena Sarabhai's demise, in 2012, the school has been in transition to keep up with rapid changes in the last decade, while still trying to hold onto the visions, ideals, and practices. The school also frequently opens its door to the wider community of the city by offering access to its museums, running a variety of extracurricular activities, during the evenings and holidays, to children and adults alike (e.g., swimming, cooking, and horse-riding classes), and providing space for public activities, including theatre, plays, and concerts.

Notable highlight from my visit: I was struck by the school's integration with nature, its open design, and architecture. The school is based in the heart of the city but has sprawling green cover, a Miyawaki forest as well as various animals and birds on the campus. The school's architecture[6] leverages and promotes the connection with nature with the various buildings and rooms interspersed through it, classrooms windows overseeing the various trees, and various activities spread out under the trees. The open-ended design and open-style design lead to a feeling of being connected with the nature around. Children played around the trees, especially an incredibly old banyan tree; at one instance I had noted nearly 50 children playing around the one tree. The nature provided various learning opportunities, where teachers leveraged different spaces for the classes, children studied nature through nature walks, and nature contributed to children's social emotional learning and wellbeing.

[6] The school was designed by renowned architects Balkrishna Doshi (considered one of the leading architects around the world, who has designed several institutions and won numerous awards, including the Pritzker Prize) and Kamal Mangaldas.

Rishi Valley School, Chittoor, Andhra Pradesh
RVS is in Southern India and was founded by Jiddu Krishnamurti in 1926. The primary school experiments with various different curricula, while the high school is affiliated with the Indian Certificate of Secondary Education. The residential school is based within and surrounded by forests and hills. The school maintains a high degree of rigour across all their learning areas: academic and extracurricular. The school leverages various progressive pedagogies in the classroom, including participatory and experiential learning. Once a year, students engage in a month-long project to explore in-depth a particular educational area through multiple transdisciplinary perspectives. The school emphasises the importance of teachers questioning and constantly reflecting on the purpose of education and their processes. They have strong systems for promoting questioning, reflection, and continued development, including through regular reading circles, daily discussion meetings, and several types of planning meetings. The school is notably also referred to as the Rishi Valley Learning Centre, considered as being a learning centre for both students and teachers. The school is also associated with the Rishi Valley Rural Education Centre, which has several rural schools and its educational model for activity-based learning has been scaled up to millions of public schools across several states in India as well as several countries beyond (Shailaja Fennell et al., 2016). A recent challenge that the school has been facing, is the increasing urbanisation around the campus (and an increasing presence of relatively unknown people who come to the area, as new colleges have and construction sites have sprung up), which has meant the school has had to start fencing the extremely large campus, thus separating it from the various hills, plains, and other forests around.

Notable highlight from my visit: The school is situated within a valley and has a thriving forest. Students do not specifically need to go into a forest, but rather they are in one all day long. Some classes happen within four walls, some in alternative learning spaces like huts, some under trees, and some while walking around. Additionally, students frequently engage in bird watching, long hikes, cycling treks, and daily silent walks atop a hill to watch the sun set. They also had a strong understanding of nature around them ranging from identifying, relating with, and appreciating nature (trees, birds, animals, flowers, etc.). The children have an extremely deep appreciation of nature; students frequently spoke to each other through phrases like "look, how beautiful is this tree", "this is a wonderful rock", and "the hill looks very beautiful [as it is struck by sunlight]". They were able to connect and communicate with trees sensing when they were ill or when they felt low. Similarly, they weren't scared of snakes, and once when one wandered onto a *verandah*, students commented: "[O]h do not worry it's just come out to take the sun it will go away soon".

Patha Bhavana, Santiniketan, West Bengal

PB is in Eastern India and was founded by Rabindranath Tagore in 1901. The school is affiliated with the West Bengal State Board of Education, but still has considerable freedom because of its stature, reputation, and its positionality as an alternative school. The school holds a strong appreciation for aesthetics education, where students are encouraged and supported to engage in various forms of art. Students and teachers frequently take part in singing, dancing, theatre, poetry, art, and crafts. While the school has specific classes to help develop these skills, they also have daily assemblies with extended singing, weekly poetry evenings, arts and crafts exhibitions, and theatre performances and the school has various forms of arts embedded all across the campus (including wall paintings, paintings, and sculptures). The school embodies an open environment: all learning happens in open spaces (further described in the noted highlight); parents frequently join in with morning assemblies, weekly special morning meditation, and weekly poetry sessions; and there is a sense of freedom for students to attend/not attend sessions. While education is very subject-specific, teachers experiment with varying pedagogies within the classes. Interestingly, teachers teach across very diverse grades (e.g., a given teacher can potentially teach grades 2, 5, 8, and 11) as a means of continuous development and developing an understanding of broader child development. A recent challenge the school is facing is related to the increasing pressures to follow a state-prescribed curriculum.

> **Notable highlight from my visit**: Most of the classes in the school happen under trees. While the school has a building, it is rarely used (mostly during the monsoons or when specific tools and materials are required, e.g., for specialised craft sessions). At other times of the year all teaching and learning take place in the open compound under large trees with students sitting in a circle around the teacher who sits at the base of the tree. This means that there is no real border between the classroom and the world around; children can see, observe, and interact with the birds, nature, soil, and animals. Teachers actively encourage this and do not perceive children as being distracted when they are observing birds or playing with a cat or dog that has walked into the 'class'.

Mahatma Gandhi International School, Ahmedabad, Gujarat
MGIS is in Western India and was founded in 1998. It has a formidable reputation for its emphasis on freedom and autonomy, for both teachers and students. The school has an extremely limited hierarchy and leverages ideas of non-positional leadership (Bangs & Frost, 2015; Frost, 2017), with teachers frequently making autonomous decisions and, at times, directing the school leaders. The school follows the International Baccalaureate and the Cambridge International Examinations, which allows them significant freedom in their curricula and pedagogy. The school engages in Project Based Experiential Learning and Generated Resource Learning (GRL) pedagogies; all learning takes place through projects, which typically last at least a month. GRL was developed by Chazot (2006) and Musafir-Chazot (2019), being inspired by Dewey, Erikson, Freire, Gandhi, Krishnamurti, Piaget, and Vygotsky. The syllabus is co-constructed by teachers and students of the given grade, with

students informing the key topics (e.g., the space, waste management, and football) that they would like to explore and teachers mapping various age-specific competencies and learning objectives against the selected topic. Additionally, the school embodies a culture of dialogue and collaboration, wherein teachers, students, as well as teachers and students together engage in projects and group work. The school has a triadic structure such that it not only acts as a space for learning for children, but also as a centre of action research, experimentation, and teacher training. Over the last few years, the school members have been involved in training thousands of teachers across the country in experiential and GRL pedagogies. A recent challenge the school has been facing, despite being one of the model schools for the Right To Education Act (one of its clauses requires all private schools to provide free education to 25% students from marginalised backgrounds), is increasing government regulation around fee caps; however, school parents have come together with the school authorities to push back against this.

Notable highlight from my visit: The school is deeply invested in project-based learning. The projects last a minimum of a month and frequently much longer (some are one-year-long projects). The children's day is structured in 2-hour blocks instead of the typical 40 minutes periods. All academic content, target skills, and competencies to be developed were woven into the project. The projects offered students the unique opportunity to engage with each other on topics that they were passionate about and to understand the relevance and application of the content covered. The project topics are decided upon by the students and involve extensive collaborative decision-making between students. Thereafter, (groups of) teachers map out their learning objectives for the various subjects against the project area.

Mirambika Free Progress School, Delhi
MBK is in Northern India and was founded in 1981. The school follows ideologies of The Mother and Sri Aurobindo, who emphasised the importance of integral education (which includes an education for several interconnected aspects, including mental, physical, vital, psychic, and spiritual). The school is not affiliated to a board of instruction and instead follows ideas of free progress, where students progress at their own pace. They take

ideas of student autonomy and freedom much further than other schools (including MGIS), such that students not only decide upon the project areas, but also do so regarding the curricula, including the objectives of the year; the content that they want to learn; the cognitive, physical, emotional, and behavioural skills that they want to develop; and the outputs they want to create throughout the year. This involves collaborative decision-making between the students and teachers, with there being enough freedom for individuals to pursue some degree of independent objectives. Much like MGIS, the school leverages project-based learning, with projects typically lasting several weeks or months. They included aspects of cross age group activities, social action components, and integral education. There are no exams whatsoever and instead students engage in ongoing self-reflective practices to map their own development, while teachers draft elaborate reports to support students' development and their achievement of their objectives. The school used to have a strong supporting parent body, who would come into the school, volunteer their time, and partake in various activities. However, this was disrupted for a couple of years, but is now being reconstituted. The school has faced some major challenges in the recent years, including being forced to change school buildings, and installation of CCTV cameras as per government mandates.

Notable highlight from my visit: The school is based within a *spiritual ashram* and most of the teaching body comprises *ashramites*, teacher trainees, and volunteer parents. The school deeply emphasises the importance of teachers' own holistic, integral, and spiritual development. This is facilitated through various processes, including teachers joining prayer and meditation sessions before school begins (many students and parents came to school earlier to join these), engaging in deep daily reflection after the school day has ended, joining weekly reading groups, participating in planning meetings, sharing their progress and practices during monthly sharing sessions, as well as consciously working on and learning a new skill (e.g., woodwork, musical instruments, dance, and yoga) every few years. The school is seen as a space for development for all; one of the teachers notably suggested, "[T]he day I stop growing inwards I will stop coming to the school". The teachers constantly strive to incorporate ideas of education for harmony within their own ways of living and being.

Conclusion

The modern education system takes a very narrow, instrumental lens to the vision, purpose, processes, and systems of education. The chapter has reviewed various Indian thinkers' calls for a substantially different education that brings about inner renewal and social change through a child-led holistic education. These thinkers have directly and indirectly informed various local, national, and international thought, policies, interventions, and movements. Their ideas have also led to the establishment of a series of alternative schools that aim to deeply imbibe and embody visions for education for harmony. Moreover, the chapter has provided a short overview to some of the alternative schools. While the descriptions do not provide a complete picture of any of the schools, I would invite the reader to explore documentaries on alternative schools in India. I would also like to invite you to think about other alternative schools, within your contexts, which attempt to bring about education for harmony. What are the school-wide processes they adopt? What are the various relations within the school community like? What kind of classroom processes do the schools pursue? And how do the children experience such an education?

CHAPTER 4

Learning to Live Harmoniously: an Essential Aim of Education in the 21st Century

My personal experiences and readings on the various educational thinkers led to me narrowing down on what *Kelavani* could look like. I strongly resonated with ideas of education as a means of inner renewal and social change. Such an education would not only support students in developing a deep scientific and spiritual understanding of their own selves, the community, and nature, but also a moral commitment to the understanding and wellbeing of the society and nature. Education, and not just schooling, would become a process of transformation of one's ways of perceiving, living, and being, such that one learns to live in harmony with oneself, others, and the nature. Such an education would be spiritual, holistic, and transformative. In this chapter, I look at what these alternative visions for education of the heart and its equivalents can mean in the twenty-first century. Furthermore, I explore the role of active harmony and peace in building active communities and democracies.

Education of the heart is a broad umbrella term that has been widely used in India to encapsulate the aforementioned ideas. It has also been used in several other contexts beyond India, especially colloquially within schools (Schonert-Reichl & Hymel, 2007), referring to a wide range of concepts, including Social Emotional Learning (CASEL, 2003), character education, moral and virtues education (Schwartz, 2007), Global Citizenship Education (Oxley & Morris, 2013; UNESCO, 2014a), and Learning To Live Together (Delors et al., 1996). Different ideas have

© The Author(s), under exclusive license to Springer Nature Switzerland AG 2023
J. Patel, *Learning to Live Together Harmoniously*, Spirituality, Religion, and Education,
https://doi.org/10.1007/978-3-031-23539-9_4

developed differently across different contexts; however, many of them have resorted to perceiving these ideas as content/knowledge to be transferred or skills and competencies to be developed. This contrasts with Indian thinkers' visions for education, who instead have envisioned education of the heart as a different way of living and being. Do note that the first half of the chapter serves as a broad literature review and takes a deeper dive into literature; and I recognise practitioners may not find the chapter as engaging as others, however, I hope it is equally valuable.

ALTERNATIVE PURPOSES OF EDUCATION AROUND THE WORLD

A Sustained Emphasis on Education of the Heart in India

There has been a long-standing interest in value-based education in India, with many notable thinkers having called for a shift to more affective mind-sets and governmental interventions targeted at such education. Education of the heart and its equivalents have been recognised by several Indian educationists and philosophers, including Mahatma Gandhi, Aurobindo Ghose, Jiddu Krishnamurti, Dalai Lama, The Mother, Sarvepalli Radhakrishnan, and Rabindranath Tagore. Indian philosophers have emphasised the role of education for equality, peace, justice, harmony, unity of life, freedom/emancipation, and self-realisation (Patel, 2021b). As noted previously, the ideas of the various Indian thinkers have strongly informed various policies, interventions, curricula, and teacher training initiatives (see Chap. 3 for further details). In more recent times, these ideas have informed two of the most important policies in India. First, the Indian National Curricular Framework 2005 (NCERT, 2005; Rajesh, 2002) and its approaches to peace education (NCERT, 2006). It notably weaved ideas of education of the heart as a means of developing cultures of peace and peaceful ways of living and being.

> Living in harmony within oneself and with one's natural and social environment is a basic human need. Sound development of an individual's personality can take place only in an ethos marked by peace. A disturbed natural and psycho-social environment often leads to stress in human relations, triggering intolerance and conflict. We live in an age of unprecedented violence—local, national, regional, and global. Education often plays a passive, or even insidious role, allowing young minds to be indoctrinated into a culture of

intolerance, which denies the fundamental importance of human sentiments and the noble truths discovered by different civilisations. Building a culture of peace is an incontestable goal of education. Education to be meaningful should empower individuals to choose peace as a way of life and enable them to become managers rather than passive spectators of conflict. Peace as an integrative perspective of the school curriculum has the potential of becoming an enterprise for healing and revitalising the nation. (NCERT, 2005, pp. 6–7)

Second, the New (Indian) Educational Policy (NEP, 2020) resonates with some of the ideas, albeit with a reduced emphasis, reaffirming its commitment to "develop[ing] good human beings capable of rational thought and action, possessing compassion and empathy, courage and resilience, scientific temper, and creative imagination, with sound ethical moorings and values. It aims at producing engaged, productive, and contributing citizens for building an equitable, inclusive, and plural society as envisaged by our Constitution" (NEP, 2020, pp. 4–5). However, the policy document is steeped in ideas of twenty-first-century skills and being much more focused on other areas. Furthermore, education of the heart is treated as an add-on, delimiting it to knowledge developed through reading 'fun fables' and the constitution and putting it off till higher education institutions where students can opt for credit-based courses on community engagement, value-based education, and environmental education. Despite these it would be unfair to judge the policy just yet; the policy has a much broader scope and many others reckon it to have unprecedented emphasis on equivalents of education of the heart. The national curricular framework and various positions papers have now been commissioned and should follow in due course of time. Promisingly there are position papers being written on health and well-being, value education, and inclusion and going by the emphasis on value education in the elementary national curricular framework (the first framework to be released) these may inadvertently build on NCF's (2005) integrative and holistic approach to education of the heart.

In the past five years, there has been a notable large-scale intervention in government-run schools, wherein the happiness curricula (Delhi State Council of Educational Research and Training, 2019), drawing on spiritual Indian ideas, were proposed as an add-on subject for developing socioemotional competencies. The programme is currently being replicated across many other states in India. In more recent times, the Delhi

Government have taken the idea a step forward and built in an emphasis on integration across other subjects and on building teachers' own socio-emotional competencies. While the intervention still treats education for happiness as development of certain skills and knowledge, it is continuously evolving and hopefully will develop into emphasising a different way of living and being through more holistic school-wide approaches.

Learning to Live Together Proposed as One of the Four UN Pillars of Education

In my explorations of what education of the heart means, it was frequently referred to as a large umbrella term with limited conceptual frameworks and guidance on how to convert these philosophies into practice. This led me to exploring other related international ideas and conceptualisations, such as Learning To Live Together (LTLT), Social Emotional Learning (SEL), Emotional Intelligence (EI), and Global Citizenship Education (GCE). I found a certain resonance with the ideas of LTLT, which had also influenced the Indian National Curricular Framework 2005 (NCERT, 2005, 2006). LTLT, whilst stemming from a report to UNICEF and based on modernist ideas, had been co-opted by Indian educationists and was referred to and rephrased as learning to live together harmoniously (Ajit Mondal & Jayanta Mete, 2014; NCERT, 2006). Furthermore, recently, there has been a renewed emphasis on LTLT with the SDG 4.7, sometimes termed "learning to live together sustainably" (UNESCO, 2018), aiming to bring about global citizenship education and education for sustainable development, and the Council of Europe's (2017) conference on 'Learning To Live Together'. Within the Indian context it is important to extend the idea to learning to live together harmoniously (Patel, 2021b). This resonates with other Indian thinkers, who see education as a means of building harmony and strong communities; for example, Radhakrishnan (1964) noted, "The importance of education is not only in knowledge and skill, but it is to help us to live with others".

Delors et al. (1996) notably expanded the ambit of education to "learning throughout life", to include four pillars of (lifelong) education: learning to know, learning to do, learning to be, and learning to live together. It is important to note that the Delors Report was written to the UN as a basis to drive policy reforms. Furthermore, it is also pertinent to note that Jacques Delors, the head of the commission drafting the report, was the previous president of European commission. The report in and of itself makes several important points and has been quite humanistic in nature due to its consideration of the whole person, rather than education as a tool for driving economic development. The report proposed LTLT to be the most evocative pillar of education, introducing notions of discovery of oneself, recognition of others, and social cohesion. Delors et al. (1996, p. 92) conceptualised LTLT as an effort to alleviate, resolve, and prevent conflict by "developing respect for other people, their cultures and their spiritual values". Delors et al. (1996) and UNESCO (2014b) advocate two complementary paths: discovery of others (a more static path) and learning to work together (and a more dynamic path), as ways to combat prejudices, cater to biases, and resolve conflict. These, in turn, will lead to experiences of shared purpose. Moreover, Delors et al. (1996, p. 93) propose a sub-objective of "understanding of the self", as a prerequisite for LTLT:

> If one is to understand others, one must first know oneself. To give children and young people an accurate view of the world, education … must first help them discover who they are. Only then will they genuinely be able to put themselves in other people's shoes and understand their reactions.

Similarly, Nussbaum (1997) argues for education of democratic citizenship, which involves individuals developing capacities for critical and reflexive self-reflection (aligning with discovery of the self), a 'narrative imagination' that will allow them to position themselves as others (aligning with discovery of the other), and a moral commitment to the human community (resulting from learning to work together and resulting in experiences of shared purpose). LTLT has a certain resonance with education of the heart equivalents as it hints at a different way of living and being. While it is important to note the modernist and universalist underpinnings of LTLT, Delors, and the iNGOs supporting these ideas, it does not necessarily take away from the ideas proposed (that too by a commission composed of various diverse authors from diverse cultures).

Since the Delors Report (1996), LTLT has frequently been used to refer to a range of ideas, including GCE, education for sustainable development, peace and conflict resolution, tolerance, value education, human rights, humanitarian action, and civic responsibilities (Sinclair, 2013). In the past two-and-half decades there has been a notable shift in the perceived purpose of education and international development through it. The report informed policy debates, international development objectives, and led to initiatives in more than 50 countries (Carneiro & Draxler, 2008). LTLT is also embedded in the discourse of twenty-first-century skills (within life skills, one of the three domains of the twenty-first-century skills framework).

Rising Interest in Other Synergetic Equivalents

Across other subfields of education research there has been a discourse for the need for education for more holistic purposes. This has led to an emphasis on LTLT, SEL, EI, GCE, education for sustainable development, peace education, and human rights education (Sinclair, 2013). Following Dewey's (1916) philosophical stance that education is a nation-building process, there have been several research discourses focusing on ideas similar to LTLT, including (a) education for international development, which includes the UN's pillars of education and LTLT, GCE, education for sustainable development, and twenty-first-century skills; (b) peace (and peace education) research through its emphasis on transrational and aesthetic peace; (c) psychology relying on EI; and (d) school improvement research emphasising SEL (for an in-depth comparison of the fields refer to Chap. 5, Fig. 5). Whilst these perspectives had different initial motivations, all of them involve children exploring how they can manage their emotions, understand others, and work/live together. The following paragraphs focus on the significance and relevance of the equivalent concepts.

The international development research inquiry into LTLT began with "what is the purpose of education?" and its role in a good life (Delors et al., 1996). The Delors Report was perceived as being "more profoundly humanistic [...] and less market driven" (Cougoureux & Sobhi Tawil, 2013) than other international development reports, one which recognised education as an end in itself as opposed to other discourses of means to an end (Power, 1997). However, others like Bhola (1997) note that the report still perceived education as an instrumental vision for preparation for the future as opposed to praxis for the present. Meanwhile, international development has also had a strong interest in GCE, referring to an education that shapes a global citizen with a sense of belonging to common humanity and the global community, leading to solidarity, collective identity, and collective responsibility (UNESCO, 2014a). GCE has been conceptualised through three different approaches (Hunt, 2017; Oxley & Morris, 2013): (a) global competence—people need to be prepared to live and work in a jobs market in an interconnected global world; (b) cosmo-politan—in a global community it is important to understand each other and respect the similarities and differences; and (c) advocacy—it is important to challenge and uplift social conditions in the unequal society. UNESCO (2014a), drawing on the cosmopolitan and advocacy approaches to peace education, notes that GCE aims to "empower learners to engage and assume active roles, both locally and globally, to face and resolve global challenges and ultimately to become proactive contributors to a more just, peaceful, tolerant, inclusive, secure and sustainable world". However, it is important also to note that, historically, GCE has been linked to liberal ideas of citizenship and often aligned with colonial ideas of a civilising mission (de Oliveira Andreotti, 2011). Moreover, recently GCE has been used very broadly and Pais and Costa (2017) question whether it makes it a global project that everyone from different perspectives is able to champion to suit their own needs, masking the various internal tensions. For example, many consider GCE as helping to develop marketable employees that can work across contexts, while others use it to encourage development of tolerance and global understanding (e.g., Khoo & Jørgensen, 2021).

Peace studies, in the light of wars, started enquiring about education for a co-operative society, helping students to be agents of peace (Page, 2008) and proponents of "positive peace". Galtung defined positive peace as peacebuilding processes based on resolving structural and cultural violence as opposed to threats and punishments (Galtung, 1969). Page (2008, p. 158) stated that "if we believe that peace, that is, harmonious and co-operative relations between individuals and societies, is a beautiful thing, a valuable thing in itself, then we should not be reticent in encouraging this as a stated objective for education". Peace education research has explored various notions of "peaces" (stemming from the discourse of many different types of peaces; Dietrich, 2012) and peace education. Moreover, recently there has been a noted emphasis on the ideas of aesthetic peace, transrational peace, and co-poesis, which resonate with LTLT and the various Indian equivalents of education of the heart, introducing ideas of spiritualism. Page (2008) described aesthetic peace pertaining to eastern ideas of peace as embodied, spiritual, and affective dimensions of peace that stem from within. Gurze'ev (2010) put forward the idea of co-poesis as togetherness, characterised by openness, responsible co-improvisation, and relations with others without aspects of self-centrism or self-sacrifice. Dietrich (2012) explained transrational peace as being concerned with inner transformation and as a form that integrates eastern ideas of spirituality and rationality. He developed a 2x2 matrix of internal and external peace along with the individual and collective aspects of engagement, which he later (2013) extended to a multi-layered pyramid with inter- and intra-personal layers.

Psychology research inquiring "how children develop" conceptualised EI (Goleman, 1995; Krathwohl & Bloom, 1964; Salovey & Mayer, 1990). Salovey and Mayer (1990) coined EI, referring to "the ability to perceive and express emotion, assimilate emotion in thought, understand and reason with emotion, and regulate emotion in the self and others" (Mayer et al., 2000). Goleman (1995) popularised EI, proposing a model (now called the mixed model) based on a wide range of competencies categorised into self-awareness, self-regulation, social skills, empathy, and motivation. Other EI models include the ability model (Mayer & Salovey, 1997), which is based on perceiving, using, understanding, and managing emotions and the trait model (Petrides & Furnham, 2001), which focuses on self-perception of emotional personality and behavioural dispositions. The ability and mixed models have been most widely used, whilst the trait model has been criticised for being very generic (not having a framework) and subsuming EI as a personality trait.

School improvement (and now co-opted by psychology) conceptualised SEL, which focuses on "youth development programs for drug prevention, violence prevention, sex education, civic education, and moral education" (CASEL, 2003). SEL "involves children's ability to learn about and manage their own emotions and interactions in ways that benefit themselves and others, and that help children and youth succeed in schooling, the workplace, relationships, and citizenship" (S. M. Jones & Doolittle, 2017). McKown (2017) defines SEL as "the thinking skills, behavioral skills, and regulatory skills needed to interact effectively with others, and to make, form, and deepen relationships". There are also several frameworks for SEL, which S. M. Jones and Bouffard (2012) compared and conceptualised three competencies of cognitive regulation, emotional processes, and interpersonal skills. While CASEL (2003) identified five competencies of self-awareness, self-management, social awareness, communication and relationship skills, and responsible decision-making. SEL and EI are both understood to be crucial to students' wellbeing, self-regulation, relations with others, and being engaged citizens (Greenberg et al., 2017; OECD, 2015).

These relatively synergetic conceptualisations, albeit stemming from different initial epistemological positions, point towards the apparent need for a different educational system. For example, the OECD (2015, 2018), drawing on LTLT and the synergetic concept of SEL, has highlighted the importance of the latter in the development of skills, knowledge, and attitudes towards individual wellbeing as well as capacities to manage one's emotions, work together, and become responsible and engaged citizens. The OECD (2015) report is also notably titled 'Skills for Progress; the Power of Social and Emotional Skills'. However, the various conceptualisations take different approaches, ranging from those that perceive them as knowledge to those referring to them as skills of competencies. They also stem from an instrumental vision for education (education for better future returns and/or for better academic outcomes) as opposed to a more intrinsic one (e.g., education for the sake of education and education for these equivalents for their own sake and wellbeing), which has been adopted by several aforementioned Indian thinkers, and advocated by Brighouse and Unterhalter (2010) and Kumar (2010a). I invite the readers to explore and reflect on whether the education for these various equivalents would look any different, if pursued for the intrinsic value in them. In either case, the interest in these concepts has not been restricted to researchers and policymakers, for it can also be found in practitioners and to a certain extent it could be argued that many of these concepts have been driven by them, who have consistently focused upon and emphasised these equivalents.

International Interventions Transforming Educational Systems

There has been a range of interventions that have been developed targeting LTLT, GCE, and SEL for children. LTLT and GCE have been promoted by international bodies, like UNESCO. Between 1996 and 2008, the Delors Report led to initiatives in more than 50 countries (Carneiro & Draxler, 2008) and since 2008, organisations such as Arigatou International (they run an international programme referred to as Ethics for Education), in collaboration with UNESCO, have been leading various programmes, including teacher training and curricular development for LTLT. Since 2012, UNESCO has been actively engaged in using GCE, especially with the launch of the Global Education First Initiative and thereafter, with the SDGs (Torres & Bosio, 2020). However, most GCE implementation has remained limited to inclusion in curricula through special subjects or through integration into certain ones (Davies, 2006; DfID & DfEE, 2000; Oxfam, 1997; Oxley & Morris, 2013; Reimers et al., 2016), while SEL has found strong interest in North America, with many interventions being developed across the USA and Canada (Weissberg et al., 2015). S. M. Jones et al. (2017) reviewed 25 of the most prominent interventions (also reviewed in Durlak et al., 2015), including (a) within classrooms, involving interventions through a specific subject or coverage under other subjects (Zins, 2004), with some teacher support to use the materials (notable programmes include Social Emotional and Ethical [SEE] curricula, Second Step, RULER, and 4Rs); (b) school-wide interventions targeting policies, conflict resolution, and creating safe spaces (notable programmes include Caring School Communities, SECURe, and latter models of RULER) (Oberle et al., 2016); and (c) community-based interventions, which bring about parental involvement and providing other opportunities to practise (e.g., community service programmes and parental engagement in the aforementioned programmes) (Durlak et al., 2010). Over the past decade, there has also been a rise in the number of programmes involving meditation (Luberto et al., 2018), mindfulness (Berry et al., 2018; Diamond & Lee, 2011; Emory University & SEE Learning, 2019; J. P. Miller et al., 2005; Schonert-Reichl & Roeser, 2016), and compassion training (Luberto et al., 2018). These, in turn, have led to various curricula and extra-curricular interventions across the world, notably government trials across 224 schools in the UK (Hayes et al., 2019; Magra, 2019). Furthermore, in India, over the past five years a range of SEL interventions have been developed by various state and non-state actors, with the Happiness Curriculum being one of the most notable changes.

There have been several studies that have studied the impact of these interventions and education for these broader objectives, suggesting a positive impact on a range of learning outcomes, including academic outcomes, cognitive skills, prosocial behaviours, and communication skills (Durlak et al., 2011; Weissberg et al., 2015), as well as predicting success at school (Zimmerman & Bandura, 1994; Zins, 2004) and work (Caspi et al., 2002; Hanushek et al., 2011; D. E. Jones et al., 2015). Education for SEL has also been implied to promote democratic and engaged citizenship, reduce criminal behaviour, and lead to improved mental health (D. E. Jones et al., 2015). Various SEL programmes have been shown to improve social emotional outcomes, including promoting positive attitudes and relations with oneself, others, and at times the larger community, while reducing problem behaviours and depression (Durlak et al., 2011; Sklad et al., 2012).

EDUCATION OF THE HEART AS A PRIMARY PURPOSE
OF EDUCATION: A TEACHER'S PERSPECTIVE

The previous section demonstrated increased recognition of the relevance of various education of the heart and LTLT equivalents. Many of the equivalents have had a lasting impact and have resulted in interventions around the globe, including in India. Deeper exploration and comparisons lead me to realise that conceptualisations like SEL, EI, and GCE treat education of the heart as knowledge and skills about the society. Their proponents believe in transferring content and practising certain skills through one-off sessions in the classrooms. While these are valuable, how can we go beyond perceiving education for togetherness and harmony as gathering certain knowledge or developing certain skills to transform one's ways of thinking, living, and being? I believe that *Kelavani* would need to be a deeply transformative process for a different way of living and being. And exploration of this question led me to visit alternative schools founded/inspired by the aforementioned Indian thinkers to understand their perceptions and practices of education. I spent nearly 10 months through an ethnographic study at 5 such schools and visited 13 others through short one-day trips. In this section, I explore teachers' perceptions of the purpose of education. The teachers foregrounded education of the heart and its equivalents as their primary focus, with 52% sections of my data exploring teachers' perceptions of purposes of education coded for education of the heart equivalents, while there were limited references to other purposes, like children's wellbeing (22% codes), holistic education (13% codes), knowledge (6% codes), finding one's interest (5% codes), career (1% codes), and other (1%) (Fig. 4.1).[1]

Limited Emphasis on Career and Knowledge

Is my purpose in life to get through the exams and get a job and lead a comfortable life, or have I come here with a specific purpose and [the purpose of education should be] to find the purpose [of life]? We often end up

---

[1] It is important to note that a few teachers questioned if there must be a predefined purpose of education. They strongly believed that having predefined purpose of education is hierarchical and therefore delimiting. Instead, they advocated for a form of mindful purposelessness, being led by students and their visions and being led for one's love for children. This resonates with ideas of Educere-ing and is further discussed in Chap. 9. However, upon further discussion the teachers described their approach as one resonating with that of education of the heart and its various equivalents.

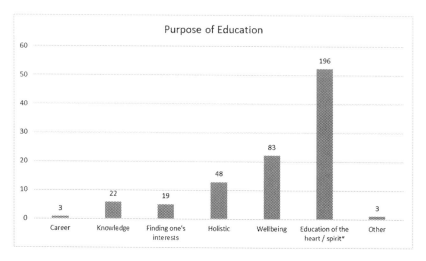

Fig. 4.1 Purposes of education. Represents the frequency of coding for the various purposes of education that the teachers discussed. *Education of the heart/spirit includes various other contextualised equivalents, including education of the psychic, education for flowering in inner goodness, and for a good human being

> looking at very inconsequential things. Things that do not really matter. How does it matter in the long run whether I get this or that? How does it matter if I do not learn the rules of grammar? How does it matter, if my students are weak, let us say in maths or they do not remember history dates? What should be more important is whether they can look at their school and say because of that I am a better person. I have learned how to locate myself. (Aaditya[PB])

Education for building a student's future career was mentioned rarely and that too only in passing, with teachers clarifying that the "primary aim of education should be to develop your human qualities and human aptitudes". While knowledge as a goal had a wider spread of importance, ranging from not important to one of the primary goals: (a) as something that was not relevant or important, through notions of "it does not matter; it is just a context why we engage with each other" and "we do not care about academics"; (b) in passing as a secondary goal, for example, "mastering knowledge and all is nothing [not important]" and "it's only a stepping stone to get to where I want to"; or (c) as important and a given, with one teacher suggesting, "The first one is how the children learn, because we are educators". However, those that emphasised knowledge also clarified that their primary goal was centred around the child's wellbeing and education of the heart.

Teachers frequently questioned the modern systems of education, for example, "purpose of education ... as it is practised nowadays in society, I do not agree (with) ... memorise and cram the memory with all this information, data, that is useless" (Baren[MBK]). While another expressed, "Whether the child is achieving what's been set out is not important. ... There are lots of opportunities to come back to things. So, actions will be done in 5th, 6th, 7th, 8th. So, it may slow down at some stage, but that's okay" (Tanuj[RVS]). Furthermore, teachers questioned the role of some of the more competitive exams, considering them to be the irrational way of evaluation, leading to stress and anxiety and ultimately promoting individualism and dividing society, rather than promoting cooperation.

Some Emphasis on Finding One's Passion

> The experience of flow where you lose a perspective of time when kids are so engaged. We do not want a break. That is very important, that means you are happy doing this, you are connected with that thing. (Anju[MGIS])

Teachers frequently emphasised the importance of finding one's passion, referring to ideas ranging from building curiosity and interest, openness to novel ideas, exploring interests beyond academics to ideas of helping students find their *dharma*. Dharma in this context meant finding one's purpose of life, finding something that really drove them, and/or finding something that led to sense of flow (Csikszentmihalyi, 1990). Furthermore, finding one's true passion was discussed in terms of students' current and future wellbeing. They emphasised the need to give students the opportunity and freedom to find and develop their interests and for these to evolve over time.

An Emphasis on Holistic Education

All teachers emphasised holistic development, at times referring to it as "all round development", which included the development of thinking skills (creating, organising, critical and creative thinking), soft skills (multitasking, articulating ideas, communicating them, negotiating, team working, leadership skills), attitudes (towards subjects, other people), creativity (through hands or the mind; not limited to crafts or sports), and the development of a 'complete human being' (linking to ideas discussed further below in the education of the heart equivalents section). They frequently referred to ideas of education of the head, heart, and hands. The ideas of holistic education were later developed into integral education, where the three were seen as an integral whole; not as three parts that came together, but rather as a single whole, with the arbitrary segregation of heart, head, and hands just being used to support conceptualisation and communication.

Wellbeing as an Essential Goal of Education

The purpose of education to come back to that is who am I? Why am I here? And they do enjoy this experience of school life discovery, expression, and the joy in learning so when we started the school, we have stated the two objectives to start in the school. I mean for the public, we said the first objective is the child should be happy and the final objective is the child should be autonomous. (Anju[MGIS])

Children's wellbeing was considered important and **widely discussed** at all schools. Teachers emphasised the role of education and schools to promote both hedonic (e.g., where students felt good) and eudemonic (e.g., where students were driven by a sense of purpose) wellbeing of students both in the present and in their future. While mental, emotional, and spiritual health along with feelings of happiness, joy, and satisfaction were commonly associated with wellbeing, teachers also placed emphasis on ideas of acceptance, belonging, and freedom. They believed that happiness was thought to be brought about by, first, freedom to pursue one's goals and that the purpose of education was to free students from their own behavioural patterns and conditioning, external oppression, as well as social and cultural violence in the wider society. Several psychologists (Ryan, 1995; Ryan & Deci, 2000) have emphasised the importance of autonomy and autonomous decision-making, while the teachers extended these discussions to Foucault's (1977) and Krishnamurti's (2000) ideas of 'deconditioning', whereby students learn to recognise and counter 'societal conditioning'. Second, they iterated that happiness was brought about by a sense of acceptance and belonging wherein every child felt included, heard, respected, and valued for the people that they are. Several psychologists (Leary, 2010; Ryan, 1995) have stressed the role of relatedness, acceptance, and belonging in developing meaningful relations and wellbeing. Hargreaves et al. (1996) and Osterman (2000) have emphasised the importance of reforming schools into better and caring communities, where students feel a sense of belonging. Third, teachers emphasized the notion of '*atmasantosh*', a deep form of satisfaction by doing the best that one can, meaningfully engaging in the community and/or living in the community. This also resonates with experiences of 'flow' (Csikszentmihalyi, 1990), where one loses perspective of time as one engages in something that one finds meaningful and "in sync with one's interests, passions and the soul" (Anju[MGIS]).

Education of the Heart Equivalents as the Primary Goal of Education

[One] clothes the ideal or the absolute he seeks to attain with different names according to the environment in which he is born and the education he has received. The experience is essentially the same, if it is sincere; it is only the words and phrases in which it is formulated that differ according to the belief and the mental education of the one who has the experience. (The Mother, 1977)

The **most discussed** purpose of education were equivalents of education of the heart, including education of the spirit, for flowering in inner goodness, for being a good human being, and/or for psychic education. These phrases were generally highly localised and stemmed from the contextualised difference (the schools are inspired by different philosophers and have different historic traditions depending on their geographical locations). Teachers used different phrases depending on local contexts, school context, and philosophies, as well as personal backgrounds, albeit largely synergetic, referring to similar notions of compassion, kindness, and care leading to "good/better/wholesome human beings", "a balance between the inner and outer worlds", "living a truly sustainable life", and "harmonious living" (summarised in Table 4.1; Patel, 2021b). Moreover, all the teachers held that education of the heart equivalents were one of the major goals and '*swabhavik*', an obvious implicit condition that does not need to be stated, for example, "real education develops the heart and the spirit" and "education without values is useless".

Table 4.1   Conceptualisation of education of the heart equivalents

Conceptualisation	Key concepts	Indian educational thinkers
Education of the heart	Deep understanding of oneself, inner peace, simple living, being free, and not pressurised (societal or peer), experiencing happiness and joy, developing values, being empathetic and compassionate, becoming a better human being, and harmonious and inclusive living.	Gandhi, The Dalai Lama
Education of the spirit or psychic	Peaceful and harmonious living, emotional regulation, spiritual understanding of the self/soul, deep satisfaction ('atmasantosh'), balance between the inner and outer world ('samta'), sensitivity, awareness of beauty, cooperation in nature, non-judgemental respectful relations, oneness with everyone around, community living, and contributing to society.	Aurobindo
Education for inner flowering	Critical inquiry and reflections as a means of better understanding oneself, harmonious living, and breaking away from conditioning and divisive frameworks; leading to sensitivity and 'sensibilities', selflessness and egolessness, kindness, and care and compassion to others.	Krishnamurti
Education for wholesome/better human being	Developing values, critically analysing one's own self, behavioural and emotional regulation, responding as opposed to reacting, being open and sensitive to others, accepting others, compassion, and a feeling of oneness with all of humanity and community living.	Tagore (1962) coined "wholesome human being"

Adapted from Patel (under review)

They notably did not see education of the heart as an add-on, but rather as the fundamental and key goal of education, which also under-pinned the school vision for education, the school-wide systems and ethos, teaching-learning processes, and interactions amongst school members. Teachers frequently suggested that education of the heart cannot be brought about through singular sessions, for it must be embedded in the individual's lived experiences and relations, such that it leads to learning to live differently (for both the teachers and the students).

Eastern Perspectives of Education for Harmonious Living

Building a Focus on Harmony; Learning to Live Together Harmoniously

The teachers explicitly emphasised education of the heart equivalents and LTLT and how their deep understanding of these localised equivalents led to a different, more spiritual, vision for education. Much like various Indian thinkers they strongly called for education for emancipation, equality, empathy, compassion, gratitude, peace, and harmony (Patel, 2021b). While I started my exploration of alternative purposes of education with the goal of unpacking learning to live together and education of the heart, further readings, interactions with teachers, and lived experiences at these school led to the realisation that many of the teachers and thinkers were aiming for a deeper purpose of education, for example, education for harmony. Teachers strongly emphasised harmony, which is shared by the various Indian thinkers, for example, the "highest education is that which does not merely give us information but makes our life in harmony with all existence" (Tagore, 1917). Other Indian philosophers have discussed ideas of harmony and harmony through education, referring to harmony as both inner harmony and harmonious communities (non-discriminatory, inclusive, just, and egalitarian). I have come to understand harmony as being associated with deep spiritual understanding of oneself and the larger world, going beyond ideas of tolerance, diversity, and acceptance of deeper ideas of diversity-based oneness. Diversity-based oneness was suggested to include an appreciation of the uniqueness of various living and non-living things and a simultaneous recognition of their interconnectedness and interdependence. Harmony was perceived as something that both required active efforts and existed naturally. Active efforts were required to deconstruct various individual and societal conditioning to allow for more natural ways of harmonious living and being.

Peace, togetherness, and harmony should be considered active forms of the terms, which are not conceptualised as the absence of conflict, separation, and chaos, but rather as the presence of justice, commitment to mutual wellbeing, and consciousness of interdependence (Cremin & Archer, 2018; Galtung, 1964; Gharse & Sharma, n.d.; Morling & Fiske, 1999; Patel, 2021a, 2021b; Regnier, 1995). For example, Gandhi (Gharse & Sharma, n.d.), like Galtung (1969), differentiated positive and negative peace, with the former being based on the presence of justice, coopera-tion, inclusion, oneness, harmony, and respect, whilst the latter pertains to the absence of conflicts (between races, nations, religions, and castes). However, harmony and chaos do not need to be mutually exclusive, for at times harmony can rely upon dissent, separation, conflicts, and chaos to bring about social justice (Patel, 2021a). Additionally, harmony is per-ceived as something that naturally exists, but one's "social conditioning" (Krishnamurti, 2013; Krishnamurti & Martin, 1997 or Foucauldian "nor-malisation") prevents one from experiencing it. Hence, achieving har-mony requires conscious and active efforts to transcend boundaries, both within and outside/beyond oneself.

Practitioners in India have emphasised education for harmony (within oneself, with others, and within the larger society) as a major goal of edu-cation. They have extended ideas of harmony beyond human society to nature and even non-living things. They have discussed notions of 'active' harmony and peace, which were based on ideas of transformation of ways of living and being that foreground understanding of interconnectedness, social justice, inner harmony, and inner peace, and overcoming sociocul-tural violence, rather than a mere absence of conflicts, disagreements, and chaos. For example, "[I]t is like silence; silence is not absence of sound [but rather about tranquillity or being calm and at peace]" (Shreya[PB]). Furthermore, they suggested harmony and harmonious societies should not become about pacifist unity, but rather should include and rely upon disagreements, dissent, and non-violent conflict to allow for differing per-spectives to be engaged with through active dialogue (Patel, 2021a). They notably reconceptualised Learning To Live Together as Learning To Live Together Harmoniously (LTLTH). They commonly emphasised that, while currently communities do live together, this might be within unjust systems or with individuals isolated from each other and instead **living together in harmony** is more important. Differences of opinions, con-flicts, and separation are essential to community building as long as they are accompanied with notions of a commitment to mutual wellbeing, sys-tems of engaging in dialogue and conflict resolution, and embedded with ideas of *satyagraha* (where the actor and the act idea are seen as separate). These are further discussed in below.

Similarly, harmony has been foregrounded by various holistic education scholars and defined as learning to not just be in harmony with oneself and others, but extended to being in harmony with the nature (Cajete, 1994; Culham et al., 2018; Lin et al., 2019; J. P. Miller et al., 2018). This emphasis on harmony relates with some of the underpinnings of the Delors Report, wherein harmony was also mentioned several times and many of the contributors stressed notions of it throughout the report. Regarding which, Myong Won Suhr (Delors et al., 1996) noted, "Living together in harmony must be the ultimate goal of education in the twenty-first century". LTLTH extends the ideas of LTLT, social emotional and ethical curricula, SEL, EI, and peace education to include deeper notions of transrational and post-critical peace. It includes ideas of deep inner peace, harmony, community responsibility, and living along with just and equal societies. LTLTH includes harmony within oneself (balance between the inner and outer world), with others (meaningful engagement with those around including people, living beings, and non-living things), and across the human and non-human societies (countering systemic, structural, and cultural violence against others that one is not directly connected to). I explore what LTLTH means and develop a potential framework to explore this in the next chapter. LTLTH aims to transform students' perceptions, attitudes, as well as ways of living and being to move beyond fragmented ways of looking and relating with oneself, others, and interconnected communities of all living beings, thus moving towards an inner sense of oneness and harmony.

The Role of LTLTH in Building Active Democracies

LTLTH can allow for building harmonious communities, active democracies, and a compassionate world. Drawing on earlier definitions of active harmony, building harmonious communities require a potential social transformation, which could be supported by LTLTH. It would allow the communities to embody the following four major principles as a means to counter various sociocultural injustices. First, a commitment to each other, the larger community, and social justice. Dewey (1916) suggested that such a commitment to empathetic understanding and wellbeing of another would be foundational to building a democracy that is not just merely a means of governance, but rather a 'mode of associated living, a conjoint communicated experience'. Second, systemic and structured processes of dissent, empathetic understanding, dialogue, as well as democratic and equitable decision-making. Several thinkers (Dewey, 1916; Freire, 1970; Gandhi, 1968; Guha, 2016; Thapar, 2021) have emphasised institutionalised systems of participation, dialogue, dissent, and conflict resolution for all members as being foundational to equitable and active democracies.

Furthermore, such systems along with the aforementioned commitment would allow for the empathetic understanding of each other and each other's lived experiences (Nussbaum, 2010; Patel, 2021a). Third, social action against issues of social justice, with Indian thinkers having commonly proposed challenging oppression, transforming oppressive societal structures, and bringing about social upliftment as a major educational outcome (Gandhi, 1968; Krishnamurti, 2000; Prasad & Bilgrami, 2020; Tagore, 1929). Teachers suggested that action against issues of social justice need to be embedded within day-to-day living and not just through large movements of social change. Fourth, the ability to differentiate the actor from the act in itself. Gandhi emphasised *satyagraha* and while the literal translation means polite insistence of truth or sustained dissent, he called upon everyone to engage in social action and dissent against the act but not the actor/oppressor (Patel, 2021a; Thapar, 2021). Resonating with Thapar (2021), teachers held that difference of opinions and voicing them is necessary and a sign of a healthy community that is engaged in constant dialogue, irrespective of its outcome, where individuals may arrive at an agreement, agree to disagree, or simply just understand and explore a different perspective. Notably, Kamala[MBK] suggested that conflicts are inevitable and essential for the process of LTLT:

> Fighting, disagreements, clashes, [and] groupism. Until and unless you go through all of these and resolve them, living collectively will not happen. [Students] become tolerant by conflict; by learning to know that you need not always be right and that many times you have to live with what will be partially right in your view. You cannot have it's either my way or no way attitude. … If there is no conflict, if there is kind of uniformity, then it becomes like these religious mutts.

LTLTH is both a process of inner renewal and societal transformation. It leads to harmonious living and harmonious communities through critical and reflexive self-reflection, empathetic and compassionate relations, understanding of each other, a commitment to the larger community, and experiences and understanding of shared purposes (Nussbaum, 1997). LTLTH, fundamentally, involves emancipation of one's own self and others in the community. It would allow for freedom from one's own emotions, prejudices, societal conditioning (or normalisation), and oppressive behaviours/habits, while at the same time also leading the transformation of oppressive sociocultural systems, structures, and practices. Historically, education in India has been thought to be emancipatory (see also Chaps. 1 and 2) and much like Freire (1970), emphasising praxis, critical thinking, and social change. Regarding which, Radhakrishnan (1959) noted, "It is through education that we acquire the passion and perspective to fight caste prejudices, class privileges and group antagonisms. ... Education has to give us a second birth, to help us to realise what we have already in us. The meaning of education is to emancipate the individual."

CONCLUSION

The chapter has highlighted both the intrinsic and the instrumental value of education for LTLTH. I call upon the reader to explore education for LTLTH as a process of, both, inner renewal and social transformation. While education for LTLTH will help build more harmonious communities, democracies, and a global world, the teachers, various Indian thinkers, and I—resonating with Brighouse and Unterhalter (2010) and K. Kumar (2010a)—believe in the intrinsic value of LTLTH for its own sake. Furthermore, I call upon the reader to explore LTLTH as a purpose of education, rather than a set goal or a set process. I invite the reader to explore whether education needs to have a purpose and if so, what should that be? What does harmony mean to you, and do you recall instances when you experienced it as child? What have your experiences of education of harmony been like? How do you imagine an alternative educational system that brings about education for harmony?

The rest of the book explores whether and if so how LTLTH can be conceptualised and the potential processes that it could draw upon. However, I would like to reemphasise that there is no single path/way to LTLTH and instead it needs to be perceived as an overarching purpose with multiple paths towards its fulfilment.

CHAPTER 5

Conceptualising Learning To Live Together Harmoniously

In my continued exploration of education of the heart and education for togetherness and harmony, I questioned, "[B]ut what does it really mean? It cannot just be a constellation of descriptive words?". I recognise that these are complex ideas only when they are interrogated fully can a more nuanced understanding of them be acquired. I acknowledge that it may or may not be possible to completely understand these ideas, but I believe(d) that a detailed exploration would allow for deeper understanding and perhaps open other layers of complexity that are currently unseen. Treating these visions as just broad objectives, without a supporting conceptual framework or deep exploration, can lead to ambiguity and vagueness, frequently leading to it being systemically overlooked. Furthermore, it can also communicate the lack of its importance and lead to it being sidelined, ignored, or being treated as an ad-hoc goal. In this chapter, I explore the challenges of conceptualising education of the heart and its equivalents and then draw upon various international conceptualisations and Indian teachers' perceptions to build an initial conceptual framework for LTLTH. This can, hopefully, serve as a prompt for readers to deepen and develop their own contextualised understanding of LTLTH.

© The Author(s), under exclusive license to Springer Nature Switzerland AG 2023
J. Patel, *Learning to Live Together Harmoniously*, Spirituality, Religion, and Education,
https://doi.org/10.1007/978-3-031-23539-9_5

A PROBLEM OF CONCEPTUALISATION

A Broad Umbrella-Like Term

LTLT has frequently been used as an umbrella term covering GCE, education for sustainable development, peace education, SEL, conflict resolution, value education, human rights, and civic responsibilities (Sinclair, 2013). The use of LTLT as an umbrella-like term has led to a fuzzy conceptualisation without clear aims and target (Sinclair, 2013). Similarly, its Indian equivalents of education of the heart are also treated as umbrella-like terms, which are partly owing to the holistic understanding of concepts and reluctance to break these down into conceptual fragments (Gandhi, 1968b; The Mother, 1977a). The local conceptualisations are broadly referred to in terms of their ultimate outcomes, including those of freedom/emancipation, equality, peace, harmony, unity of life, and enlightenment (self-consciousness and self-realisation). However, these broad objectives, without a supporting conceptual framework or deep exploration, lead to vagueness and difficulty when it comes to translation into practice. Additionally, the extant framework(s) are ideological and not based on practitioner voice or classroom practices, thus making it even more difficult to translate them into practice.

One can argue that the lack of conceptualisation could be by design to prevent piecemeal efforts; however, the local conceptualisations were proposed as broad visions by thinkers, who were engaged in multiple pursuits and could not necessarily build on the aims further. These need to be unpacked either through descriptive and narrative efforts or through an interconnected framework. The Mother (1977a) endeavoured to generate a conceptual framework for education (in general), coining the term "integral education", to include dimensions of physical, mental, vital, and psychic (with the vital and psychic being akin to LTLT), with detailed discussion on each of the components. However, education for the psychic was still perceived and presented as something that could not necessarily be conceptualised, because it involves education for/connection with "greater consciousness beyond the consciousness of his normal life … what the human mind does not know and cannot do, this consciousness knows and does" (The Mother, 1977a, p. 133).

Non-describable/'Indescribable' Conceptualisations

Several teachers and local educationists who I met held that ideas of education of the heart cannot be put in words and "it cannot be said; it has to be felt". There were strong ideas of: (a) the moment it is articulated it ceases to be what it is. For example, one senior non-participant teacher[RVS] said, "[S]ilence is what it is. The moment you speak about it, it is not silence", while Srila[MBK] suggested, "The more you speak about it, the more you mentalise it, then it stops being the psychic. So [it] cannot really be spoken about, but just has to be lived." (b) There is no need for a definition, because one knows what it means: "[Y]ou do not have to define what a brother is, you just have to say this person feels like a brother to me and the idea is communicated straight away, which to me means that inside us we already know what this is, so you do not need the definition" (Atul[RVS]). And (c) there is a need to practise these (ideas) rather than talk about them: "[T]eachers are doing it, they do not say these words, but they really try to live" (Baren[MBK]). Jayanthy[MBK] expanded on points (a) and (c), explaining "in either case we do not speak about it now, because we think we should know about it [first]", thus linking to ideas of it needing to be practised and lived rather than spoken about. She went on to say, "[B]ut the moment we know about it, again we won't speak about it because there is nothing to speak about [as it would cease to be what it is once put into words]".

However, Atul[RVS] suggested the need for articulation when saying:

> The reality is obviously something in itself, but it can be expressed in words, and it can be communicated … otherwise we get into this trap of the truth is not communicable and then, what are you doing here [as a teacher]? And this communication that the 'truth is incommunicable', where did that come from? That should be incommunicable too.

Similarly, The Mother (1977a) notes, "[A]ll formulation is only an approximation that should be progressive and grow in precision as the experience itself becomes more and more precise and coordinated". As is evident, there is definite tension around trying to articulate what education of the heart equivalents could mean, which partly also stems from the overarching nature of the terms, difficulty in unpacking them, and the lack of research on them. Over time, I came to realise that, perhaps, there could be no one global answer as to what education of the heart means and rather it must be an individual exploration of what it means to oneself.

In this chapter, I draw upon teachers' voices to explore what education for togetherness and harmony means to me and hope that it prompts a similar contextualised enquiry for the readers.

Multitude of Incomparable Frameworks of Various International Equivalents

While there are limited frameworks for education of the heart in Indian contexts, there have been several international attempts at creating conceptual frameworks for some of the education of the heart equivalents, which make up components of the LTLT umbrella (CASEL, 2003; Dietrich, 2012, 2013; Goleman, 1995, 1998; Mayer & Salovey, 1997). Blyth et al. (2018) suggest that the spectrum of frameworks leads to a challenge akin to putting together a puzzle with pieces from multiple different ones of which two have the same shaped pieces. This, once again, leads to problems in translating frameworks into practice and measuring and evaluating already hard to measure competencies (Stecher & Hamilton, 2017; Unterhalter, 2017). In this chapter, I start by exploring some of these as a potential starting point to exploring education for togetherness and harmony.

In this chapter, I build a holistic framework exploring what education for togetherness and harmony means to me (the framework is merely a tool that allowed me to develop a deeper understanding of LTLTH). It is aimed at prompting readers to question and explore what education of togetherness and harmony means to them (rather than just accepting the proposed framework here) and aiding teachers in translating the 'fuzzy' ideologies into practice.

BUILDING A CONCEPTUAL FRAMEWORK

Exploring Extant Frameworks

Chapter 3 introduced LTLT as having the three broad components of discovery of the self, discovery of the other, and learning to work together. There are several synergetic international conceptualisations which could be used to provide better understanding as to what these components mean (Fig. 5.1).

Dietrich (2013), SEL and Goleman's (1995) EI share a strong overlap with the three LTLT components, while Dietrich (2012), GCE, and Mayer

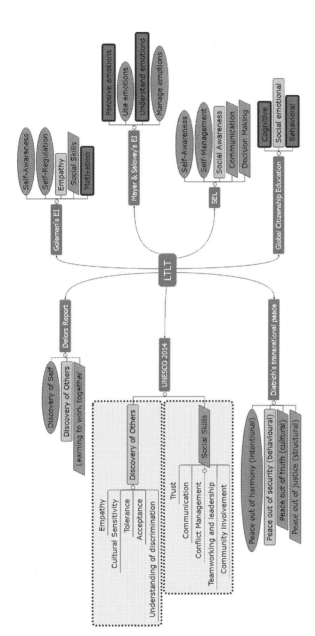

Fig. 5.1 Conceptualisations of LTLT. Taken from Patel (2021b). The various conceptualisations and their synergies: orange (elliptical), yellow (rounded rectangle with thin border), and green (parallelogram), respectively, represent discovery of self, discovery of others, and social skills, while red (rectangle with thick borders) represents concepts that do not necessarily resonate across the three components (Color figure online)

and Salovey's EI frameworks are harder to compare with LTLT, because they refer to dimensions that cut across various domains referred to in LTLT components. GCE discusses the dimensions of cognitive, socioemotional, and behavioural to include aspects related to both the inter- and intrapersonal. Mayer and Salovey's (1997) notions of perceiving and understanding emotions cut across discovery of the self and others. Similarly, whilst Dietrich (2012) initially suggested dimensions of harmony, security, truth, and justice, later (Dietrich, 2013), he built on the model to include intra- (persona, sexual, socioemotional, mental, spiritual, and transrational awareness) and interpersonal (family, community, social, political, and global) layers (akin to Delors' domains). In sum, Dietrich (2012), GCE, and Mayer and Salovey's EI frameworks propose dimensions, while Delors, Dietrich (2013), SEL, and Goleman's EI frameworks propose domains. Both the types of frameworks have similar aims and cover similar aspects; however, the use of fundamentally different perspectives, domains versus dimensions, makes direct model-based comparisons harder.

In the next subsections, I draw upon Indian teachers' voice to develop a novel conceptual framework. I develop a nuanced, interconnected model, with three domains (of discovery of the self, other, and the world) and six dimensions that cut across the domains (awareness, caring relations, sense of purpose, change in perspective, compassionate action, and meaningful engagement). For a more detailed exploration of what these domains and dimensions entail, see Chap. 6 in Patel (2020).

Three Domains

Teachers' descriptions of LTLTH lead to the adaptation of the original three component structures of LTLT. I make two adaptations: first, I add a new domain corresponding to discovery of the world (including the wider human society, other living beings in nature, and non-living things), referring to discovery of those one does not have direct connections with (the three domains are further discussed below). The differentiation of domains of the other and the discovery of the human and natural world resonate with many Indian traditions. For example, Dalai Lama and Hougaard (2019) distinguish compassion from extended compassion, which extends towards all 7 billion humans. This also aligns with Dietrich's (2012) matrix, whereby the "interior aspects of the individual" correspond to discovery of the self, "exterior aspects of the individual" correspond to discovery of others, and "interior and exterior aspects of the collective" correspond to discovery of the community. Second, learning to work together (at times also referred to as social skills) has been subsumed within the dimensions that intersect the domains.

Teachers generally perceived the three domains as highly interconnected; they believed that the various aspects were inseparable and interacted with each other. The domains were described as being in a continuous flux, whereby each helped develop the other, for example, 'using others as mirrors to understand oneself', 'extending compassion from people one knows to the wider community', and the 'conflicts in society are reflection of conflicts within one's own self'. Also, within the Indian context there is a common understanding that deep discovery of any of the domains will eventually lead to discovery of other domains, for example, through discovery of self one can realise the interconnectedness with others and the whole.

Discovery of the Self

Across the literature there is a strong emphasis on discovery of the self, with the Delors Report (1996) stating, "There is … every reason to place renewed emphasis on the moral and cultural dimensions of education … but this process must begin with self-understanding through an inner voyage whose milestones are knowledge, meditation, and the practice of self-criticism" (p. 17). Similarly, Dietrich (2013) called for internal peace and included an intrapersonal layer, while both EI (Goleman, 1995) and SEL (CASEL, 2003) place emphasis upon self-awareness and self-regulation. Self-awareness is considered to mean knowledge of one's emotions, strengths, weaknesses, needs, values, and understanding of one's behaviour. While self-regulation refers to regulation of emotions, thoughts, and behaviours to manage and redirect disruptive emotions and impulses. Similarly, various Indian philosophers have strongly emphasised notions of discovery and understanding of deep spiritual/'inner' world. For example, Krishnamurti (1981) stated, "[W]hat one is inwardly will eventually bring about a good society or the gradual deterioration of human relationship. … This harmony cannot possibly come about if our eyes are fixed only on the outer … the inner world is the source and continuation of the disorder." Additionally, Krishnamurti recommended choiceless awareness or critical looking (akin to self-awareness) as a form of self-discovery (Krishnamurti & Martin, 1997). Similarly, other Indian thinkers have frequently emphasised changing oneself as a means of changing the world, with Gandhi notably calling for being the change that one wants to see in the world.

All the teachers who participated in the study strongly emphasised the importance of self-regulation, with most believing knowing oneself as being extremely salient, while some went to the extent of saying that it is the starting point to allow for everything else. Teachers referred to a range of ideas: awareness and responsibility of inner and outer worlds, becoming a free soul, understanding the inner self or soul, finding who one is, finding one's *swadharm* (a purpose of life) or why one is here, self-regulation, self-governance (and autonomy), discipline referring to ideas of inner discipline or the discipline of the spirit, and understanding and managing emotions. Teachers also referred to self-compassion and inner peace. Most of these ideas could be categorised as awareness, understanding, acceptance, responsibility, regulation, and self-compassion. Education for this domain was brought about through reflection, meditation, discussions, and feedback from others.

Discovery of Others
Within the literature, all conceptualisations of the various LTLT equivalents have stressed discovery of others. Delors et al. (1996) emphasised the need for developing understanding of others' emotions, history, traditions, and values, further advocating the importance of building an awareness of the similarities between people and interdependence of all. While UNESCO (2014b) conceptualised it to entail empathy, cultural sensitivity, and tolerance. During primary schooling years, children may not necessarily be expected to understand the different histories and traditions of others; however, an understanding of others' emotions (empathy) would reflect discovery of others. Developing empathy at school was suggested to influence adult social life by helping people understand other points of views and avoiding the lack of understanding that leads to hatred and violence (Delors et al., 1996). Empathy can lead individuals to appreciating and celebrating different perspectives as well as recognising, understanding, and feeling different people's emotions, thus allowing for possibilities of working together and leading to experiences of shared purpose. Empathy is understood to have two components: first, affective empathy—experiencing and feeling others' emotions—and, second, cognitive empathy—understanding others' emotions and perspectives (Decety & Jackson, 2004; Feshbach, 1975). Empathetic responses can lead to sympathy (involving a feeling of care, sorrow, or concern), personal distress (self-focused behaviour leading to discomfort and anxiety), or compassion (motivation to act), depending on the activation of affective and/or

cognitive empathy (Eisenberg, Eggum et al., 2010). Compassion is brought about through a balance between both affective and cognitive empathy.

Indian philosophers discuss discovery of others in the context of right relations, referring to sensitivity (empathy), non-discrimination, and compassion. Krishnamurti (1977) emphasised an individual's relation with society and one's responsibility for establishing a 'good' society. He further referred to ideas of deconditioning (freedom from ways of being and living imposed by society), freedom from false barriers, and harmony across socioeconomic and religious divides. Similarly, Gandhi, Tagore, and Aurobindo (Gandhi, 1968b; Gharse & Sharma, n.d.; Tagore, 1929) commented on overcoming divides: class, caste, religion, socioeconomic, and national, with the potential for education to aid in the process.

Most of the teachers from alternative Indian schools described discovery of others as extremely important. They referred to rising/going beyond the individual self, sensitivity to others and their needs, 'right relations' with others and with the environment, empathy, compassion, mutual understanding, interconnectedness between people, a feeling of oneness, and developing a multiplicity of views (and perspectives). The ideas were centred on sensitivity and awareness, empathy (as opposed to sympathy) and respect-based relations, and compassion towards the immediate surroundings, including people, other living (like plants, animals, and birds), and non-living things (buildings and physical spaces). Pedagogical practices for this domain included reflection, dialogue, project- and group-based learning, peer learning, conflict resolution, various behaviour regulation routines, and lived experience of living together.

Discovery of (Human and Natural) World
Most of the literature on LTLT equivalents has primarily focused on the development of social skills instead of discovery of the human and natural world. However, I propose a new dimension, wherein one discovers people, nature, and non-living things that one is not directly connected with. There is a strong resonance with the SEE curricula (Emory University & SEE Learning, 2019), which introduced the domain of systems. Emory University & SEE Learning (2019, pp. 18–19) describes the systems domain, "We do not solely interact with each other one-on-one. In our increasingly complex world … [we require an] understanding of the wider systems within which we live." Discovery of the natural and human world that one is not directly connected with will allow for understanding the interconnected and interdependent nature of the world, thus fostering the creation of truly harmonious communities. Additionally, it will also lead to

the discovery of various issues of sociocultural and structural violence. Peace education has commonly emphasised the importance of understanding and resolving sociocultural and structural violence, with Dietrich (2013) designating two of the four components of his model to it. Similarly, several sociologists and Indian thinkers have highlighted the importance of understanding, dissenting, taking action against, and transforming systems and societal structures of oppression as a major educational outcome (Gandhi, 1968b; Krishnamurti, 2000; Prasad & Bilgrami, 2020; Tagore, 1929). Furthermore, it is important to note that the domain (like the previous one) includes the larger natural world; several Indian (Mani, 2009, 2013), indigenous (Cajete, 1994; Four Arrows, 2018), and holistic education (Four Arrows, 2018; Miller et al., 2018) scholars have emphasised the recognition of the interconnectedness with (and within) nature and the development of a sacred view of this.

All teachers (except Anita[MGIS], Joona[MGIS], Hema[MGIS], and Surojit[PB]) focused on notions of understanding a wider community that one may not have immediate links with. In different contexts different phrases were used to describe this, including 'a larger family' and 'a collective'. They referred to notions of responsibility to the inner and outer worlds, being good or responsible citizens, building or living as a collective or a 'larger family', understanding interconnectedness, breaking away from conditioning, community living, being proactively involved in taking community responsibility, bringing about a change in the wider world, and making the world a beautiful place. The ideas were centred on understanding of interconnectedness, influencing a change, and living as a single family with extended surroundings (including people, nature, non-living things, and ideas across various boundaries). Education for the domain was brought about through dialogue, field trips, adaptation of content to focus connectedness with the wider society, and integration of social action projects as an important aspect of project-based learning.

It is important to note that the framework goes beyond the anthropocentric worldview and appreciates/emphasises the importance of learning to live in harmony with the natural word. This is in terms of both the discovery of the other and the discovery of human and natural world domains. This emphasis on nature **within the framework (and not as a separate domain)** fundamentally integrates and extends our ontological understanding of the world as not just the human world, but rather a larger world, which human society is a small part of. While modern education system has predominantly focused on the human world, it is important that we not only learn about nature (beyond extractive/exploitive purposes), but rather learn how to live in harmony with nature. Furthermore, it is important to note that many of the teachers thought of the nature as one of the biggest educators (for more details see Chap. 7, Cremin, 2022; Patel & Ehrenzeller, under review); they believed nature helps students understand and experience a deeper connection with one's own soul, inner peace and harmony, and interconnectedness.

Six Dimensions

Teachers described six dimensions (awareness, empathetic and caring relations, sense of purpose, change in perspective, compassion, and meaningful engagement) that intersect the three domains. Figure 5.2 depicts the frequency of coded data, while Table 5.1 outlines the key concepts within each of the dimensions.

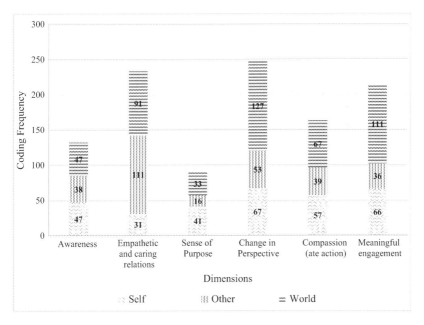

Fig. 5.2 Coding frequency across the framework. Reproduced from Patel (2021b). Represents the frequency of coded data across the 18 components (6 dimensions for each of the 3 domains). Wavy orange lines represent discovery of the self, green vertical lines represent discovery of others, and blue horizontal lines represent discovery of the community

Table 5.1 Key ideas within LTLTH framework

		Domains		
		Self	*Other*	*World*
Dimensions	Awareness	• Self-awareness • Understanding of conditioning and beliefs • Distancing from self • Living in the present	• Sensitivity • Empathetic understanding • Awareness of prejudices • Distancing from self	• Unrestricted sensitivity across boundaries • Cultural diversities • Interconnectedness
	Empathetic and caring relations	• Non-judgemental acceptance • Patience	• Non-judgemental acceptance • Care • Mutual love and respect • Not imposing/being imposed on	• Equity • Care • Individuality within communities • Teamworking and communication • Not imposing/being imposed upon
	Sense of purpose	• Sense of purpose (quest for happiness/inner self) • *Swadharm* (inner purpose) • Responsibility of self	• Empathy • Similarity between people • Family-like relations	• A sense of purpose for the collective • Kinship; one family • Doing something because it's right

Dimensions		Domains		
		Self	Other	World
Dimensions	Change in Perspective	• Identity • Who am I? • Critical self-reflection • Balance between inner and outer worlds • Impermanence (*anityata*) • Understanding the cycle of emotions • 'Minisculity' of problems	• Appreciating multifaceted identities • I to other (or us) • Appreciating and celebrating diversity • Similarity between people • Others' perspective • Illusion of separation • Impermanence	• Absence of prejudices and stereotypes • I to we (mine to ours) • Ideological plurality • Diversity-based oneness (seeing the beauty in the diversity) • Common humanity • Interdependence • Impermanence • Respecting different paths
	Compassionate action	• Self-regulation and self-governance • Deconditioning • Self-compassion • Self-transformation • Dissolving the ego	• Compassion • Helping others • Responding (non-reaction) • Gratitude • Self-transformation	• *Sewa* (social/divine work) and uplifting others • Peacebuilding • Community responsibility
	Meaningful engagement	• Inner joy, peace, satisfaction, and harmony • Connection with *paramatma*/soul • Equanimity (*upeksha*) and balance (*samata*) • Transcending divisive perspectives	• Meaningful relations • Engaging as equals • Unconditional love (loving kindness; *metta*) • Transcending boundaries of the self and other (oneness) • Open-hearted • Non-attachment	• Community living and onus • Extended compassion (wishing everyone is free of suffering; *karuna*) • Empathetic joy (*mudita*; finding joy in that of others' joy or sharing one's joy with others) • Universal oneness/brotherhood

Adopted from Patel (2021b)

Awareness

Teachers suggested awareness to include aspects of 'empathetic understanding', for example, deep understanding based on empathetic relations. Regarding which, Kamala[MBK] stated, "I wish ... we could be little more open to each other's needs without the other person saying so". Teachers frequently also discussed notions of unrestricted sensitivity (unrestricted by national, geographical, political, religious, and socio-economic boundaries) as seeing beyond 'superficial' or 'man-made divides'. This was described as helping students understand similarities and differences between groups as well as multiple perspectives of vastly different people in society as shades of grey, with none of them being correct or incorrect. In addition, this included an understanding of the possibility of various strands of the different perspectives, ideas, behaviours, and actions also being present in one's own self. The teachers fundamentally held that students need to understand interconnectedness and learn to see things holistically beyond 'arbitrary' divides. For example, Atul[RVS] commented:

> Sometimes we have designed things so poorly that lots of connections are invisible. See, like many city children, they have no idea where milk comes from. It comes from the door in the morning, where the milkman hangs the carton and he goes, Cows give us milk, no cow gives us milk, **we take** the milk ... They should know that cows are milked, and you do not get milk just like that. And [similarly when we ask where water comes from, children will respond] water comes from the tap.

This resonates with Rosenberg and Cullen (2013), who stressed that compassion, care, and concern all begin with awareness, sensitivity to others, and mindfulness. Similarly, Nussbaum (2010) emphasised three key values of citizenship (education) that can be encompassed in the awareness dimension: (a) critical thought about one's own tradition; (b) narrative imagination (described as being able to put oneself in another's shoes); and (c) understanding oneself as a member of a heterogeneous nation. I conceptualise awareness as going beyond awareness of one's own emotions to resonate more with Krishnamurti (2000), who emphasised the need for understanding the social, economic, and political systems that condition one's consciousness and behaviours.

Empathetic and Caring Relations

Teachers placed emphasis on relations based on care, respect, trust, and love. A leader at Rishi Valley School noted, "Good education focuses on developing the right relations with others [and] with environment". Meanwhile, Kamala[MBK] held relations to be central to LTLTH, as

> (Togetherness) is not something that will be built by imposition. It has to come by building each individual's faith and trust in being themselves and adjusting to the others [and] respect[ing other]. Lots of work has to be done in doing that kind building mutual respect in each person, which is not just for show, but genuine.

Teachers frequently emphasised: (a) not judging oneself, others, and groups of people harshly for actions and identities as people have a multi-faceted identity, which keeps changing; (b) not judging the actor, but the act, in resonance with Gandhian ideas of 'hate the sin but love the sinner'; and (c) not making definitive statements as everything keeps changing. Ideas of non-discriminatory and non-judgemental relations were extended to the wider community through notions of egalitarianism, equity, appreciating (and celebrating) differences, and transcending arbitrary divides between people.

Schools in India generally embody notions of competition, comparisons, and discrimination; however, the sampled schools aimed to build an environment of cooperation, where throughout the 10 months of field-work, competition was only referred to once (that too a competition to save water during a past drought). Competition was generally perceived as (a) blinding, as Anju[MGIS] shared, "if you view the others as competition then … you are going to be in this dog world"; and (b) leading to loss of wellbeing and self-esteem, with Tanuj[RVS] explaining how "competition can make them lose their sense of wellbeing easily. Outward yardsticks become more important than their inner sense [of accomplishment and of learning]."

The dimension shares strong resonance with Noddings' (2003) ethical caring, Rosenberg and Rutsch's (2012) culture of compassion, and Freire et al.'s (2016) emphasis on humanising education, involving sensitivity to one's own and others' needs and aspirations. However, holistic education takes the role of relationship a step forward by emphasising it to be a key goal of education, including relationships between the soul, oneself, the community, and the Earth (de Souza, 2018; de Souza et al., 2016; J. P. Miller, 2007). Furthermore, notions of equity, mutual love, and acceptance have been discussed by all Indian education philosophers (previously discussed in Chaps. 1 and 2). For example, Buddhist philosophers talk about openness in *Samaya*: a vow to openness and acceptance to all situations, emotions, and people (Chödrön, 2012). Similarly, Tagore (1917) wrote, "[W]e may become powerful by knowledge, but we attain fullness by [empathy].[1] The highest education is that which does not merely give us information but makes our life in harmony with all existence. But we find that this education of [empathy] is not only systematically ignored in schools, but it is severely repressed." There is also a strong resonance with empathy such that it can also lead to self-awareness. Ramachandran (2011) suggests that the mirror neurons involved in empathy (Gallese, 2001) can 'turn inwards' or lead to the development of a sense of commitment to other's wellbeing (further discussed below).

Sense of Purpose

Teachers emphasised the importance of finding one's *swadharma* (purpose of life) and it leading to a meaningful and natural way of life. They frequently referred to it also as "life work", "divine work", "inner calling"—something that one pursues as a quest for meaningful life, rather than as a 9 to 5 job. Teachers suggested that empathy and a sense of kinship lead to a commitment to the wellbeing of others and the wider world. Anita[MGIS] narrated an incident, where a student commented, "[H]e is just like me. He also minds that [if/when] he is pushed", while Bharat[SF] narrated how students shared what they had, even when they themselves had very little, based on ideas of "how can a classmate go thirsty or hungry". Empathy, kinship, and a sense of responsibility (as opposed to duty) were suggested to drive action and bring about LTLTH '*swabhavikpane*' (as a naturalistic way of being and living).

Finding one's own *dharma* resonates with Moore's (2018) call for the care of the soul. He suggested that the neglect of the soul leads to being

---

[1] The original quote mentions "sympathy"; however, "empathy" was only coined in 1909 and sympathy was commonly used to refer to empathy around the time Tagore wrote this.

lost, not finding one's calling or purpose, and not feeling the sense of belonging. Teachers understood the sense of purpose and *swadharma* to be based on ideas of responsibility and 'commitment'. This taps into Sen's (2005) ideas of commitment and pursuit of goals based on others' wellbeing and interests, while also resonating with Tagore's vision for "a world where multiple voices were encouraged to interact with one another and to reconcile differences within an overriding commitment to peace and mutual interconnectedness" (O'Connell, 2003). Similar ideas of 'will to act', 'motivation to act', and 'empathetic concern' have been explored by compassion and mindfulness researchers (Berry et al., 2018; Rosenberg & Cullen, 2013). Berry et al. (2018) suggest that compassion is more than noticing (and empathising) someone's suffering, for it requires a will to act. The will to act also gets emphasised in Noddings' (1986) differentiation of "caring for" as "an act that demonstrates care" from her initial definitions of "caring about", which reflects "a certain benign neglect" that does not manifest itself in action. Additionally, the sense of purpose also forms the basis of eudemonic happiness (Niemiec, 2014).

Change in Perspective
Teachers frequently used ideas of a change in perspective referring to changes in ways of being, thought patterns, and attitudes, in line with paradigm shifts related to looking at 'a larger/bigger picture'. Teachers questioned who one is, one's purpose, and multifaceted identities of oneself and others. They believed that human beings are holistic and labelling anyone fragments them. Anju[MGIS] explained:

> (Labelling) is very dangerous, because then you enter a hierarchy and a gradation of intelligences [and] you are fragmenting it more and more. Human intelligence is a composite intelligence; I am not only left or only right, but I am also kinaesthetic [and] visual, and I am also this and that … [else] it becomes a bit simplistic and reductionist. And also, we are changing [all the time].

Additionally, teachers advocated transcendence of dualities and dichotomies, to seeing the world as a continuum with strands all existing in everyone. Teachers discussed interconnectedness and interdependence (within and across human and natural worlds); they perceived boundaries as unending, that keep fragmenting people until a single person is left isolated. Teachers extended these discussions of interconnectedness to highlight the role of every living being in the society, questioning structural and cultural violence, promoting an egalitarian society, and developing a sacred view of nature. For example, Aaditya[PB] suggested:

> There is of course one way of looking at a problem that is something that happened, but it does not affect me, so I am good. Then, there is the other way of looking at it' whatever happens I am kind of involved [directly or indirectly] and I am responsible.

Teachers perceived tolerance as limited and instead proposed appreciating and celebrating diversity. All stressed the need to recognise, value, and appreciate different ways of life as equally 'valid'. They discussed a **holistic (not just pluralistic) epistemology, where different perspectives coexist, complement, and build on each other**. This was best captured in Baren's student's comment that a "scientist may not consider Pluto as a planet, but artists do". They suggested that, despite the differences, there are many similarities that bind us together: across the schools and the teachers there was an attempt to foster diversity and maintain unity and oneness. This idea of a diversity-based oneness is quite different from notions of enforced uniformity through uniforms, bells, and predefined streams; instead, it is established through shared experiences, efforts of harmonious living, and a commitment to each other.

One's worldviews and perspectives, which are picked up from various experiences across time, underpin and inform all our actions. This dimension calls for changes in perspectives to more holistic ones, as previously described, which in turn, will help address problems of fragmentation and to transcend boundaries. These ideas of change in perspective are linked to Freire's "conscientization", Greene's "wideawakeness", and Dewey's "extraordinary experiences". Additionally, the understanding of interconnectedness and structural and cultural violence within human societies resonates with peace researchers (Dietrich, 2013; Page, 2008) and Noddings' (2003) "sense of justice for the larger community", which is central to extending compassion to the 'discovery of the world' domain. Many of the quotes on appreciating and celebrating diversity resonate with Giroux (1992), who wrote: "[D]emocracy is a celebration of difference". The dimension also resonates with emancipatory ideas of the Indian philosophy (*sa vidhya ya vimuktye*; i.e., knowledge that liberates). For example, Radhakrishnan (1959) noted that "it is through education that we acquire the passion and perspective to fight caste prejudices, class privileges and group antagonisms. Education has to give us a second birth … to emancipate the individual." Whilst Krishnamurti (2000) emphasised the ideas of deconditioning one's own self (freedom from ways of being and living imposed upon by society), freedom from false barriers, and harmony across socioeconomic and religious divides. Furthermore, these holistic perspectives strongly align with what several indigenous scholars (Cajete, 1994, 1999; Four Arrows, 2018) have referred to as change in the worldview to a non-anthropocentric one. They and similarly Indian thinkers (e.g., Jinan, Lata Mani, and Tagore) have called for developing an understanding of the sacred and interconnected view of nature.

Compassion (ate Action)
Compassion was generally understood as an action that results from empathy; it was seen as a culmination of the rest of the dimensions, which in turn also cyclically bring about the other dimensions. Compassion(ate) *sewa* (social action) was described as doing something or 'being there for' the other person, because of the person rather than for oneself. Teachers emphasised the importance of the underlying intention and whether it was to genuinely help the other or because one would feel good about themselves. All teachers discussed notions of self-transformation and self-governance as the basis for compassion. For example, Anita[MGIS] remarked "that's compassion—first that you control yourself; I do not care how [angry/frustrated you are]". Self-transformation included ideas of understanding and quietening the mind, freeing oneself from conditioning and eventually freeing oneself of ego. While, self-governance drew on notions of inner discipline, whereby the discipline was based on actions being driven by the inner spirit/soul as opposed to external rules. Teachers proposed community responsibility-taking as a form of compassion, where they contrasted responsibility-taking and building a sense of onus and trusteeship against duties, where the lattermost was perceived as top-down imposition and a 'burden', while the former two were described as stemming from a sense of love. Trusteeship is another Gandhian idea where teachers believed that one does not own anything, but rather is responsible for taking care of certain things. The word was associated with material things that one would otherwise possess, including money, house, school, tables and chairs, water, food, so on and so forth. It was generally perceived that given that we cannot own anything and are mere trustees and that one must treat the things with responsibility. This is a different way of

living and being that does away with ideas of ownership and control, instead perceiving humans as transient caretakers of the material and nature. This ontological perspective is fundamentally also linked to other previously discussed indigenous perspectives and ontologies. This, in turn, prevented attachment, possessiveness, greed, competition, and misuse.

Compassion has been widely emphasised in recent years, with the rise of EI, SEL, and various initiatives for students and adults alike, including those in the global north, for example, Compa ssion Cultivation Training (Stanford University), Making Caring Common (Harvard University), and Cognitively Based Compassion Training (Emory University). The ideas of compassion as action, social service, and self-governance resonate with Dalai Lama's (2014) and Gandhi and Kumarappa's (1953) ideas of compassion through a sense of oneness, self-governance, and community service. Gandhi (1968b) and Tagore (1929) both contended that compassionate action is one of the crucial aims of education; they advocated an education that would empower and motivate students to bring about social uplifting. It is important to note that, for many Indian thinkers, compassionate action comes about *swabhavikpane* (i.e., as a natural way of living and being). Regarding which, Ramana Maharshi (1985) stated, "[A]s the activities of the wise person exist only in the eyes of others and not in [one's own],[2] although one may be accomplishing immense tasks, one really does nothing. ... For one knows the truth that all activities take place in their mere presence and that one does nothing. Hence, one will remain as the silent witness of all the activities taking place" (p. 137).

Meaningful Engagement

Teachers emphasised the importance of a shift in one's way of living and being, such that one embodies notions of inner peace, inner joy (*anand*), deep satisfaction (*atmasantosh*), harmony (*samata*), equanimity (*upeksha*), unconditional love (*metta*), extended compassion (*karuna*), empathetic or vicarious joy (*mudita*), and universal oneness. The dimension was seen as a long-term impact that may or may not manifest itself during schooling years for all children and at times be like sowing seeds of change that come to fruition after school lives (further discussed in the next chapter). There were strong notions of universal oneness, and transcending false boundaries within oneself, between oneself and others and between people. For example, Hema[MGIS] explained a classroom incident:

---

[2] The original quote used the phrase "man exist only in the eyes of others and not in his own" instead.

She (a fourth-grade student) said something like she is a human, she is not this or that [referring to religions] but only a human. ... I was, like, pretty shocked that this fourth grader came up with that ... it's so important to teach children to move beyond all these boundaries that everyone has in terms of they belong to this and that and maybe this larger circle ... [but] she was just like there are no circles and it's just like I am human; that means I am part of every group.

Teachers extended the discussions on community responsibility to community living, which was based on ideas of *swabhavikta* (a natural state of being), "people do good without knowing they are doing good" and to be truly alive means living as being connected with everyone.

The dimension draws on Indian and Buddhist spiritual values, which have also been emphasised by Miller (2010), in education of the whole child. Several eastern thinkers and spiritual leaders have called for a spiritual transformation, and while teachers recognised that these maybe life-long journeys, education could help 'sow the seeds'. Buddhist philosophy holds that compassion and wisdom are two wings of a bird, both of which are equally important (Siegel & Germer, 2012). Both deeply draw on notions of spiritual wisdom and interconnectedness, these also being emphasised by J. P. Miller (2010) and J. P. Miller et al. (2005), with their description of holistic education of the whole child. A key point to highlight is that the dimension, much like Noddings' (1988) relational ethics of caring, is not based on Kantian ideas of moral duty or conformity-based rules, but rather on love, oneness, and a sense of commitment. Aronson (1947) described Tagore's ideas of meaningful engagement as "fruitful co-operation among human beings based upon the awareness of one's own individual separateness and of one's responsibility towards the society in which one happens to live and towards all the other societies that constitute humanity". It is important to note that individuality, perceived as understanding one's soul, is not seen as an opposite of community living or notions of oneness. Teachers suggested a nuanced understanding based on the idea of non-duality, where oneness and individuality coexist. Moreover, the goals of discovery of the self, the other, and the world at large are related through people's responsibility and meaningful engagement with each other (Patel, 2021b) (Table 5.2).

Table 5.2 Learning to live together harmoniously framework

		Domains		
		Self	*Other*	*World*
Dimensions	Awareness	Self-awareness	Sensitivity and empathetic understanding	Interconnectedness
	Empathetic and caring relations	Non-judgemental acceptance	Mutual love and respect	Equity
	Sense of purpose	*Swadharm* (inner purpose)	Empathy	Kinship
	Change in Perspective	*Anityata* (impermanence)	Illusion of separation	Interdependence and common humanity
	Compassion (ate action)	Self-governance	Compassion	Community responsibility
	Meaningful engagement	Equanimity, balance, and inner peace	*Metta* (unconditional love) and oneness	Universal oneness and *karuna* (extended compassion)

Conclusion

The chapter has demonstrated the complexity of conceptualising LTLTH and education of the heart equivalents. While many of these ideas were suggested as broad ideological directions, the chapter has explored what these could mean by drawing on practitioners' voices. While the proposed framework appears to be neat (organised in a matrix), it has an inherent 'messiness' and opens other layers of complexity, which are further explored in the next chapter. The framework is aimed at helping other practitioners and researchers better understand LTLT, rather than being utilised as an evaluative tool. Furthermore, given that all models are a simplification, they break a continuous whole into components (albeit interacting) and reduce lived experiences into a few words, I recommend perceiving the proposed framework as a potential way to deepen our understanding of LTLTH. I hope that the reader takes the onus to see the interconnectedness, recreate the whole, and more importantly hope that it prompts readers to explore what ideas of education of togetherness and harmony could mean in one's respective contexts.

I call on the reader to explore the following reflective prompts: what does meaningful (spiritual) engagement mean to you and what can it look like within children? What would the framework look like within your context; how would you extend and/or adapt the framework? How can I overcome the limitations of showcasing complex ideas in 2-dimensional space? How would you transfer these ideas into practice within your homes, schools, and communities? How could you support a different, more meaningful, way of living and being that is fundamentally different from our more modernistic ontologies, epistemologies, and ways of living and being?

CHAPTER 6

Learning To Live Together Harmoniously (LTLH) as a Way of Living and Being-Nuances of an Interconnected LTLTH Framework

The popular maxim, "all models are wrong, but some are useful", suggests that all models are approximations that simplify reality into a few key concepts in the frameworks. Furthermore, it is important to understand what information a given model fails to convey and the implications on how it can be perceived and used. The previously proposed framework, while quite useful, must be perceived not as an evaluation tool or a blueprint, but rather as a means of deeper exploration, understanding, and contextualisation. While using it, it is useful to be mindful of its several nuances. It is a highly interconnected framework, where the various domains (and similarly dimensions) are linked with each other. While they are segregated to allow for a conceptual understanding, these separations are arbitrary. Any changes in ways of living and being will prompt a cyclical change across various other components in the framework. It is difficult to convey this kind of interconnectedness in a simple-to-use, 2D, matrix-based model. This chapter explores three major nuances of the framework, including its inherent interconnectedness and need to avoid piecemeal efforts, perceiving LTLTH as a way of living and being rather than a short-term activity, and educational processes and lived experiences as being seeds for lifelong LTLTH.

© The Author(s), under exclusive license to Springer Nature Switzerland AG 2023
J. Patel, *Learning to Live Together Harmoniously*, Spirituality, Religion, and Education,
https://doi.org/10.1007/978-3-031-23539-9_6

INTERCONNECTED FRAMEWORK

The inherent messiness within education for harmony allows for pluralistic and diversified efforts to achieve its broader objectives. As previously discussed, LTLT, education of the heart, and their equivalents have been perceived as umbrella-like terms. I have now come to see **some** insight in it being treated as such. Whilst umbrella-like terms can lead to fuzzy conceptualisations without clear aims and targets and difficulty in translating these into practice, it prevents 'piecemeal efforts' and instead promotes bringing about education of the heart as a form of lived experience. This perspective prevents any 'fragmented' or prescriptive efforts of developing a specific subject, expectations of linear learning trajectory, and pursuits of quantitative measurement. Shreya[PB] exemplifies this while expressing her hesitancy with defining education of the heart and creativity:

> (Like education of the heart) there is no definition of art and creativity; over here, the purpose is to activate the senses. The moment you define creativity you are delimiting individuals and the community too. By giving a definition of creativity, actually, you are limiting the notion of creativity. We just cannot fix a parameter and then start doing it. We have to let it be (and an understanding develops) with the time and individually (for each child). I think that's important for me personally; I do not define, I do not want a fixed aim and an objective structured position.

Definitions and frameworks can understandably delimit our perception of what education for harmony could entail and more importantly draw boundaries on what it does not include. Moreover, neat frameworks, at times, lead to the perception of singular paths to predetermined outcomes. Teachers believed that education of the heart/for harmony is a non-linear journey, without a predetermined outcome or a singular path (further discussed below). They believed that it was difficult to define a singular set of characteristics of a person who is educated to live harmoniously and instead they suggested a constellation of different characteristics that one may develop depending on who they are and their individual journey. They frequently believed that some of these characteristics cannot be segregated and are overlapping in nature and that if over time some of these are consciously developed, then the rest will follow suit.

LTLH Through Education of the Head, Heart, and Hands

While I primarily hoped to explore education of the heart and what that means in the Indian context, I realised that the head, heart, and hand were intrinsically connected. Initial analysis of the LTLTH framework suggests a connection with Indian notions of the head, heart, and hand, with (a) awareness and change in perspective corresponding to the head; (b) will to act and action, compassion, and *sewa* being associated with the hand; and (c) right relations and meaningful engagement being associated with the heart. It is understood that LTLTH would involve aspects of critical thinking (commonly proposed by Freire, 2005; Giroux, 1983) and creativity, while notions of community action have commonly been understood as the education of the hands (Gandhi, 1968b; Tagore, 1929). However, further analysis of the data suggests that all dimensions involved education of all three: heart, head, and hands, with Bodhirupa[PB] commenting that they are like three pillars of a given structure; all pillars are equally important and only when they come together do they hold the structure together. In the east, heart and mind are not seen as separate, but rather as very much interwoven, while the differentiated terms are only used as a means to conceptualise and communicate. As Gandhi (1968b) noted:

> Man is neither mere intellect, nor the gross animal body, nor the heart or soul alone. A proper harmonious combination of all three is required for making of the whole man... they constitute an indivisible whole. According to this theory, therefore, it would be a gross fallacy to suppose that they can be developed piecemeal or independently of one another.

In contrast to Descartes, Anju[MGIS] suggested that "Indian philosophy speaks of *Advaita*; it speaks of non-duality [and how the heart, mind, body, and soul are all interlinked]". It was a commonly held understanding amongst the teachers that practices for the development of any of the components are overlapping. For example, Surojit[PB] expressed, "Through arts, painting, music, dance, woodwork; it is not about the final performance but the process. It allows space for the mind's development. It creates a different kind of mind (creative, observant, and sensitive). Mind develops through hands." Likewise, in India, many frequently colloquially comment that restlessness in the mind manifests as restless in the body and a common way to deal with restless minds is to engage with physical exercise and sports. Similarly, in peace education literature there has been a noted shift towards integration of the various aspects, with Cremin (2016) suggesting innovative approaches to such education that integrate the body, mind, heart, and spirit. This, in education, means that we learn through our bodies, emotions, soul along with our minds. We need a holistic education that trains not the parts of oneself, but rather the person as whole. Various piecemeal efforts are based on arbitrary separation within a person and fail to acknowledge that the whole is much greater than the sum of its individual parts.

Interconnected Framework

The framework, as demonstrated previously, is highly interconnected. Srila[MBK], discussing components of LTLT, remarked, "[I]t cannot be split into parts …; you have to see things as whole and interconnected." Many other teachers also commented on the inherent interconnectedness of the various domains and dimensions. They commonly suggested that: (a) regarding the three domains, the inner (the self and the soul) and outer (other and community) are indivisible, intrinsically linked, and highly interdependent (e.g., self-awareness and self-transformation are foundational for empathy and compassion for others and the community, while others and the wider community can act as a mirror to help one better understand oneself). (b) The dimensions are interlinked and the development of one of these could also lead to that of others or a single teaching-learning process could target multiple dimensions. This interconnectedness across the various components of the framework can be demonstrated best by the following example. Schools commonly involved students in group social action (*sewa*), which led to understanding of interdependence and development of team working skills, which, in turn, fostered a better understanding of others' and one's own conditioning. This results in an understanding of similarities between oneself and others and a shift from I to we mindsets, finally leading to increased motivation for *sewa* and/or various forms of meaningful engagement.

This form of interconnectedness was embedded in teachers' own ways of living and being and their classroom practices. For example, Kamala[MBK] commented:

> I am blessed that I am not poor or not hungry or I am not ill clothed, but there are so many around me who are, and as long as they are I am also poor, I am also ill clothed and I'm also hungry, so I have to feel that pain and I

cannot wish it away, because I do not see it, or I am not in it. ... You have got to somewhere feel that you are responsible for what happened. It's not that there are murderers in society, and I do not know them [and therefore I do not care]. So, those people who are murdered are unfortunate and those who murder are sick and so they should put in mental asylum. No. When anyone hurts other, do I feel the pain? Am I troubled by it? Can I take away that pain in anyway?

LTLTH as Purpose of Education Rather than a Predetermined Goal/Objective with a Singular Path

The teachers made a further distinction, whereby LTLT was considered as a purpose, rather than a set goal or a set process. They commonly explained how there is neither a predetermined goal nor a single path, but rather a guiding purpose, which allows for both varied and a multitude of different paths and manifests in diverse ways of living and being, depending on students' backgrounds and interests. They believed that every individual has a different journey, where individuals may pick paths as diverse as themselves and progress through them at a vastly different pace. Furthermore, they recognised that, at times, this could lead to a seemingly distinct set of characteristics, and rather than seeking predetermined paths or singular or even measurable outcomes, they called for understanding individuals as a whole and allowing for individualised progression through their own educational journeys of togetherness, harmony, and spirituality. The recognition, appreciation, and adoption of pluralistic understanding of education for harmony allowed for diverse approaches being adopted by teachers depending on the students they worked with and who they themselves were.

In practice, this meant that teachers developed an ethos of harmonious living through shared lived experiences and teacher-student relations, created spaces for students to reflect and deeply understand themselves, created opportunities to engage and dialogue with each other and the larger community, sought teachable moments that resulted from everyday interactions, and maintained detailed qualitative behavioural reports for each child. This strongly links to the idea of promoting and preserving students' diversity and allowing for the pursuit of diverse goals and trajectories, rather than a monoculture-based approach to developing a certain pre-set value system through a predetermined singular route. This contrasts with increasing efforts to develop curricula with predetermined learning trajectories, and quantitatively measuring emotional intelligence, SEL, happiness curricula outcomes, and SDG 4.7 outcomes.

EDUCATION FOR LTLTH AS A WAY OF LIVING AND BEING

Education for togetherness and harmony, while overlapping with various international perspectives and outcomes, notably contrasted with several of them by being fundamentally pluralistic (discussed above) and not being about knowledge or skills, but rather as a way of living and being.

LTLTH as Knowledge, Skills, and/or Virtues, Values, and Attitudes

It is important to explore whether education for harmony is a form of information that is transferred, a set of application and understanding-based knowledge that is developed, a skill that can call upon, a set of attitudes or habits that one develops, values/virtues which underpin attitudes, what people prioritise and their decisions, and/or (a process of transformation of one's) way(s) of living and being. This exploration will underpin what LTLTH means, if and how a framework for it can be used, and how it can be practised in the classroom.

Internationally, the various LTLTH equivalents are fundamentally different concepts, which have led to them adopting different approaches and processes within the classrooms. The cosmopolitan approach (Oxley & Morris, 2013) of GCE focuses on building a knowledge set (of understanding different people in a global community) and at times values of understanding, tolerating, and respecting each other. However, the awareness or knowledge does not always translate to changes in behaviour or ways of living and being. Meanwhile, SEL (OECD, 2018; Trier, 2002), GCE within the global competence approach (Oxley & Morris, 2013), and positive psychology-based ideas, like grit (Duckworth, 2016), are frequently considered as skills (Chernyshenko et al., 2018; OECD, 2015) or competencies (Trier, 2002) that one develops. Moreover, as with any other skill one is free to choose to use or not to use them.

In contrast, character education has gone beyond these by perceiving character as a way of living and being. For a long time, there have been calls for education for character development and/or virtues (like wisdom, kindness, gratitude, and compassion). For example, in ancient Greece Socrates and Aristotle called for education for a virtuous and good life. Similarly, education in various other cultures has also emphasised the importance of character education, for example, Confucius calling for *ren* (love and goodness). In more modern times, Seider (2012) developed a character compass of moral character, performance character, and civic education. While such character values are difficult to measure and are influenced by many factors (H. A. Alexander, 2016), they underpin people's behaviours, passions, and choices. Similarly, J. P. Miller (2018b), commenting on holistic education, suggests that education should not just be about the mere transfer knowledge or building of skills, but rather should pertain to the engagement of teachers and students' souls.

Aristotle thought of virtues as a state of being instead of a feeling, capacity, or tendency to behave in specific ways. For him, character was about a way of life whereby one actively pursues certain virtues (like the golden mean). Furthermore, for Aristotle, living virtuously is a continuous process, where there is no one right answer, but instead one is constantly engaged in the process of finding the correct balance between two extremes, for example, the balance point between cowardice and bashfulness would be confidence, whilst between fear and fearlessness would be courage. He importantly suggests that it is a continuous process, where one does not have a pre-set answer, but rather the more one practices being virtuous, the more they improve at balancing two different extremes. Similarly, teachers suggested that for education for harmony, this does not have a pre-set answer or path and instead is a continued exploration and engagement in trying to live harmoniously; this in turn will lead to a more nuanced understanding and decision-making, opening new planes of complexity, and transcending from pursuit of outcomes to pursuit of processes.

Whilst LTLTH draws upon some aspects of knowledge and skills, it goes beyond this to a way of a living and being, much like education for virtues. It goes beyond a mere understanding of facts, ability to do things, or behavioural patterns. A simple example can be taken through any of the commonly experienced emotions, let us say anger. One can have the full knowledge and understanding of why one should not get angry, its ill impact on others and oneself, and its limited 'usefulness' and yet still one does get angry. Someone might have certain skills to regulate their emotions, for example, deep breathing, however, if and when triggered, they may not always be able to apply the skills. Instead, LTLTH would call for a shift in change of living and being to more empathetic, loving, and compassionate ways of living and being. Similarly, in one of my reflections I recently noted:

> I was preparing for a lecture for a set of undergraduate students. I had finished sooner than I had anticipated and had at least two hours before the lecture to eat lunch and cycle to the faculty. I was not keen on getting another task done in the meantime and decided to slow down. As I was having lunch, I reflected on the nature of slow living; I have known, believed in, discussed, and shared about the benefits of slow living, but the past fortnight had been extremely busy, such that I hadn't had any chance to live it. Over lunch, I was finally practising slow living just as a technique or a small part of my daily life; it was wonderful—I became more aware of what I was eating and, later as I was cycling, I became aware and connected to the various chirping birds, the trees, and the way that a stream meandered through the meadows. I felt more like myself and was closer to the present moment. I had several insights, including for the lecture, this book, and a teachers' community of practice that I support. However, I was quick to get lost in my regular rushed way of living and being when I did the dishes, packed my bag and walked through the faculty. Perhaps, I had just used slow living as a technique (and that too arguably imperfectly) to slow down a bit, but it did not transcend into a way of living and being.

Education for harmony is highly process-oriented and is aimed at bringing about a different way of living and being 24×7 rather than over short durations of time. Its process-oriented focus can be observed, firstly, in terms of its conceptualisation. Regarding which, Delors (1996) foregrounded processes and experiences by suggesting it should involve discovery of the self and others and experiences of shared purpose. Teachers described it as entailing notions of discovery, lived experiences, building relations, meaningful engagement, and a way of living.

A Non-dualist Approach to LTLTH as a Way of Living

Advaita emphasises non-duality and I have previously highlighted how it is difficult to separate the head, heart, and hands and similarly it is equally difficult to segregate the various interconnected components of the LTLTH framework. Furthermore, in Chap. 4 I explored the role of chaos, disagreements, dissent, and conflict within harmony. This can also be extended to deeper ideas of spiritualism, as Suzuki put it:

If śūnyatā (nothingness) denies or rejects everything, tathatā (suchness) accepts and upholds everything; the two concepts may be considered as opposing each other, but it is the Buddhist idea that they are not contradictory. ... In truth, tathatā is śūnyatā, and śūnyatā is tathatā; things are tathatā because of their being śūnyatā.

Therefore, LTLTH goes beyond notions of various perceived opposites, and it is important to note that education for harmony is not about transcendence of our current reality, but rather a complete experience and flowering of humanity.

Teachers frequently championed and practised LTLTH as a way of life. However, this raises an even more pertinent question how does one 'live differently' or rather, how does one 'live more holistically'? In my own spiritual journey, I have always questioned "how does one really transform one's ways of living and being?" and found it to be extremely difficult. In India, scriptures recognise that there are numerous spiritual paths that can broadly be categorised into four types: *dhyana yoga, gyana yoga, karma yoga,* and *bhakti yoga.* I have personally come to believe that one needs to develop an understanding of all four paths at some point of time in their own journeys. While I recognise that each of these paths lead to short-term spiritual experiences, I believe the real question is about how does one live/be differently 24×7, as their natural way of living and being. I can perhaps exemplify this from one of my own reflections of my past few years. Within my exploration of the *karma yoga,* I started with the belief that I was a *nimit* (medium) for a larger energy (which I tend to refer to as existence/universe) to bring about a change in the world around, the team involved, and myself. Luckily, I haven't struggled with associating the times when we experienced some modicum of 'success' (again I question what success really means, but I resort to using the term to allow for a more pertinent reflection) with it being driven by the 'universe'/'existence' rather than perceiving myself as the doer. However, whenever I have struggled and faced challenges, especially with the pandemic, or fell short of my own arbitrary measures of success, I have been quick to lose my internal harmony. I re-established (or found) the harmony over time; sometimes it took a handful of moments and at other times months. I would rely upon various tools, including reasoning, reflection, reminding myself of being the *nimit* (and not the doer), meditation, and/or insights from the meditations/the higher intellect. However, maintaining, finding, and re-establishing (whatever we might want to call it) my sense of harmony required a constant conscious effort as opposed to it being a natural way of living and being. This contrasts with my observations of *Brahmavedantji* (the spiritual leader from the ashram I have spent a considerable part of my life at), who truly embodied various ideas of harmonious living in his own ways of living and being. I imagine he would have pushed me to stay engaged in the process, rather than looking at the outcomes, questioned my narrow perceptions of what I understand as success or lack thereof, and have suggested that perhaps even completely unsuccessful attempts (including processes and outcomes) might have various ripple effects, and pushed me not to get bogged down in moments of paralysis. I imagine that each of us must individually explore, if and how, we can truly transform ourselves and our ways of living and being.

Teachers called for LTLTH to be a way of living and being (both for themselves and for their students), whereby it would not be practised for short spans, intermittently, but rather, something that was practised every moment. Teachers **consciously tried** to practise aspects of LTLTH in their daily lives (further discussed in Chap. 9). One school administrator-[RVS] asserted that "teachers require a constant inward gaze", while many teachers referred to the ideas of "it has to be a way of life" and "the philosophy of LTLTH has to be a living thing and should not become an ideology". Similarly, Lange (2004), discussing transformative learning theories, suggested that perspectives of interconnectedness between oneself, the wider community, and nature need to extend beyond epistemological processes (changes in worldview) to ontological ones (changes in ways of being). This resonates with Aristotle, who suggested that living virtuously is not a mere process of habituation, but rather a process wherein one enjoys living virtuously. Furthermore, indigenous education revolves around changes in ways of being by focusing on establishing and maintaining relationships with oneself, the community or tribe, and physical place/space (Cajete, 1994). Similarly, LTLTH, as a way of life, resonates with Noddings' (2003) notions of cultures/ethos of care and Rosenberg et al.'s (2015) cultures of compassion, where they called for these ideas to be embedded and embodied in the classroom ethos and various lived experiences.

LTLTH as a way of life leads to the interesting notion of "carrying peace and harmony where they go" (Jyothi[RVS]) and similarly a senior teacher at RVS explained:

> Now, another form of harmony could also be a state of being, rather than a quality ... because you can be in physical distress, and you can still be in harmony. ... [In the community living context] if you are in the state of harmony, then you would not perceive things around you as disharmony, you would start seeing the interconnectedness of things over time and you would see this is how it is.

In this regard, peace is not seen as a momentary experience, but rather as a state of being that one is in, holds on to, and carries with him/her. Teachers suggested that people can embody values 24×7 to the extent that they become synonymous with these values. This resonates with Krishnamurti and Osho's ideas of "Do not shake, but become shaking" and "Do not love, be love", while also being reflected in common language in terms of the use of phrases like "be happy" and "are you happy?" as opposed to "are you feeling happy/happiness?". LTLTH as a way of life was also captured in notions of (a) *swabhavik* (natural response), (b) in "doing good without knowing they were doing something good" (Senior teacher[RVS]), and (c) a sense of commitment bringing about togetherness and compassionate as opposed to actions due to a sense of duty or responsibility. For example, "the tree naturally knows when to shed leaves, no one needs to tell it to do so, it is not doing so to put on a show for anyone" (Santharam[RVS]). This idea of a natural response was also captured in "[c]hoiceless awareness—there is no choice but to be aware; you are aware all the time and hence, it is not a choice; there is no other way of being that you can live by" (Senior teacher[RVS] quoting Krishnamurti).

A Different Non-anthropocentric Epistemology

The current educational systems are based on a modernist, consumerist, universalist, and anthropocentric epistemology. While I have previously already discussed the origins of the modern education system, LTLTH calls for a fundamentally different ontological and epistemological approach to education. For example, western approaches towards the nature have usually entailed seeing the natural resources as materials to be exploited for individual/societal development: forests being chopped for their wood, mountains being mined for rocks and precious minerals, so on and so forth. These epistemologies put the individual/society and his/her/their interests at the forefront. These epistemologies consider others (including non-living things, other non-human beings, and other human beings as different) as being objects that can be ravaged, exploited, and polluted as they are foundationally separate from one and are there to serve oneself. This gets transferred to other human beings and even more easily across various divides (social, economic, race, caste, gender). This strongly contrasts with epistemologies from the global south, for example, indigenous communities frequently regard nature (including non-living things like mountains, rivers, lakes, oceans, stars, planets, and moons) as living spirits that, both, protect the human world and one should protect. Similarly, in India, nature and the earth have been commonly associated with being a mother, with whom the human society shares a reciprocal, love-based bond. The anthropocentrism and ego-centrism in the modern world is also seen in our language construction with phrases likes "I burnt my finger" as opposed to more indigenous ways of communication, like "my finger was burnt", or modernist ways of communicating directions, where colloquially one talks about turning left or right, going straight forward, or turning backwards as opposed to indigenous communication being based on going east, west, north, or south.

It does not matter whether the epistemologies are true or not, I do not believe it is possible to gather rational proof to support one or the other epistemologies. Instead, it is more important to recognise that children brought up in educational systems and communities with different epistemologies will be vastly different from each other. This leads to vastly different people and societies, for example, in the modernised society, faced with a plethora of adverts that drive consumerism and material gain learns to see buying and possession of material things as the only way to bring pleasure and joy to one's own self. In contrast, Buddhists had walls painted with prayers for wellbeing of all sentient beings (human, non-human, and beyond human). Similarly, Gandhi's Talisman was all about thinking about the wellbeing of the 'last human being'. Indigenous and spiritual ways of living and being constantly see a difference between pleasure and happiness; they suggest that the constant seeking of pleasure is one of the root causes of suffering. Instead, they call for working towards more meaningful forms of happiness based on inner joy, peace, and harmony.

LTLTH calls for an epistemology different from the current one underpinning modern educational systems. An epistemology that moves away from the current anthropocentric, modernist, and reductionists ways of thinking to those based on southern and eastern wisdom traditions (Four Arrows, 2018; Macy & Brown, n.d.; Santos, 2014, 2018; Sheldrake, 2018), which are much more holistic in nature and based on ideas of sacred interconnectedness (Cremin, 2022; Mani, 2009, 2013; The Mother, 1977a). Furthermore, western epistemologies have frequently been linked with and based on power dynamics, where they have frequently been seen as the only singular and (ironically) civilised way to live life. In contrast, the teachers discussed, embodied, and helped students develop a holistic (not just pluralistic) epistemology, where various perspectives coexist (with not one being true or untrue), complement, and build on each other; for example, Kamala[MBK] noting:

> The different paths, they exist. And to work in harmony is a call to build that beautiful weave between eccentric paths; it is the purpose of existence. And the paths are all [equally valid and] eccentric.

Seeds for Lifelong Learning

In this section, I apply the previously described harmonious, southern, holistic epistemologies to explore whether and if so how the framework can be applied to education. Teachers fundamentally called for moving away from thinking of the various components of the LTLTH framework as pre-set outcomes to be attained through standardised linear paths and instead, as previously explained, they called for constantly pursuing them as larger goals of education. In this section, I specifically explore the role of educational systems within education for harmony.

Children are Intrinsically Good

Teachers believed that students develop LTLTH through a variety of factors, including by birth, school, home, and the community (this was encased in a nature-nurture debate). Aligning with Rousseau, Froebel, and Tolstoy, teachers believed was that LTLTH is intrinsic, quite natural (*swabhavik*), and that every child is intrinsically good. As Jyothi[RVS] explained:

> There is goodness in the children and there is no doubt about it. Children are there for each other, whichever manner you see that. ... I think most times it is about preserving what is already there, and not bringing things which may obstruct that, but not to say that children are all angels [always], but those are different things, but there is goodness in all of them, and I think it's more about conserving that.

They believed that, many a time, all that was needed was actively limiting top-down suppression of children's ways of living and being. More recently, educationists calling for radically different educational systems have commented on pedagogies of no-teaching (Jinan, 2022). While such approaches can be extremely powerful for education for harmony too, I remain cautious in suggesting them for school-aged children. I recommend that as educators we try and reduce the 'conditioning' that we ourselves, parents, and the wider society may bring in and allow space for children to flower in the inner goodness. Furthermore, practically, children can form cliques, ostracise others, tease or bully others, be mean or harsh to each other and at these instances teachers need to actively work with children on LTLTH (building or preserving harmony). However, this does not take away from their belief that children have an inherent capacity to be/do 'good'.

Teachers' notions of children being intrinsically good were related with examples of children demonstrating sensitivity and care to others (all teachers), sharing even when they had little or nothing, and unprompted social action (e.g., RVS children cleaning a stretch of plastic-ridden 3 km path on a trip and opposing the school management's decision to separate the dining hall for support staff). Additionally, teachers also believed that, at times, students lived more harmoniously than teachers (they were frequently far more accepting, forgiving, and loving). I believe all of us, in one way or another, would have appreciated the children's abilities of curiosity, wonder, joy, acceptance, and love. During my time at some of the schools I was also struck by their abilities of intuition, deep reflection, and spiritual insights.

Seeds in a Non-linear Journey

Teachers believed that learning is not linear. Surojit[PB], quoting Tagore, suggested that exams and assessments can be pointless (especially even more so for LTLTH), because of the non-linearity of learning. He commented, "If you water a plant and then go and see if it has flowered, then the plant will have failed. It will flower in its own time." School leaders and teachers acknowledged and appreciated that every individual (student and teacher alike) is on his/her own spiritual journey and at different phases appreciating that it can take time, constant effort, and, frequently, it is a lifelong journey. While it might take time for the outcomes to show (if at all during school years, however, I found innumerable examples of students exemplifying this while at school), teachers believed that it was their responsibility to support the journey. There was a strong notion of just sowing seeds, which might flower or not. Regarding which, Baren[MBK] said:

> It's a starting point that teachers and schools provide and when the time is right, in a certain situation or when certain deeper existential questions arise, they would know where to start from. ... I feel these (lived experiences at the school) are the things without knowing ourselves, without being mentalised they will carry them for the future. These are the seeds; these are the sparks.

Teachers believed that these seeds flower much later in life and they shared instances of where school alumni had grown older and started to live harmoniously. Tanuj[RVS] explained that what matters is that teachers did what they could, without expecting any impact, which may come immediately, in the future, or not at all. The teachers believed that they had to follow their own *dharma*.

> Finally, what happens and does not happen is really [immaterial/insignificant]—some take it. It may happen with some; it may not happen with others. One just does not know. That journey is [unpredictable] ... all you can do is give the inputs and what finally is going to come out of it is not predictable—like, I put A, B, C into this X, Y, Z should come out of this. I think we can only say what I am putting in is the right thing, that can be examined, but not the [outcome].

I believe that spending multiple years at schools targeting education for harmony with teachers engaged in reflective journeys allows for students to develop certain understanding, skillsets, epistemologies, and ways of living and being, which they carry with them after they complete schooling. They may or may not realise it or even practise it, but it is always with them and should one choose to live differently much of the foundations are already in place to support the same. Furthermore, I believe it's important not to expect pre-set outcomes and instead to appreciate that every individual is on their own journey and that they will flower not just at separate times, for they will also probably develop and flower differently (from each other and the educator). I believe that education for harmony is a lifelong journey and about constantly engaging in terms of processes, rather than obtaining some abstract knowledge, skill, or behavioural outcomes. It is an ongoing process of learning, unlearning, relearning, experimenting, reflecting, and exploring what living harmoniously means for themselves.

A Fine Balance Between Letting Children Be, Deconditioning and Conditioning to a Separate Set of Cultural Norms

There is a fine balance between letting children be who they are and flowering in their intrinsic goodness, actively working towards deconditioning the ways of living and being children would have picked up from other adults and the society, and conditioning them into a set of values and beliefs that we as educators may hold. While I do not have a simple answer to what one could do, many of the teachers constantly reflected on the balance between the three: they questioned if, when, and how to intervene. They were wary of shaping children into one's own self or someone that the teacher holds as being a 'good student', with Srila[MBK] stating, "My thing for students is that they become independent; they become independent of me! You become who you are and do not become Srila[MBK]" and similarly Aaditya[PB], suggesting:

> What Reema is doing is something that is part of her swabhav or nature and one way of making her stop, it would be to give her an ultimatum. That way, she would be a very different girl altogether. … The moment you tell Reema to not do that, she would not be Reema.

Additionally, teachers and students pointed out that teaching for LTLTH introduces "a danger where teachers can act like spiritual leaders with spiritual knowledge that they might impose" (alumni[RVS]). One senior teacher expressed concern in this regard, stating: "Perhaps this whole idea of children should be sensitive is something that we are imposing on them and conditioning them with. There should be no should and should nots."

If and when teachers stepped in, they merely drew students' attention to different realities, certain behaviours, and patterns. [1] Frequently,

---

[1] For younger children more support was required while teachers frequently let older children be: allowing them to take in what they wanted to and to reject the rest. Teachers remained mindful to not impose (with the exception of certain non-negotiables). All teachers held certain, albeit a small number, non-negotiables (e.g., causing no harm to each other) and they put their foot down if and when, these were not followed.

teachers themselves were engaged in trying to live more harmoniously and they carried this energy with them, which, in turn, stimulated the same in children. However, it could be construed that what teachers drew children's attention to and their exposure to certain ways of living and being could be a form of conditioning too, albeit with different norms! This is where it is important to note the schools and teachers' emphasis on critical and postcritical pedagogy as well as that on the development of children's own independent and critical thinking. These can help children overcome any unintended conditioning by the teachers. It is also important to note and understand the cultures and ethos of these schools; all these interactions are embedded within an ethos of deconditioning and emancipation (even from the teachers), autonomy and autonomous decision-making. While there might be some degree of conditioning to a different way of living and being, the emphasis on independent thinking, autonomy, freedom, and emancipation appeared to have allowed for students to be critically aware of this and, hence, were able to choose what to adopt and what not to.

Conclusion

Education for harmony calls draw on Southern perspectives and requires to be understood holistically. The chapter has demonstrated that the previously presented framework is deeply interconnected and must be perceived from a harmonious, holistic, and interrelated perspective. Subsequently, I explored how education for harmony goes beyond narrow goals of the development of specific knowledge, skills, or character traits to transformation of epistemology and one's ways of living and being. I would like to invite you to specifically explore what does education for harmony as a way of living and being mean to you and within your contexts. How can/have you develop(ed) a non-anthropocentric way of living and being? Is such a way of living and being intrinsic or does it need to be taught? Can it be taught, and if not, then how can one support children in developing such ways of living and being? How would you balance the importance of deconditioning children and not conditioning them into another set of norms? Throughout the chapter, I have presented how teachers at the alternative schools adopted a similar worldview to their own visions, purposes, approaches, and practices for education for harmony. They notably believed that children are intrinsically good and frequently lived far more harmoniously than teachers, and that their role as educators was not necessarily to change students, but rather to let them be, to prevent conditioning from themselves/undo conditioning from others, and to engage in transforming themselves (not just as educators but rather as human beings).

PART II

Classroom Practices for Togetherness and Harmony

Lived Experiences as Teachers

Do we not already live together?
Do we not learn through the moral value and citizenship education classes?
Parrots sharing well-mannered greetings 'good morning' and 'thank you'.
But do we live harmoniously?

Perhaps it's a different kind of education that we need,
An education that liberates, frees, empowers and emboldens
From one's ownself and societal structures.
But how do we teach without caging the bird in a new cage?

Perhaps it's a different kind of education that we need,
An education that shapes gazelles, lions, peacocks
Something foundationally different from mice preparing for rat races.
But how can it done through a system designed to train faster mice?

Perhaps it's a different kind of education that we need,
An education that embodies freedom, love, equity, compassion and harmony;
Shapes a different way of life; a humane way of life.
But how do we learn to internalize these values?

Perhaps it's through shared lived experiences with trees, birds, animals and humans;
Shared pursuits of life-long learning for a different way of life;
Shared reflections, introspections and meditations;
That we may find the balance and holism of the yin and yang koi fishes.
~Jwalin Patel, 2020

This part explores how theories and philosophies of education for harmony could be translated into practices. I draw upon practices used by several holistic educators in India and hope that these case studies will help others to find ways to create contextually appropriate ways to bring about education for harmony into their respective practices.

I have been intrigued by whether and how education for harmony can be translated into praxis. However, before I delve into it there remains an even more important question: is it the role of the school to bring about education for harmony or is it something that parents or the larger community needs to do? In my own experience, education for harmony for me took place at home, within ashrams, and within our housing society (where my friends and I played outdoor games every day), while schools were a place for academic learning, to play sports (semi-professionally), and to become exposed to various forms of extracurricular activities. While I was fortunate to have spent my early childhood in a school that aimed to bring about all-round development, they, at least in my time and in my memory of the school, trained each part of the student, rather than the student as a whole. The stark differences between the school and experiences in the ashrams and at home led to several 'conflicts', where I struggled to understand how to apply my ways of living and being within the school settings. Over the 12 years at school, I came to understand that, perhaps, it was not the role of the schools to engage in education for harmony. While I remain grateful for the academic training I have received through several academic institutions, my experiences running an education reforms organisation forced me to question the purpose of education, the role of schools, and the narrow visions of academic or all-round development. It led me to seek out other, alternative, more holistic schools that engaged with education for harmony (and that too not just as an add-on, but rather as an integral and primary purpose of education), wherein teachers managed to integrate education for harmony in all their practices.

EDUCATION FOR HARMONY IS CAUGHT RATHER
THAN TAUGHT

There has been an ongoing debate around the character and virtues education: whether aspects of education for the heart can be taught or whether they are caught (from peers, teachers, parents, and the wider community). Many Indian and ancient Greek and Roman thinkers commonly suggested that aspects of character education are not teachable. Similarly, recently a colleague was reflecting on his discussion with a leading peace researcher and suggested that "[aspects of peace education] It cannot be taught with words and resolutions but rather has to be lived with examples". Social cognitive theory suggests that students develop behaviours, skills, and attitudes by watching others around them and modelling behaviours is an important aspect of teaching-learning processes (Bandura, 1986). Similarly, Goleman (2006) described the phenomenon as "limbic resonance", whereby teachers' own affective state strongly influences that of their students. Neuroscience and social psychologists have shown that emotions, like empathy, involve mirror neurons that help an individual "mirror" or mimic another person's behaviour (Gallese, 2001). For example, teachers' own behaviour is considered to affect students' Social Emotional Competency (Bar-On, 2011; Gandhi & Kumarappa, 1953; Tagore, 1929).

There are a wide range of SEL, GCE, and character education interventions, ranging from those that teach for the development of these aspects through a specific subject, to those that aim to integrate these aspects in curricula across multiple subjects and, finally, those that aim to bring about a school-wide change by foregrounding and embedding these aspects in the school-wide ethos. The question as to whether education for harmony can be taught or not boils down to how we perceive it; if it's knowledge, then it can be taught and if it's skills, then they can be developed. However, if it is related to ways of living and being, then these are difficult to transfer and, instead, need to be inculcated through facilitation, reflection, and shared lived experiences. I understand education for harmony primarily to be a way of living and being. Hence, while curricular interventions can be helpful, I would call for a more holistic school-wide implementation that goes beyond treating it as a separate subject or an add-on: one that foundationally integrates the emphasis on it across its various approaches, policies, systems, and practices.

All teachers commonly held that LTLTH is mostly 'caught' and not 'taught'. They generally held that students see, observe, and learn from the school systems and teachers' lives and behaviours. [1] They emphasised how they could only model behaviour, draw children's attention to certain aspects, and question realities, but its internalisation into their lived practices could not be imposed or forced. The teachers further nuanced the discussion on internalisation, suggesting that it might be dependent on their receptivity. For example, in a discussion with two senior teachers[RVS], one commented, "Some students are naturally sensitive, some a little more selfish; school sets the environment and provides example. It is caught and not taught; some students have the antenna wired for it." All teachers questioned whether teaching for LTLTH only impacted students receptive to it or all children. They generally opined that it is the latter; however, they contended that those who were inherently sensitive would benefit more.

THE PEDAGOGICAL PROBLEM

The alternative epistemology of education for harmony brings up several pedagogical challenges that need to be considered and kept in mind as we go on to explore potential practices that can be ad[o]apted.

First, education of the heart has commonly been proposed to be indescribable, immeasurable, and deeply contextualised. This leads to difficulty in not just describing what education of the heart (or education for harmony) means, but also, in observing it, let alone practising or measuring it. While I advocate against the hegemony of testing (especially high stakes and competitive), accountability-regimes, and valuing only that which can be measured, I recognise that it is important to observe the development of students to inform next educational steps. Recently, there have been several attempts at developing quantitative, universalised measures for various equivalents, like SEL and GCE, but these, inadvertently, end up measuring students' knowledge or the development of narrow competencies like social literacy. I believe that the use of detailed qualitative behavioural reports (by both teachers and students) can help understand students' ways of living and being as well as informing further educational practice.

Second, education for harmony is focused on transformation of one's ways of living and being. It goes beyond narrow goals of gathering

---

[1] While the book focuses on classroom practices, other aspects of children's lived experiences are extremely important including the school-wide environment, parents/at-home environment, and the larger community.

knowledge or developing certain skillsets and instead emphasises the primary purpose of education as being about drawing on knowledge, competencies, commitments, and attitudes to inform one's approach to life and ways of living. This is a much larger ask than transferring knowledge or training to use certain skillsets. It requires deep understanding of oneself and the student, the development of meaningful relations, and deeper engagement with the students and the educational processes.

Third, as discussed in the previous chapter, education for harmony has been suggested to be a nonlinear process, with individuals being on their own respective journeys and several LTLTH components manifesting over long timespans and frequently after schooling years. This has two implications: it requires teachers to make provisions for students to pursue their individualised journeys, rather than expecting the whole class to follow a certain set of pre-set outcomes and predetermined paths or for each child to develop, according to arbitrary, homogenised, common set of ways of living and being as defined by a curriculum or even the teacher themselves. In addition, it calls for educators to engage in the process themselves, working on their own ways of living and being as well as supporting students without expecting predetermined results. The seeds of harmonious living may or may not germinate and flower during school life.

Fourth, there is a widespread nature versus nurture debate, which questions whether harmonious ways of living and being are intrinsic or whether they can be developed. I believe that it involves both; however, nurturing education for harmony begs the question as to whether it is something that can be taught or can only be caught. Furthermore, it raises the matter as to whether it should be the role of a school to inform students' ways of living and being. I believe that this would depend on how we understand education and the difference between it and schooling. Education needs to go beyond mere schooling, where schools attempt to integrate parents, the community, and nature into the educational process as opposed to teaching being limited to short timespans, within four walls, with limited relevance and application to children's lived realities and the world beyond.

BLACKBOX OF PEDAGOGY

There are several programmes and interventions that focus on content and school-wide changes to bring about LTLTH, directing teachers *what* to teach (various curricula-based interventions, including Reimers et al.'s, 2016, Global Citizenship Education; Arigatou International's LTLT curricula; and SEL interventions like Social Emotional Ethical curricula, RULER, second step, and the 4Rs). However, there has been a limited amount of empirical research on *how* to teach for LTLTH. There remains a theory-practice gap within the literature for education of the heart and LTLT. R. J. Alexander (2001) and Hardman (2015) suggest that studying the pedagogy is central to improving the quality of education, especially in resource-constrained contexts. They contend that there is not enough evidence on teaching-learning processes, whilst Prophet (1994) refers to this as the "black box" of teaching and learning. This has resulted in (a) various global development reforms skipping the 'black box' of pedagogy and focusing only on access to education, (b) curricular reforms, and (c) reduction of teaching-learning processes to transference of the learnt concept, with teachers being treated as technicians (Istance & Paniagua, 2019). This book is aimed at identifying teaching-learning practices that can be used to bring about education for harmony.

Internationally, there have been some notable efforts to frame teaching-learning practices for SEL. Gillies (2011) coined the term "emotional pedagogy" as comprising teaching pedagogy, teacher behaviour, and classroom routines that lead to the development of Social Emotional Competency. Similarly, UNESCO (2014b) suggests teaching for LTLTH as being dependent on teaching pedagogy (Hattie, 2009; Yoder, 2014), teachers' behaviour (Power, 1997), and Teacher Student Relations (Perry, 1998, Hattie 2009). Notably, Noddings (2002), with a specific focus on education for care, happiness, and moral education, developed a four-component framework: (a) modelling—teachers model caring, behaviour rather than preaching to students, or providing texts to read; (b) dialogue—classroom dialogue as a means of critical examination of ideas, deep understanding of other perspectives, reflection, and teachers modelling care in communication; (c) opportunities for students to practise—opportunities for students to practise care within and beyond their classrooms, including community service opportunities; and (d) confirmation and affirmation—teachers appreciating something admirable in each student, 'confirming' and valuing each individual, as opposed to imposing a single ideal of high expectation. In India, teaching pedagogy and Teacher Student Relations (TSR) comprise two parts of the eight key indicators of quality monitoring tools (R. J. Alexander, 2008; National Council of Education Research and Training, 2003), while the National Council of Educational Research and Training (2012) lists ethos, behaviour management, pedagogy, and relation and modelling as four of the nine dimensions in the framework for value education (the others include school leadership, school-wide activities, evaluation, teacher development, and home-school-community partnerships).

In the next chapters, I draw upon my case studies and the broader literature to explore how education could be brought about by classroom pedagogy and ethos. This is also informed by TSR, behavioural regulation, and teachers' own ways of living and being. I explore ways in which schools can engage other educators—including the parents, the wider community, and nature—to transcend from being a school for young people to being a centre of education for all, and communities for harmonious living. I would like to draw the readers' attention to two points as they go through this part of the book: first, the separation of content between the chapters is theoretical but in praxis I believe all of them would be highly interlinked and interdependent. As Aaditya[PB] noted, "[T]hese components, in fact they very much go together. I would like to believe that on certain days, at least, all these work together, even if very briefly." Second, I find that all the systems and practices must run through the whole school and have to be implemented for both teachers and students. Given education for harmony is a lifelong education goal it is applicable to both teachers and students, alike. For example, if we expect teachers to emphasise autonomy for their students, then they themselves need to be allowed to make autonomous decisions. While this is beyond the scope of this book, it includes several instances that exemplify this.

A Few Examples of the Outcomes Observed

I have previously described the process as being nonlinear and like sowing seeds, which may or may not flower across multiple years. However, I would like to point out that within the schools that I visited I observed innumerable instances of students living harmoniously. Students regularly demonstrated mutual care and sharing, challenged the societal status quo, demonstrated a sense of fairness and justice, and were inclusive of everyone around. This had become their natural way of living and being, rather than their following a prescribed set of dos and do nots or being driven by fear of 'consequences'. Students frequently engaged in various social action projects, and these were integrated into their approach to life, for example, while on fieldtrip all the students decided to pick up waste that was littered on the 3 km stretch of road that they were walking on. Similarly, Jyothi[RVS] narrated how "children quickly saw that because it is a continuum … you cannot really label anybody this way or that way, but strands of all these exist in us". They were also engaged in a deep process of inner renewal, with several classroom discussions revolving around deep existential discussions or reflections on the spiritual self. This was demonstrated when students intuitively talked about the emotions and health of trees, wrote extremely deep and insightful poems, and wrote reflection notes on *andar ka dost* (the friend inside). Additionally, classroom observations picked up various phrases that students used, such as "we are all in the same boat", "*koi ne apva ma apne khushi thay, ane juthvi lidhu toh apne pastavo thay* (we find happiness/anand in giving to others, and guilt if one steals)", "peace will wipe out evil", and "life is nothing but an illusion". Similarly, students' art pieces included deep fundamental ideas of harmony of religions (a painting where various religions started from the corners of a page and met in the centre), the Earth as a living being (a 3D model made of pottery clay that depicted a landscape as a woman who nurtured the people and animals living in it), and harmony between humans and animals (a painting of a man reading seated under a tree and telling stories to animals and birds around him; which was followed by a discussion about how a tree, much like humans, also has eyes, arms, and a stomach).

CHAPTER 7

Experiential Learning Pedagogies and Practices

The schools and the teachers generally perceived that students 'caught' LTLTH through a continuum of harmonious lived experiences that were embodied through the pedagogy (this chapter), classroom ethos (Chap. 8), and teachers' own ways of living and being (Chap. 9). These lived experiences were frequently described as shared, being shaped by both students and teachers. In this chapter, I first explore the potential (albeit limited) role of content in education for harmony. Thereafter, I probe various pedagogical practices that can provide opportunities for education for harmony. Furthermore, I expand on this to develop a theory of lived experience-based (or experiential education) pedagogy that holistically integrates education for harmony in various processes. I emphasise that education for harmony needs to be integrated within students' lived experiences of the classroom, rather than as something targeted by certain content or pedagogies.

THE POTENTIAL (ALBEIT LIMITED) ROLE OF CURRICULA

Increasing Numbers of Curricular Interventions

Both formal and hidden curricula influence not only what children learn but their identities and ways of living and being. Frequently curricula have been manipulated and shaped to assert a certain national identity and has contributed to propagating structural and cultural violence through

J. Patel, *Learning to Live Together Harmoniously*, Spirituality, Religion, and Education, https://doi.org/10.1007/978-3-031-23539-9_7

excluding certain people, narratives, and ideas (NCF, 2005). And in contrast curricula can be made more inclusive, counter structural violence, promote understanding of root causes of violence, and provide necessary tools (NCF, 2005). Efforts to create more inclusive curricula that promote cultures of peace have tremendous potential.

In addition, many curricular interventions have been developed that aim to introduce a new subject. These have included curricula interventions across the various LTLTH equivalents, including Reimers et al.'s (2016) GCE curriculum; an LTLT curriculum developed by Arigatou International; and several SEL curricula, such as Social Emotional Ethical, RULER, second step, and 4Rs. In India, in the last five years, notably, there have been two large-scale SEL curricula: first, Social Emotional and Ethical (SEE) learning (2019), and second the happiness curricula (SCERT, 2019) along with its contextualised various equivalents. SEE was inspired by his holiness Dalai Lama and developed at Emory University, while the happiness curriculum draws upon CASEL and A. K. Nagraj, a spiritual leader in India. The happiness curriculum entails a daily class being committed to SEL and it is currently run across tens of thousands of public schools in India. It was initially developed by the Delhi government and a group of NGOs, having now been scaled up and replicated in other states.

Some of these curricular interventions conceive LTLTH equivalents as knowledge that can be transferred and/or skills that can be developed through exposure and repetitive practice. While education for harmony is primarily a way of living and being, it could include some aspects of knowledge and skills; and would potentially benefit from a specific subject. There would be a significantly deeper impact through a creation of an inclusive curriculum that is integrated with various ideas of education for harmony. It is important to note that content and curricula can provide teachers and students a context and structure to engage with and delve deeper into ideas of education of the heart, creating opportunities for training specific skills. In such instances, I believe that, rather than mechanically following a syllabus, leveraging various classroom-based incidents is more desirable. Unfortunately, in our current system, if something is not measured or emphasised in the curriculum it is ignored. It is important to note that the teachers in these alternative schools believed that education for harmony was the primary goal of education. While such an education may not be measurable through objective tests or assessments, its development can be tracked through students' self-evaluation and/or detailed descriptive behavioural reports written by teachers.

Limited Relevance of Content Within Alternative, Holistic Schools

In my study, there were a multitude of views on the importance of academic curricula for LTLTH, including it can be helpful, it is secondary, and it does not matter. The language teachers generally believed that content was important and they leveraged it to introduce new perspectives and bring about dialogue. However, other teachers opined that it was secondary, and in practice, they adapted the content to weave in LTLTH or they brought about LTLTH, despite the curriculum. Many teachers, especially those with restrictions regarding what they taught (due to teaching high school children), believed that the mainstream aspects were irrelevant and needed changing. Regarding which, one non-participant senior teacher[PB] said:

> Our curriculum does not promote us to care for our environment; they will study [about] bees' life cycle not of the dogs around; no history of Shantiniketan; no map of Patha Bhavana; students cannot name the trees around. … Maybe we need a curriculum that is flexible, that allows for contextualisation.

There were generally no special classes or curriculum for value education, with RVS being an exception, where they had 'culture classes': a discussion space for LTLTH. There was no predefined curriculum and instead the topics for discussion were determined by classroom incidents. Teachers generally believed that LTLTH-teachable moments arose naturally and that they needed to be aware and leverage those moments. Joona[MGIS] opined, "[W]e do not have moral science classes, which is also not needed, honestly. We will talk about values. No, it would not be there, it will only flow, something will happen in your class and suddenly you will stop, and you will leave what you teach." Teachers leveraged various lived experiences, classroom incidents, and other content to explore and delve into education for the heart. Higher-grade students (16- and 17-year-olds) regularly engaged with texts written by various philosophers; however, teachers were wary about this for younger children based on their reluctance to impose belief systems on them. There was surprisingly little use of Social Emotional Competency (SEC) language, a commonly recommended practice by various SEL interventions. Researchers and various programmes recommend helping students label and recognise emotions, while teachers (except for Anita[MGIS], who used nonviolent communication language tools) hardly ever did so. The focus/emphasis of the practices was on feeling, experiencing, and living, rather than labelling. This difference in approach from the global north could be attributed to a difference in cultures (India is a high context culture). Teachers also suggested labelling emotions as being very reductionist as one usually experiences a myriad of emotions and reducing these to a single one can do harm. Instead, they helped students holistically to understand how one feels and empathetically understand how others feel. Moreover, teachers normally refrained from direct instructions of dos and do nots. They did so only in rare instances, when students would have harmed themselves or others around them, usually through one-on-one behavioural (dialogic) discussions with certain students. These discussions were used as a last resort; teachers frequently let students be, provided different perspectives, and helped students to be aware of their behaviour. Dos and do nots were seen as a form of imposition, and as Srila[MBK] explained, "I also am not overly preachy, be like this or that, that's my expectation. I would rather want to go by children's expectations." Teachers, at times, provided reminders for students to be more aware of their behaviours and the behavioural goals that they had set. They recognised that, at times, students (and adults) could find it difficult to self-regulate and at these instances gentle reminders from others can be useful.

Stories as a Means of Real-Life Connections

A few teachers frequently leveraged content-based stories, especially for language learning. However, Joona[MGIS] and Kamala[MBK] weaved in stories around science content, and they and Surojit[PB], Shreya[PB], and Bharat[Shreyas] narrated first-hand experiences to build relations and real-life connections. Teachers contended that the content-based stories had to be based on students' lives, include active reflection, debriefing before and after the stories, and that the text must be related to oneself, the wider community context and other pieces of texts. The following interaction with a senior teacher[RVS] encapsulates the process of bringing in content-based stories:

> What [another teacher] told me [an incident amongst children], yesterday, it just gave me a lovely opportunity to take the story to class, but a story is never introduced without a few leading questions. I ask them the leading questions and then we move on to the story … [then] we explore it by con-

textualising it. 'So, this has happened in the life of a selfish giant, how does it show in your own life and in the life of others who are very close to you?'. So, that is my way of looking at the morals, you know, without directly talking about the morals. Sometimes you do not even have to lead them, when they see selfishness. There are always a few students who catch it and then, they say, 'akka sometimes I see in my own life'. … And then I do some reflective writing. It's easy for them I think to express their feelings in writing.

Teachers contended that stories helped them to grasp students' attention and to discuss practical issues within the class through their reflection (distanced reflection on the story and then self-reflection). The stories were a way of reaching the 'students' hearts', allowing for content to 'sink in' as opposed to students being preached at. While participatory learning was foregrounded in these alternative schools, it was not always possible to do so at PB, where the classroom sizes were slightly larger. However, stories frequently brought about engagement and active participation through 'narrative transportation', especially when interspersed with discussions (Sinclair, 2017).

Teachers were against using stories that were disconnected to classroom incidents. Hema[MGIS] explained that "if it is presented as okay, I am going to tell you the story and it's going to teach you a lesson about life and how you should lead it. Then, that probably affects how you receive the story, but if it's just within the flow of things or it connects to other things that they are learning about then it's a very natural kind of flow." Additionally, some teachers were vocally against explicit discussion on the moral of the story; they believed that the students understood the implicit meaning. Bharat[Shreyas] held:

> When we tell stories there is absolutely no need for a teacher to ask the students for the moral they have learnt. Every child takes a moral of the story. They understood the story and started crying; that is the answer, there is no need to explain it further. Shreyas is like this, there is no need to give morals as the environment is such, teachers are such, and method is such that it teaches things *swabhavikpane* (organically or naturally).

CLASSROOM PEDAGOGIES

How teachers teach rather *what* they teach is central for education for harmony. Comprehensive research has demonstrated teacher pedagogy as being the main predictor of teaching effectiveness and student outcomes

(Campbell, 2004; Hattie, 2009; McDonald & Elias, 1976; Sankar & Linden, 2014; UNESCO, 2014b). Research on GCE has recommended pedagogical practices for active participation, critical thinking, conflict resolution, dialogue, and creativity (Hunt, 2017; Lynch, 1992; UNESCO, 2014a). A. Skinner et al. (2013) emphasised the need for the participatory pedagogies that lead to active engagement and similarly research into SEL has stressed such pedagogies. Yoder's (2014) meta-analyses of SEL programmes identified ten teaching practices that are commonly associated with its development within six domains: (a) dialogic teaching; (b) cooperative learning; (c) self-reflection; (d) student-centred discipline; (e) competence building (modelling, practising, feedback); and (f) TSR. Critical pedagogy, based on Freire's emancipatory philosophy of education, has been argued as bringing about GCE (Skinner et al., 2013). It recognises individuals as being embedded in social contexts, promotes an open dialogue towards critical reflection, understanding of each other, as well as fostering collaboration between learners and teachers (Hooks, 1994). It emphasises learners' ability to reflect critically and change their lives.

In this section, I explore various classroom pedagogies, while the next chapter explores aspects of behavioural management, TSR, and classroom ethos. I found that teachers in the alternative schools in India leveraged a lived experience-based pedagogy by engaging in dialogic teaching, group-work, project-work, self-reflection, and meditation, as well as social action. Moreover, they drew upon an extended community of educators, including peers, non-teaching staff, parents, community members, and nature.

Dialogue as a Means of Bringing New/Different Perspectives

High quality dialogue is at the heart of critical pedagogy and research has demonstrated it to be essential for children's development in both social emotional and cognitive skills (R. J. Alexander, 2003; Skinner et al., 2013; Vygotsky, 1986). A. Kumar (2008), extending Freire's emancipatory and Gandhian participatory educational approach, recommends a dialogical education pedagogy, where learners (and teachers) not only collaboratively pose problems, but also work together to seek solutions to these. Teachers frequently used dialogic pedagogies (including for academics, behaviour management, reflection, and classroom or school-wide decision-making), where they prompted students, created a platform for different voices and perspectives, challenged biases, pointed out leaps or gaps in reasoning, and guided discussions. Many school and classroom decisions were democratic (further discussed in the next chapter) and involved an active dialogue between peers and between the teacher and students. A few teachers saw it as a form of balancing what would help students, what a given child wanted, and what the rest of the class wanted.

Teachers frequently introduced (sensitised), explained, and helped students in empathetically understanding different perspectives. Regarding which, educationist[MBK] commented: "Should we treat objects with respect or use as an object? We know how it's painful to be treated as an object." The use of dialogues as pedagogy, albeit a time-consuming process, led to increased student responsiveness, intrinsic motivation, onus taking, independent thinking, and decision-making, while at the same time it also enlivened the teachers as they found the process to be meaningful. Many of these characteristics of dialogic decision-making are demonstrated in a critical incident and its discussion in an interview with Baren[MBK]:

> There were seven presentations left. I asked Amar to come and write on the board. Amar responded, 'I will not come'. I said come, *aaja*, come, come, and write. He replied, 'Then why me?' I said okay, no problem. Let us do alphabetically. Then again, his name comes first, so then another child said, 'Bhaiya is very clever'. ... Then somebody says 'okay let us pickup chits'. So, Riya had made some chits earlier, I said 'okay, okay why chits?' ... I said 'stop chits, no chits. If Amar's name will come up in picking chits, then he will be unhappy, because he does not want to anyway. So, no chits and let us understand why we are doing this. What is the reason behind it? Is it to make [put/bring] you down or up? Now I am asking each one of you, so tell me why are we doing it?'. Everyone took turns and shared reasons. And then, without saying anything, Munira came up to write on the board. Next, Riya came up, next Amar came up and said, 'I will write'.

Teachers built a platform for new perspectives, by ensuring everyone was included, pushing students to find their own thoughts and opinions as opposed to 'chiming in', actively working towards 'group formation' (referring to classroom relations where students listen, accept, and understand each other's perspectives), and creating an ethos of sharing, questioning, and non-judgemental respect. The dialogic process also allowed for perspectives that the teachers themselves had not expected. For example, Kamala[MBK] reported, "[Y]ou know what this boy was just saying, 'what would happen, if firecrackers [producers] are closed down, to the people who are making them, what about them?'".

They created platforms for new perspectives through silent spaces, reflections, lived experiences, projects, stories/poems, games, and art-based activities. Hema[MGIS] suggested that the hierarchy of knowledge must be broken down to allow for building a platform for new perspectives. Teachers aimed to break down hierarchies of knowledge and create opportunities for dialogue and learning from various experiences, of one's own self, other students, the wider community, and other spaces (including nature). Teachers leveraged dialogic discussions to build connections with real life through circle time, storytelling, and the pedagogy of exploration of a text by relating it to oneself, to the surrounding world, and then to other texts that the children had used in the past. At MBK and MGIS, the contextualisation was inherent to the project-based pedagogy, with teachers weaving in personal stories and dialogic discussions. Dewey (1916) and Kolb (1984) regard critical dialogue and reflection as central to student-centred learning as it allows for new perspectives, creating meaning from lived experiences and transformation of one's ways of living and being.

Peer- and Project-Based Learning as the Core Teaching/ Learning Process

Srila's[MBK] first response to the question of how she brought about LTLTH for children was two words: "group work". Group activities engage students in practising and embodying cooperation, compassion, togetherness, and sensitivity. There were many group-work based activities in all the schools: groups of students came together to participate and lead an activity, rather than just large group activities wherein they were passively spoken to. These ranged from group work within for a single session (also usually cross-curricular in nature) to those that spanned several months and to those that brought together children across grades (e.g., at MBK students frequently collaborated on several months-long projects, sports classes, and shared meals). In addition, the boarding schools also had various student clubs that engaged students in group-work outside school hours, and group-work involving the whole school (e.g., students leading school-wide decision-making and assemblies, whilst another notable example included all students at PB creating a large mosaic work of art by sticking small pieces of coloured paper together). This led to a sense of collaboration, sharing, and oneness.

The teacher's role took the form of facilitator, who helped students to decide on a common project; created a collaborative ethos; leveraged different students' interests, skills, and past experiences; managed behaviour within and between groups; and set classroom routines. Teachers opined that project-based learning required them to build strong teacher-student and student-student relations, conduct 'group formation' activities, observe and understand the children, as well as slowly guiding them out of their comfort zones. During project-work, teachers were most actively engaged during the planning phase, where they helped students plan out the project, school-wide activities, and social action that could be integrated, discussed the academic areas' students wanted to cover, developed a timeline, and outlined objectives for a given day (usually done for younger or hyperactive children). Post the completion of planning, teachers took a more backseat role in the project, with students directing it and the former only intervening intermittently and focusing more on children's behavioural and emotional development.

Student autonomy and a sense of onus (further discussed in the next chapter) underpinned the projects and peer-work. The projects at MGIS and MBK were decided upon by students, which, in turn, meant that all teaching-learning content and the mode of teaching-learning were decided by them. At MBK, children discussed the skills, character traits, as well as the physical and mental development aspects they wanted to work on. This arrangement led to MGIS being able to hold two-hour long classes, with the students remaining engaged and on-task! The projects led to an integrated holistic education that transcended compartmentalisation of subjects. They often involved interaction with the wider community and were integrated with social action. Projects and student-work generally ended up being presented to other children within the class, members of the school (including non-teaching staff), and at times published as books (at MBK and RVS). These contextualised projects with real-life implications made the educational processes meaningful. Anju[MGIS] suggested:

> [First, the projects build independence] and children are doing projects that they would like to do. Secondly, to arrive at a state of peace and happiness you would need to do things that are meaningful and purposeful. If there is no meaning, if whatever I am doing serves no purpose, what's the point of doing it?

Meditation, Reflection, and Introspection Embedded
in Educational Processes

Teachers frequently called upon student to 'go inwards', self-reflect, meditate, feel/embody silence (physical and mental),[1] and referred to a need to
'respond not react'. MBK, PB, and RVS spent extensive amounts of school
hours, with school-wide moments of silence, prayer, and meditation at the
start (PB, MBK, RVS, and Hema[MGIS]) and end (MBK) of the day. The
schools also practised daily walks to see the sunset (RVS), silence before
meals (RVS), and class-based moments of silence before the start of a class
(Anonymous[RVS] and Aaditya[PB]). Herzberger (2018) emphasises the importance of silence and the silent mind especially for transrational education.
It is important to distinguish being quiet from silence; the former is a
physical act of being quiet, while the latter involves physical, mental, and
emotional calmness, allowing one to go beyond the mind and to connect
with oneself and others more intuitively or spiritually.

Teachers also tried to bring meditative practices to their teaching processes by engaging in visualisation (Hema[MGIS] and Anonymous[RVS]), slow-
writing/slow-thinking (visiting monk[RVS]), birdwatching and nature
appreciation (Santharam[RVS], Shreya[PB], and non-participant teachers[RVS and
PB]), writing reflective poems (Santharam[RVS]), and breathing practices when
class energies became too high (Joona[MGIS] and Anonymous[RVS]). Teachers
frequently commented that while they used certain techniques, they aimed
to transcend into the intrinsic value of meditation, rather than just the
instrumental. Regarding which, one school administrator[MGIS] suggested,
"Meditation has to be integrated, but [in other schools it] seems to be
used as a technique to manage classroom behaviour or for creativity".
Silence, meditation, or reflection was not just practised for short spans,
but was embodied through the day, which resonates with Lees (2017),
who when researching Summerhill School (an alternative school founded
by A. S. Neill in the UK) found that children were frequently allowed to
hang about, chill out, and do "nothing much", with these ideas being
embedded in the whole school all through the day.

There was constant discussion on the length of meditation or the silent
spells: some were short (less than 5 minutes, e.g., at the beginning of a
class or before meals), while others were longer (30–45 minutes, e.g.,

---

[1] Note that while a few teachers called for students to be silent, most of them called for
them to embody silence or be silence, instead of the physical act of being silent.

daily walks to see the sunset, and occasional visits to the *samadhi*). Teachers discussed whether the use of set times for meditation had become mechanical or if they played the role of a reminder to be silent and reflective all the time. They saw the latter as the long-term goal; however, the former was important as well. That is, the set times were seen as *riyaz* (repetitive practice; usually associated with Indian music) that helped students hone meditational skills and experience deeper meditational states. Some students appreciated these practices, seeing them as the best time of the day and sought to come back to school post-vacations for the silence (informal discussions with students[MBK and RVS]). As a participant observer at the schools there were some instances when I felt as if 'silence descended' across the whole school. In one of my ethnographic notes about RVS I observed:

> Silence literally immediately descends on the assembly. The students go absolutely quiet. And there is a feeling of silence and deeper connection that I sense. Perhaps it's to do with the mood/state I am in. Or maybe, the larger space offers this to everyone.

While in another, at PB, I noted:

> Many parents and students come early, and students keep playing around. But as soon as the assembly starts, they become [silent] and as soon as a small group of students start singing there is literally pin drop silence. This once again felt like a form of sacred silence that descends and engulfs everyone. At no point does a teacher ask them to not run or play around, or to be quiet. It seems to be a more natural way of being, where there is not an imposed seriousness of silence.

Lees (2012) differentiates two forms of silence: a weak one, where students in traditional schools are silenced and forced to be quiet, in contrast to a strong silence, where children have the freedom to be quiet or to choose not to do so. The schools emphasised the latter, as they believed that silence does not need to be enforced as short-spanned practices, but rather has to be felt, embodied, and 'developed from within'. This resonated with the schools and teachers' beliefs in students' autonomy, not imposing on students and letting them be. From my experiences at the schools, we need to extend this form of strong silence to a form of **sacred silence** as a deeply embodied form of silence that also extends beyond one's body and mind.

Teachers also emphasised self-observation, reflection, and introspection, claiming that these required the students to silence their minds, settle emotions, distance themselves from the self, and be still/silent. These practices allowed for consolidation and internalisation of values and conversion into lived experiences. There is a certain resonance with Bonnett (2009), who emphasised that moments of silence, withdrawal, reflection, and self-awareness, while not requiring dialogic discussions with the other, can help one experience one's own humanity. While such moments can be enriched if lived as shared lived experiences with others, they do not require others and might prevent imposition (conscious or subconscious) from others. Introspection was brought about in diverse ways: classroom council meetings (Anita[MGIS], Joona[MGIS], and Hema[MGIS]), dramatics as a means of promoting group introspection (Anita[MGIS]), one-on-one or group introspective dialogue (most of the teachers), reflection journals and diaries (oral/written; Joona[MGIS], Jayanthy[MBK], Kamala[MBK], Srila[MBK], and Anonymous[RVS]), and discussions after projects (all teachers). Teachers used critical incidents, quotes, poems, their own observations, and/or students' comments/appreciation/complaints about one another as prompts for introspection. There was a subtle nature of it being self-directed, whereby the teacher only provided a prompt and questioned, if something was true or not and then, the rest was explored by the child. Teachers leveraged the presence of other students in the reflective process as 'others are a mirror'. For example, Anju[MGIS] suggested:

> In those moments they reflect and there are also opportunities for children to give feedback to each other. I might be thinking that I am a very sympathetic listener, that I am such a good worker, but my classmates might tell me you are impossible to work with, because you really do not follow the deadlines, so we find it very difficult to work with you. … Children, like anybody else, would have a self-image and mostly it's a distorted image and because it's coming from fewer perspectives. So, one of the strategies we use in the class is to get to know the self [from the others' perspective].

Teachers put forward a couple of nuances to introspection: it should not be used as a firefighting tool after a critical incident, but as a form of regular introspection (Anonymous[RVS]) or as a constant 'moment to moment' practice (Tanuj[RVS]). Additionally, they suggested that introspection was not about the metacognitive awareness of what one thinks, but rather about why and how one thinks, behaves and lives, and be/becomes. This form of introspection allows for an extended understanding of one's ways of living and being and allows for the potential for transformation. Furthermore, Baren[MBK] contended that it should be embodied and involve emotional connection as opposed to being just intellectual, reasoning based, or involving metacognitive engagement:

> She is becoming too much mentalised; it is not living. The child has to connect to what the child is doing. … No, it has to be living; it has to be feeling. The more it is feeling-oriented that much it helps, because feelings remain long, while thinking and talking reasoning out evaporate very fast. If you have felt something negative, you will not go for it again.

Engaging Students in Social Action (as a Form of Education)

Teachers and schools promoted student social action. Teachers themselves were engaged in many social action projects (these are further explored in Chap. 9), and students frequently joined in and/or set up their own projects. As previously discussed, the projects often involved interaction with the wider community and social action. Regarding which, Kamala[MBK] commented:

> Every project must have it (social project at the end). [We should] not just [teach] science without social purpose. How can technology improve the lives of people? This has to be an ongoing project in every school. The children have to go on innovating, there is no point in saying 'I wish I had electrical drill'. It's so difficult to drill, see how hard it is when the person has to do it by himself. How would you make a cheaper functional electric drill? When there is no electricity how will the drill work?

The students engaged in a range of social action projects both within and beyond schools. Within the school this entailed cleaning it, feeding and caring for animals, waste segregation and recycling, manure production, water and electricity conservation awareness drives, as well as student-based movements for the equality of support staff. Outside school students ran/were involved in awareness campaigns (waste, education, women's health, pollution, bringing about electoral awareness), awareness films (use of leather), rural improvement drives (fundraising and making wells), street plays, community radio shows, living with and helping farmers, unprompted student-driven cleanliness efforts, as well as making and selling products (calendars and diaries) to fundraise for NGOs and during natural disasters. These social action initiatives helped transform awareness into action and created lived experiences embedded in reality. These led to their understanding different lifestyles and being more compassionate. Anita[MGIS] commented:

> We took a walk and I feel that every step they were looking at how am I responsible or what change can I make. What impact do my choices have on the lane outside of my house or in my home; so, I call this as compassion.

Various scholars have emphasised engaging students in social change. For example, Bourn (2022), Sharma (2018), and Shor (1992) have argued for the foregrounding of students' involvement in social changemaking, while Battistoni et al. (2009), Celio (2011), and Wade (1997) have called for their engagement in various social service and service-based learning activities. These ideas have also been emphasised by the various Indian thinkers, who fundamentally believe that education should inspire students to create a more socially just world, not just after completion of schooling, but also during their educational journeys. For example, Gandhi and Kumarappa (1953, p. 32) noted:

> Whilst Sir M. Vishweshwarayya has emphasized one grave defect of our present education which places exclusive emphasis on literary merit, I would add a graver defect in that students are made to think that whilst they are pursuing their literary studies, they may not do acts of service at the sacrifice of their studies, be it ever so small or temporary. They will lose nothing and gain much if they would suspend their education, literary or industrial, to do relief work, such as is being done by some of them in Gujarat. The end of all education should surely be service.

Underlying Approaches to Teaching

Embodied Learning (for Both Academic Education and Education for Harmony)

We commonly learn to live (and learn) within four walls through a narrow focus only on the mind, fragmenting our ways of knowing, limiting them to those based on reasoning, and separating one from the others and the larger world. I have always pondered, in such a system, how do we learn to connect with the human, non-human, and the more-than-human?

In the East, heart, head, body, and soul are not seen as separate, but rather as very much interwoven, being deployed to conceptualise and communicate. As Gandhi (1968b) noted:

[Human][2] is neither mere intellect, nor the gross animal body, nor the heart or soul alone. A proper harmonious combination of all three is required for making of the whole [human being][3] … they constitute an indivisible whole. According to this theory, therefore, it would be a gross fallacy to suppose that they can be developed piecemeal or independently of one another.

In contrast to Descartes, Anju[MGIS] suggested that "Indian philosophy speaks of *Advaita*; it speaks of non-duality [and how the mind, body and soul are all interlinked]." The conceptual separation of the head, heart, body, and soul gives us tools to talk about each of them. I find this interconnectedness to be deeply common-sense based; for example, it can be exceedingly difficult to cognitively focus when one is not feeling well, the body is tired, or if the 'heart is not in the task'. In the West, Rene Descartes ushered in an era of rationalism, with "I think therefore I am". However, modern day sciences, including neuroscience, have highlighted that cognition in and of itself is deeply embodied with the mind being integrated with the sensorimotor systems (Barsalou, 2007), physically interacting with an object leads to a response in the brain (and thinking about the objects also leads to a similar response). Many peace and holistic education researchers, along with several eastern thinkers, have advocated against the segregation of a human being, divides within the human society, and anthropocentrism. I believe that in the eastern thought Rene Descartes' proposition would be rephrased to "I feel therefore I am" or better still "I am because I am". Also, some Eastern thinkers might take an issue with the anthropocentrism in such statements and might instead rephrase it to "I am because we are". Over the past two decades, several thinkers across the world have noted the importance of moving beyond rationality to post-critical and/or transrational theories. The transrational philosophy attempts to recognise, value, and integrate several ways of knowing and being, including the rational, embodied, and spiritual aspects (Cremin et al., 2018; Echavarría Alvarez et al., 2018). They draw upon Eastern thought not simply to reject rationality, but rather to combine the diverse ways of knowing, being, and living dynamically (Cremin, 2018; Cremin et al., 2018; Dietrich, 2013, 2018).

---

[2] The original quote used the word "man" instead.
[3] The original quote used the word "man" instead.

Teachers recognised that learning happens through the whole human being: the body touches and responds to things around, the heart and emotions are affected by events, people, and memories, and the soul is potentially linked with the nature and others around; whilst the mind is also being driven by curiosity and intuition. Teachers frequently promoted 'slowing down' through activities like 'slow observation' and 'slow walks' as a means of creating space for more embodied and transrational learning. Over the centuries, various practices like yoga, chanting, meditation, tai-chi, and fasting have been used as ways of connecting to the soul, healing the body, calming the mind, learning, and transforming one's ways of living and being. Various scholars—including Jinan (2022), J. P. Miller (2010, 2018), R. Miller (1991), Neill (1960), Rogers (1979), and Yoder (2014)—have called for the embodied education of the whole child. Similarly, in peace education literature there has been a noted shift towards integration of the various aspects, with Cremin (2016) suggesting novel approaches to such education that integrate the body, mind, heart, and spirit.

Teachers, resonating with Macedonia (2019), noted that education is very multisensorial; students are constantly learning through seeing things, visualising things in their minds, touching various objects, manipulating objects, moving around, listening, speaking, smelling, tasting, feeling, and intuitively sensing. At PB, all classes were conducted under trees (the classrooms were only used when it rained), while at RVS teachers frequently used various teaching-learning spaces, including those under trees, on the sports ground, and in the forest. These were seen as spaces where real learning took place (the role of the nature on the campuses is further explored below). At all schools, learning took place through being in the real world and interacting with the community. I made a noted observation/reflection:

> Surojit[PB] was telling a story about birds to the class. … As usual, during such story telling sessions students have a lot of freedom to listen, scribble, close their eyes, look around, and potentially daydream. [I decided to focus on] a boy who was apparently not listening; he seemed to be looking around and not necessarily following the story. … [After a couple of minutes, he] commented "Surojitda even the birds are listening to the story". (Classroom observations of Surojit[PB])

Interestingly, I had probably lost touch with what the story was really about, despite being a participant observer and listening intently. The child's comment helped me realise that the story was about birds. And in actuality there were so many birds around us; interacting with each other and potentially with all of us too. Perhaps the boy was following and really understanding the student; while I was the one who was distracted.

Music and art were recognised as an integral part of education and were strongly integrated into all projects at MBK and MGIS, while at PB and RVS they were seen as part of the main curricula; PB recognised them as a way of life. Tagore, the founder of PB, believed that in developing an aesthetic sense, this would eventually lead to harmony. Surojit[PB] opined that "one who truly understands poetry can never be dishonest, because he has a different sensitivity". Music and art were integrated into daily life through projects, public art displays, and special classes. I frequently found students singing or rehearsing as they walked around the campus. Teachers suggested that music and art helped calm the mind, connect to one's heart, understand one's own self, develop a distinct perspective, empathetically connect with others, bring together people irrespective of differences, and develop an inner silence. There was a constant notion that mind develops through hands. For example, Surojit[PB] suggested:

> Through arts, painting, music, dance, woodwork … it is not about the final performance, but [the journey or] the process. It allows space for the mind's development. It creates a different kind of mind (creative, observant, sensitive). Mind develops through hands.

There was a strong focus on everyday experiences of beauty, stillness, and feelings of connection with the human and the more-than-human; this resonates with the spiritual ideas of recognising beauty around us and living a beautiful life (thinkers, like Eckhart Tolle, Confucius, and other Buddhist and Indian thinkers have repeatedly called for learning to see the beauty in everything). Teachers emphasised recognising, valuing, and connecting with the beauty of the environment and seeing it in 'small things', like dew on flowers, grasshoppers, and butterflies. A visiting alumni[RVS] commented on the intricate features of a nearby hill, while many students frequently commented on trees, hills, sunsets, shadows, snakes, and birds, with phrases like "[L]ook, how beautiful is this tree!". This appreciation of beauty around us leads to a very different way of living and being; I believe it moves students from an anthropocentric, extractive ways of living and being to more humane, sustainable ways of living and being. I doubt a person who inherently values and sees the beauty in trees would waste wood, not reuse, and not recycle it. Similarly, the recognition of the beauty in diversity leads to deep-rooted valuing of every living being in the community (irrespective of all kinds of boundaries) and prevents certain community members or living beings from becoming invisible, being ill-treated, being treated as objects, or being taken for granted. Similarly, seeing beauty in everything around one also went beyond seeing beauty in living beings, non-living things, and/or phenomena to include beauty in ideas and perspectives. There was a constant emphasis on recognition and appreciation of different perspectives and ways of life as equally 'valid' and transcendence of dualities and dichotomies. For example, Shreya[PB] noted:

> It's like the idea of seeing the beauty and harmony in diversity, seemingly diversity seems to be very chaotic, everyone is so different, so many different viewpoints.
>
> I think nature gives you that example—nature in front of you might just—these mango trees, it's not proper, but if you properly analyse and critically look into it, then every leaf has a proper place. So, it might look chaotic, but there is a pattern.

An Extended Community of Educators—Peers, Community, Nature, and the Wider World as Educators

Mass education systems frequently adopt a banking like model, whereby teachers merely transfer knowledge that they hold. In contrast, historically, all living beings have always been learning over many millennia through a variety of ways of embodied learning within the world (Jinan, 2021). Learning happens 24×7 and is a natural process, while academic learning is optional. The teachers recognised that there are numerous sources of knowledge and ways of learning (including nature, the world around, other living beings, students themselves) and believed and leveraged everything around them as educators. Teachers not only recognised the need for, but also supported and created spaces for students to learn from their parents, community members, the wider world around them, and their own deeper selves (through reflection, introspection, and meditation). Their roles as educators notably changed from that of teachers who were torchbearers of knowledge to those of facilitators of learning who created conducive environments and supported students (while promoting students' freedom to decide what and how they wanted to learn). And for most teachers their roles had further transformed to those of a co-learner wherein both the students and the teacher were engaged in a shared journey of learning from each other and everything about them. At different times, teachers adopted roles of facilitators or co-learners (but never the role of the torchbearer/holder of knowledge). They believed that children have deep and meaningful insights and wisdom, frequently more than that of the teachers themselves (some examples were provided in Part II), and teachers frequently took inspiration/learnt from these insights.

There was a strong appreciation of the home environment: teachers aimed to build a coherence of educational vision between the school and the parents (at times home environments and parents created a contrasting ethos, with some pushing for competition and/or excessive focus on academic learning). However, at times, schools leveraged the parent body and engaged them in the children's educational processes by bringing them in to give talks to the whole school, as volunteer educators as well as involving them in planning and setting up of various festivals and events. Some of the teachers actively brought in and promoted interactions with community members; examples included accounts of interactions with shoemakers, waste-pickers, school support staff, mechanics, craftsmen, musicians, and activists. They believed that not only did the community members hold deep embodied knowledge, but also helped introduce other equally valuable forms of knowledge and ways of knowing. Furthermore, there was a strong recognition of the indirect, and both conscious and subconscious impact of the wider society in which the schools were based. Teachers recognised that various marketised, capitalist, anthropocentric cultures have become predominant in society and these influence students through advertisements, popular media (news, films, TV series, WhatsApp forwards), and various discussions within communities beyond the school. Teachers aimed to moderate the impact by building awareness of these and engaging students in dialogue and questioning about the modern ways of living and being. For example, Shreya[PB] pointed out:

> They are very much into this rat race. [It is brought in via] entertainment. Everybody is much more like *jeelo apni zindagi* (live your life). That is also fact; the advertisement you see and the TV you see. The ads coming on the TV are very materialistic. The fairer you are, the more powerful you are. Fair and lovely ad. Gender [based stereotypes] are coming into the ad. Materialism is coming [into the ads]. The more you have, [if you have] a Fossil watch, the better you are. So, the brands are coming in.

Nature as an Educator

Nature was frequently thought of as a carer and educator for both teachers and students; they regarded it as being non-judgemental, loving, and caring. Nature helped both students and teachers to remain calm, feel a sense of peace and harmony, and feel connected to oneself and others. Teachers and students commented on how nature helped one feel connected to oneself and the wider world, helping one to appreciate the miniscule nature of the self and one's problems as well. Students frequently commented that the time with nature was some of the best times in their day. An alumni[RVS] commented:

> That old tree. It must have been here for far longer than I have been, and it will be there after me. Similarly, that mountain—it is quite huge. It allows you to see that you are quite tiny.

Patel and Ehrenzeller (under review) find that nature can act as a peace educator through building a sense of inner peace and wellbeing, building positive nature-student relations, and bringing about an understanding of the wider world, as well as supporting the development of skills, non-anthropocentric epistemologies, and harmonious ways of living and being. Similarly, teachers suggested that nature was an educator. Nature was frequently suggested as having its own harmony; for examples, teachers suggested that trees know when to shed leaves; they follow 'rhythms of nature', and an internal system of discipline. Immersion in nature led to the development of non-anthropocentric and ecological epistemologies and ways of living and being, where students were intrinsically sensitive, mindful, and calm.

The perspective of nature as an educator fundamentally moves away from modern educational practices, where we learn to study about the world as an object of study, instead of partnering with it to learn about oneself and the world or building meaningful relations with nature. Krishnamurti and Tagore frequently emphasised the role of nature; they suggested that it intrinsically builds an ethos of harmonious living (O'Connell, 2003; Thapan, 2001). Tagore held that developing a close affinity to nature would build sensitivity, empathy, and a feeling of oneness with the world around (Tagore, 1929), while Krishnamurti stressed its role in being human: "If you lose touch with nature, you lose touch with humanity. If there's no relationship with nature then you become a killer;

then you kill baby seals, whales, dolphins, and [human beings][4] for gain, for 'sport', for food, or for knowledge. … You probably are not related to anything, to your wife or your husband; you are much too busy, gaining and losing, with your own private thoughts, pleasures and pains" (Krishnamurti, 1982).

Classes (RVS and PB) were frequently conducted under trees, with projects (all schools) revolving around the trees and birds, whilst MBK students had produced multiple books on nature. There were several instances when animals walked into classes at PB, while snakes and other animals were commonly found in RVS. The schools are situated within forests and/or surrounded by nature. This brought about a deep immersion, where students lived with nature all the time, leading to an intrinsic way of living and being in harmony and in connection with it. This starkly contrasts with various modern approaches to building connections with nature, including studying about nature or short excursion visits into forests, farms, and the natural environment. Notably, one of the secondary data collection schools highlighted the importance of purposelessness when spending time in nature—the school was situated in a farm and students were free to wander purposelessly across the farmlands, and in the orchards, they took students for repeated purposeless weekly walks up the same hill, and they have been taking students for 2–3 weeklong, yearly visits to the same forest. All of their interactions with nature are purposeless, that is, without a pre-planned objective, itinerary, or list of things to do. In my short time at the school, I noted that the children were genuinely very happy. The city-based schools (MGIS and MBK) did not have as many opportunities to interact with nature; however, the teachers frequently sought opportunities to integrate nature into their lessons or held classes in places where students could experience it.

Notably, many schools aimed to adopt a nature-based approach to their systems, pedagogies, and processes as opposed to modern educational systems, which are inspired and shaped like machines. For example, this involved things like democratic decision-making processes, approaches to organic and nonlinear development, freedom to follow individual development trajectories, emphasis on cooperation rather than competition, and a move away from various commonly utilised assessment practices. This resonates with Cremin's (2022) call to rewild education, whereby nature-based ways are embodied and embedded within schooling systems.

---

[4] The original quote used the word "man" instead.

A Lived Experiences-Based Pedagogy for LTLTH

I have come to realise and appreciate many different forms of knowledge and to fundamentally recognise lived experiences as the greatest form. Various Indian thinkers, notably Krishnamurti (2000) and Tagore, proposed that experiences equal knowledge, that different people have different experiences, and that they construct their own knowledge. This resonates with Jinan (2021), who has been extremely critical of knowledge as solely transmitted through written works and thus has called for observing and fully experiencing the world around one as a means of understanding it. Similarly, teachers commonly held that education for harmony resulted from students' lived experiences of living harmoniously. They believed that values are inculcated through processes and lived experiences as opposed to normative, value judgements, or prescriptive statements, like 'honesty is a good value' or 'be honest'. Surojit[PB], referring to both students and teachers, suggested:

> The teaching of the Ashram [Patha Bhavana is frequently also referred to as an ashram] is to live life fully and wholly. So, it's a way of life. It's not only then a few things. … It's the way you are living. Everything becomes part of your education. It is just because everything helps you to grow up.

This resonates with various proponents of experiential education. Dewey (1938) was a strong advocate of experiential and participatory education, emphasising "the importance of the participation of the learner in the formation of the purposes which direct his activities in the learning process". Similarly, Freire (2005) emphasised lived experiences as a way of learning and praxis (and student participation) calling for "reflection and action directed at the structures to be transformed". Additionally, Rogers (1979) in *Freedom to Learn* asserts the need for meaningful, relevant experiences to be embedded within all educational processes and for experiential learning to be self-initiated and participatory. In peace education, Reardon and Cabezudo (2002) recommend a "pedagogy of democratic engagement", which is participatory, experiential, inquiry-based, and aimed at challenging societal hegemonic structures of silencing and oppression. Similarly, J. P. Miller (2010, 2016), a strong proponent of holistic education, describes it as involving integrated education of the mind, body, and spirit through experiential education. The focal schools' teaching-learning practices resonate with Kolb's (1984) 4-stage model of experiential learning, which integrates ideas of experience and reflection from Dewey and Freire. Their learning practices (academic and LTLTH) involved: (a) concrete experiences of opportunities for dialogue, stories, and further reflection; (b) reflection on incidents, experiences, and their own responses; (c) abstract conceptualisation, where students conceptually explored behavioural patterns, trends, unexamined responses, beliefs; and (d) students actively experimenting with and working towards adapting their ways of living and being. It is important to recall that students also charted and planned out non-academic, behavioural, and LTLTH-based outcomes that they wanted to work on.

Students' experiences of harmonious living included various home- and school-based experiences (content, pedagogy, school ethos, TSR, behavioural management routines, and teachers' ways of living and being). Srila[MBK], much like other teachers, suggested, "Children see how teachers behave and they grasp things as these are lived experiences that they live". Similarly, Atul[RVS] held that students seeing teachers trying to live harmoniously lead to them LTLTH:

> The Steiner school had nothing, but the students saw the challenges and they learnt something subtle—a group of people who wanted to make a change were making it, despite the adversities. They see that you are trying, and you are doing your best. ... Children see how teachers behave, how they get along, when the school is being inclusive with eating together and also, when it does not happen and when people are treated differently.

The diverse nature of the schools and classrooms, with students from different social emotional backgrounds, cultures, religions, socioeconomic status (SES), nationalities, states (language backgrounds), interests, and genders led to lived experiences of togetherness. While Aaditya[PB] expanded upon this by saying, "[W]hen you look at the composition of the [non-residential students] you have the professor's daughter, and you have a fourth-class staff, peon or messenger's children. They actually share the same space, they learn the same things from the same teacher, they grow up together right from Ananda Pathshala, and they do make a bond, which is lifelong." Teachers emphasised that whilst diversity was important, having supportive inclusive practices (as a form of 'active inclusion') was even more so, especially for the economically weaker students.

> If you do not have strategies to support inclusion, it's not going to happen. It's not sufficient to, let's say, do what the government says as positive

action … you **cannot** just create a quota, this whole thing about reservation. If you are going to create quotas without support: [without] people looking at each other and listening to each other, accepting each other's point, understanding each other's points of view, then inclusion is not going to happen. (Anju[MGIS])

Additionally, teachers were vocally against all forms of labelling and streaming, believing that the false boundaries of ability-groups created a competitive environment, led to internalisation, were based on arbitrary measures of learning, were reductionist, and hence against the core philosophies of living together. Even 'positive' labelling was perceived as harmful to the person labelled so, as it pressurises one into meeting arbitrary standards, builds a false sense of self, and lacks an understanding of *anityata* (impermanence), while indirectly telling others that they are not 'good'. All schools had students with special needs and were generally against (except RVS) labelling students with a syndrome (e.g., ADHD); they treated students as individuals, seeing everyone as individuals with a different set of needs. At RVS, the labelling was driven by the parents; however, the teachers treated children as individuals with unique needs.

It is pertinent to note that such lived experience-based pedagogy differs from 'learning by doing', in that teachers perceived that learning for LTLTH happened 24×7. The experiential education through the school ethos and lived experiences at school went beyond short-term activities and programmes (like community service-based programmes). Community service-based programmes have championed lived experiences through off-campus community service, providing holistic opportunities for social, personal, civic, and academic learning (Celio, 2011; Conrad & Hedin, 1982); however, they make up a small part of a child's lived experience. Instead, lived experience-based pedagogy includes participatory processes, classroom lived experiences, as well as engaging students in challenging power dynamics and hegemonies within and beyond the classroom (Freire, 2005; Kester, 2007; Reardon & Cabezudo, 2002). The teachers strongly emphasised the role of (classroom and school) ethos and the school-wide conditions, which resonates with recommendations for educators to create school-wide 'conditions' for SEL development (Brackett et al., 2019; Greenberg et al., 2017; S. M. Jones & Bouffard, 2012; Oberle et al., 2016). Similarly, in peace education, Page (2008) highlighted the importance of exploring the structural or cultural violence in schools (e.g., direct or indirect compartmentalisation of knowledge into subjects and of students into age, ability, or social class).

CONCLUSION

Translating education for harmony into praxis has its challenges. While curricula are important, they have limited relevance to LTLTH. Rather than developing a specific subject, I advocate for its integration into every subject, within pedagogy, classroom ethos, and the students lived experiences (further explored in the next chapter). Throughout this chapter, I have explored how teachers leveraged a lived experience-based pedagogy as a way of bringing about 'education of the whole child' through embodied and integrated education of the head, hand, and heart. Teachers commonly used several pedagogical tools, including dialogic teaching, peer- and project-based learning, meditation, reflection, and social action, in order to build a continuum of lived experiences of harmony. It is important not to consider the pedagogical practices suggested here as prescriptive suggestions or to use them with a tick box approach; I present them as a case study to demonstrate how teachers used these practices to bring about education for harmony, with their practices being underpinned by their philosophies and commitment to this end. I would like to invite you to explore and respond to the following questions: do you think LTLTH can be taught, caught, or is it a bit of both? What pedagogical practices (could) bring about education for harmony in your respective contexts? Can you share an incident (in your own life or those of your children/ students) that brought about education for harmony? PS through my several reads of the now completed book, I realise that education for harmony can seem quite daunting; however, in reality it seemed to be a lot easier, more natural, and more organic than the modern education systems. While the excessive theorising and articulation of process can make it appear daunting, in actuality, with some reflection and practice, anything but education for harmony can be far morechallenging.

CHAPTER 8

Continuum of Harmonious Lived Experiences Through Classroom Ethos, Behavioural Management Routines and Teacher Student Relations

The previous chapter raised the question about how LTLTH can be ingrained in students' lived experiences (as a continuum across time and not just temporarily through momentary experiences, interactions, and/or content). As I reflect upon my own childhood, I believe some of the aspects that moved me to live more harmoniously were related to my relations with various adults (including parents, teachers, and community members in the ashram) and the ethos of the ashram. The ashram ethos was based on ideas of autonomy, self-exploration, community living and this shaped underpinned all the interactions in the space. Unfortunately, the ethos of the schools that I went to as a child was in complete contrast. In this chapter, I first take a deeper dive into exploring the ideas of education for harmony through a continuum of (shared) lived experiences. Thereafter, I explore the contribution of classroom/school ethos and TSR to the continuum of experiences. The school ethos and TSR in alternative schools highlighted the importance of autonomous decision-making. I end by exploring the latter's role in building a sense of freedom, agency, and onus.

J. Patel, *Learning to Live Together Harmoniously*, Spirituality, Religion, and Education, https://doi.org/10.1007/978-3-031-23539-9_8

A Continuum of Lived Experiences

Lived experiences create learning opportunities (e.g., students' interactions with each other and the teacher; engagement with content; and engagement in dialogue, projects, social action and field trips, and outside learning spaces and activities). This links to the idea of the 'teachable moment', where teaching-learning takes place when students are ready. Baren[MBK] believed that such moments lent themselves to education for harmony, and when they arose, he aimed to not be disruptive (by stopping all other activities), but rather he subtly embedded teaching/learning for LTLTH. Similarly, Tanuj[RVS] held that "whenever a group of people come together, group dynamics come into play; there is bound to be power play." He further opined that it is important to wait for the right moments and to not make a huge hue and cry when they occur.

Teachers strongly believed that LTLTH must be integrated into **all** the lived experiences of both the student and the teachers. They perceived LTLTH to be long term, with non-linear objectives, which allow for individualised learning paths and journeys and reduced expectations of predetermined outcomes. This way of perceiving teaching-learning practices as lived experiences that span across spatio-temporal boundaries contrasts with typical research and practice focused on individual teaching practices and activities. There is a certain resonance with Aristotle's *Eudemian Ethics* (ethics for human flourishing or literally translated to ethics of 'well divinity/spirit') where Aristotle (2000) referred to happiness and *virtues* as something that is not momentary, but rather much like a way of life; "[virtues] will be in a complete life. For one swallow does not make a spring, nor does one day; similarly, neither does one day nor a short time make us blessed or happy." Lived experiences also underpin Noddings' (1986, 2002, 2003) care theory, wherein natural caring (for intimate others and others that one is not directly connected with) is an embodied way of living and being (over ethical caring), stemming from experiences of being cared for and lived experiences resulting her framework of strategies of care (modelling, dialogue, practice, and confirmation). Similarly, Charney (2002) suggests care can be taught only through lived experiences and school ethos, whilst Cardona (2017), in her book titled *The Very Process of Living Together Educates: Learning in, from and for Co-operative Life in Rural Malta*, holds that the lived experience of community living educates and brings about LTLTH.

A Classroom Ethos of Harmonious Living

Caring School Ethos

The schools and all their members engaged in building a school-wide ethos for harmonious living. Teachers frequently suggested that due to the non-linearity of LTLTH it could not be preached, taught, demanded, or expected, but rather a teacher should try to create an environment/ethos of harmonious living within the class/school. This ethos was created both by teachers themselves trying to live harmoniously (further discussed in the next chapter) and through classroom cultures, practices, and routines, as well as TSR: "[T]he culture in the classroom is important for any organisation, any space and there I set my culture ... they will feel the lack of being judged, which a child needs. I do not want them to feel judged" (Anita[MGIS]). Students sensed this and frequently appreciated the school ethos even long after leaving the schools. Teachers created a caring, loving, trusting, free, and inclusive ethos, which led to a noted positive affect in students towards each other and the teachers. This was expressed through smiles, hugs, physical embraces, active engaged open discussions, and meaningful (lifelong) connections.

All schools emphasised valuing, respecting, and treating children as equals; this ethos led to children living harmoniously *swabhavikpane* (naturally). This notion of equality was not restricted to just the classrooms, for it also ran across the schools to all members, including the support staff. Students not only noticed the inclusive ethos but also appreciated it. For example, students at RVS appreciated that everyone, including support staff, ate the same food with them and that everyone was equal. This fundamentally led them to respect and treat everyone as equals *swabhavikpane*. Several teachers commented on how students did not waste food, did not throw waste, engaged in active sharing and inclusion, took up social action, and so on, despite not being instructed to do so.

A Sense of Onus and Collective Responsibility

Schools generally created a democratic environment (further expanded below). They had several student-run committees that ran club-based activities, whilst also contributing to school-wide decision-making and these democratic notions of choice were also embedded in everyday activities. For example, Aaditya[PB] held a poll when there were multiple correct answers to a puzzle. Moreover, throughout the fieldwork there were multiple discussions and polls, where students weighed in decisions like the content they would like to learn through the year, the next steps in a project, and various school-wide decisions. This, and other factors, contributed to a strong sense of connectedness (McNeely et al., 2002), where students felt included and developed a sense of belongingness and onus. This is exemplified by one of Srila's[MBK] comments, "There is no hierarchy here—two children sit in the principal's seat and proudly asked what do you want?". There was a powerful sense of onus and collective responsibility (as opposed to "I do not care" or "it's your problem" attitudes). The schools promoted and maintained an environment of collective responsibility, where students and teachers, alike, felt responsible for the school and each other's wellbeing. Kamala[MBK] said:

> To me school is a place where a collective is being built ... it's the spirit of collective effort, which is what I think is the difference here. It's everybody's problem, you know, or the children are not going [home] on time, where everybody is concerned about it or the fact that my group is using bad language or somebody in our meeting ... we all are sharing and being collectively worried about what is happening.

This sense of collective responsibility was strongly associated with the previously described ideas of commitment within the sense of purpose dimension.

Cooperation over Competition

The school and classroom ethos promoted cooperation (as opposed to competition). Teachers actively tried to 'keeping competition away' as they put forward cooperation, with a senior teacher[MBK] commenting that "[c]ompetition is from the west, but in India we have *sarve bhavantu sukkhina* (may everyone be happy)". This was reflected in their practices, where the schools did not have exams before high school and promoted cooperation and group-work. All the schools were pushing against the examination systems and MGIS, MBK, and RVS used qualitative report (behavioural) cards for children. Anju[MGIS] explained:

> We went so far as to even remove marks from our report cards, because giving marks is a system of violence, because you are judging, but to give

qualitative feedback is maybe support[ing] your child to do better ... another student told me is, that 'you know we grew up not being competitive, because you never gave us marks, because nobody was a 80% or a 60% or a 40%. Everybody was good [at] certain things and they were not very good [at] certain things, so that was okay because [there was] always something you are good at.'

During the fieldwork, I heard about a competition only once; RVS had conducted a competition, a few years ago, to save water during a local drought. Competition was understood to lead to self-centrism ("Me first, mine first, I first" ~Baren[MBK]), isolation, animosity, and poorer wellbeing (of both high and low performers). This would inevitably lead to comparison in other aspects of life (material possessions, like mobile phones and bags or physical appearances) and a sense of ownership (as opposed to notions of onus, responsibility, or trusteeship), which was considered the antithesis to the goal of building communities. Competition was also usually frowned upon, because of its arbitrary nature and weak association with learning and evaluation of learning. Instead, some teachers (Anonymous[RVS] and Jayanthy[MBK]) argued for perfection and excellence. Meanwhile, Tanuj[RVS] tried to reduce notions of competition to build the right relations with the work and where the process became an intrinsic reward:

> So that [sense of wellbeing] for me is important, because competition can make them lose their sense of well-being easily. Then, outward yardsticks become more important than their inner sense. For example, if I were to give a test, now then, they might do well, but it does not mean that they are learning well. ... So, the whole thing about connection with the subject, relating with the subject and certain way of understanding the subject ... it shouldn't just resort to just learning of techniques.

An Intangible Impact of the Space

Additionally, there was a strong notion that the physical space had something that was intangible and had an incredible impact on children. At MBK this was referred to in terms of the place carrying a sense of calm and related to the nature and ashram around, whilst at RVS it was related to the surrounding nature and at PB it was associated with the nature around, the physical space, and the art-based ethos. The places generally carried a sense of calmness and a deeper form of silence. I believe that this was brought about by the various participants in the schools and their own ways of living and being, by the nature around, and potentially by the physical space in and of itself.

Teachers' own ways of living and being (further discussed in Chap. 9) are incredibly important to education for harmony and the school-wide ethos. I strongly believe that their ways of living and being were impacted by the physical environment around. Teachers frequently commented on the intangible effect that the physical environment had on all stakeholders; for instance, Jayanthy[MBK] suggested, "In the physical space there is the reverberance of that living [harmoniously], because these *diyas* [teachers] are actively living it … once you are committed [1] to it, you are committed to it". Similarly, recently I had a similar experience that I noted down in my autoethnographic diary.

> Recently, before one of my postgraduate lectures I went to the room early. I sat down, pulled out my laptop, after going through my notes and I decided to quiet my mind. I put aside any presession anxieties, connected with my spiritual self and brought my whole self to the session. As I was doing this a few students walked in, I greeted them and continued with my own practice (with my eyes open). They continued their ongoing conversation and unbeknown to me, at some point, they went completely quiet. It must have been several minutes and then, another student walked in and commented on feeling a sense of **sacred silence**. The phrase immediately struck a chord, and I was reminded of my experiences at the schools, where I had felt a sense of sacred silence engulfing the school.

The school campuses were frequently surrounded by nature, and as previously described, this acted as a peace educator by helping promote wellbeing and at times teaching concrete concepts, skills, and ways of living and being. However, I believe that the impact of nature went beyond and it affected the school-wide ethos bringing about a sense of peace and harmony. In an interaction with an educationist, he referred to a tree on the campus as being *samadhisheel* (in the state of enlightenment and can help others reach enlightenment). Furthermore, three of the schools were also associated with spiritual activities and had dedicated space for prayer and meditation, which at times also contained relics and objects from spiritual leaders (these were mostly frequented by various adults in the school

---

[1] The original quote, in both the instances, used the word "given" instead of "committed".

and/or surrounding community members). Teachers frequently suggested and believed that these relics also had an impact. Similarly, the art-based, reflective, and expressive ethos at PB was suggested to impact on everyone around. The various paintings, sculptures, and sounds of students singing and humming and of musical instruments had an impact on everyone in the school. Surojit[PB] pointed out that, whilst there might be things that children or teachers may not understand, they can still have an impact.

> Tagore's songs, they may not understand the implications of all the words when they listen to them. Even this painting on the other side of the wall, it's not that we always see that. But it's there in the ambiance, in the environment. They all somehow or other help in building yourself, in discovering yourself, and the whole nature. ... This place is a living being. So, it's there all around you and all around you and it's not only the people who you meet. The place itself is there and it creates a kind of ambiance.

It is difficult to articulate the impact of the physical space and I believe that it must be experienced from a transrational perspective (rather than a purely rational one). Perhaps we can find simpler examples from our own lived experiences; some of the more relatable examples that I can think of from my own experience include the impact of organised desks/workspaces, visits to areas of national beauty, and walks in cemeteries.

EQUAL, CARING, AND LOVING TEACHER STUDENT RELATIONS

TSR Mediate the Impact of All Other Processes

TSR have been suggested to be significant to all learning processes, with Hattie's (2009) meta-analysis ranking it as the 11th (out of 138 influences) most important influence affecting student learning; Pianta (1999) suggesting it as underpinning the development of cognitive and non-cognitive abilities in students, including social and emotional skills; and Jaffe et al. (2004) calling these relations as the fourth R of education (along with Reading, wRiting, and aRithmetic). Similarly, at-home and in-school relations are considered to underpin SEL (Eisenberg, Valiente et al., 2010; Jones & Bouffard, 2012). Moreover, positive TSR are widely agreed to bring about a warm, positive, trust-based, and safe emotional climate that supports the development of student outcomes, motivation, self-esteem, and confidence (Baker, 2006; Hamre & Pianta, 2001; Pianta & Stuhlman, 2004).

TSR play a significant role in education of the heart. Battistich et al. (1997), Noddings (2002), and Goodenow (1993) argue that students, through their attachment, use relations and behaviours of others around them to learn behaviours and build worldviews and attitudes. Teachers held that the relations with students underpinned the impact of pedagogical processes (Chap. 7), the continuum of lived experiences, and school ethos and teachers' own ways of living and being (Chap. 9). Mutually caring, loving, and respectful relations mediate and allow for these various aspects of the classroom and school practices to impact on the students' ways of living and being, with Anju[MGIS] suggesting: "[T]eacher-student relationship is heart of it, if you are scared of your teacher, then obviously there is no happiness per se" and senior teacher[RVS] sharing, "So, for me, [TSR] is another important thing; more than the subject or anything. Once that relationship has grown and developed and then it's a beautiful learning process for both." Teachers held a strong internal belief that 'life is to be related' and relations are what makes life more enjoyable and meaningful. Alumni often kept writing letters or returning to the schools, while ex-students who moved schools or cities frequently had their parents call up teachers.

Deeply Understanding a Child

Strong TSR (and alternative pedagogies like autonomous learning) are dependent on teachers developing a deep understanding of children. Teachers were mindful of children's personal lives and home backgrounds: parents, grandparents, and friend circles. Teachers had developed a deep understanding of each child: their likes and dislikes, needs, attitudes, mental and emotional states, fears/apprehensions, levels of sensitivities, behavioural patterns, and internal dynamics between students. For example, Hema[MGIS] narrated:

> This year Sagar said 'no, I do not want a helper', but he actually likes it. He likes having someone help him and look after him, but he does not want to say it. I said that we won't have any one person be Sagar's helper, but as with everything else, whoever sees he needs help has to go and help him.

Teachers believed and constantly remembered that children are children; Surojit[PB] noted, "Child is a child is a child is a child is a child" as a main mantra. Similarly, teachers across schools were mindful of students' age, behaviours, and not to judge a child. Kamala[MBK] explained students' behaviours and her patient responses as, "Can you use the mouse on the screen? His English was being translated by these kids [his classmates were trying to put the mouse on the monitor]. Those are children that's why they are there" (Kamala[MBK]). Similarly, a senior teacher[RVS] narrated:

> "Akka, you do not seem to be carrying anything you are so normal", he asked me. I said it's because I know that your arrogance and rudeness come out of certain immaturity, so why should I be angry with you? A time will come when you will understand this, so I choose to be patient with you.

The constant remembrance of children being children was reflected in the teachers' patience, beliefs of non-linearity, and the TSR. Teachers recognised that students held fundamental existential questions and that notions of the soul or the spirit were not just for adults. For example, Anju[MGIS] stated, "[F]undamental existential questions are there no matter what the age and we underestimate the fact that children also are dealing with these existential questions", while Jyothi[RVS] held, "[C]hildren are quite aware of it, in fact, in some of the conversations one has with them I think they have innate wisdom in them [and hence we must nurture/protect it]".

Teachers used a variety of tools to understand children deeply, including meaningful (non-academic) interactions with children, home-visits (MBK and MGIS), parent-teacher meetings (all schools), and parental engagement during school functions (all schools). For example, at PB, parents frequently joined in for morning assemblies, weekly meditations, and weekly poetry evenings, while at MBK, parents frequently joined in daily assemblies, meditations, festival celebrations, and volunteer teaching. Teachers at the residential schools believed that most of the student understanding happened through observing and participating with a child outside the classroom, while at MGIS and MBK a lot of this informal space was created within the classroom through the project-based pedagogy. Teachers drafted detailed behavioural reports on students at MGIS, MBK, and RVS (and this not only helped break stereotypes, but also nudged teachers to observe and deeply understand each child), and partook in teacher discussions on student interests and behaviours (RVS scheduled meetings twice a term, whilst at MGIS and MBK this happened through informal discussions). The detailed reports allowed teachers to humanise the process and profoundly understand the child as opposed to labelling. Whilst the teacher discussion meetings led to exploring different perspectives across different teachers, who shared different relations with an individual child.

Teachers found labelling a child problematic for several reasons, including understanding that labels are reductionist, life is dynamic, behaviours are especially *anitya*, and the need to understand the 'whole child'. The non-judgemental TSR and deep concern for the child allowed for the latter to 'open up' and share their lives with the teachers. Students frequently shared 'secrets' with them. The deep understanding of the child is cyclically linked with the '*laagani*' (love)-based relations (next subsections).

Evoking Familial Bonds

Teachers were generally considered to be like older siblings, friends, parents, or grandparents, depending on their age and the grades they taught. Teachers at MBK, RVS, and PB were called *bhaiya, da, didi, aka*, or *di* (local equivalents of brother/sister).

> I love them and I see them as my own children. I also see them as my friends. It's not that I do not scold them, but … well they even accept that scolding, like your own sons and daughters. (Surojit[PB])

Surojit[PB] further narrated a story about the difference between a teacher and a mother's reaction to a child telling him/her a story about how 'a dog was chasing two man'; the teacher would correct the grammar, while the mother would laugh with the child. Kamala[MBK] took it beyond an emotional feeling to a way of life, where she believed in the oneness of humanity

> Is there a difference between my own children and the children I work with? I do not see it? I see the same struggles and I see the same sorrows, but only they live in another house and that is because my society is divided into houses, but one day that too will go.

Students, at times, had a stronger bond with the teachers than their parents. There were certain teachers that students sought out to share incidents, experiences, 'secrets', and stories from their personal lives. For example, students from across the school came to speak with Shreya[PB] whenever they got a chance. Additionally, a senior non-participant teacher[PB] spent a lot of time with residential children, and when ill, they frequently sent messages to ask him to visit them. Relation building happened inside and outside the class, especially during non-formal activities (shared meals, story-telling sessions, trips, sports, and student clubs). These non-formal spaces afforded opportunities to build a different kind of relation, where teachers became co-participants (e.g., joining in while cooking, baking, or playing a sport). These relations lead to an ethos of mutual care, love, and respect (further discussed in the next subsection).

There was little hierarchy and children frequently commented on teachers being a part of their group or like them. Teachers regularly (a) joined students in cleaning activities, extra-curricular periods, and at lunch time; (b) used words like we, us, and ours, rather than I, you, mine, and yours; (c) explained that we all are one/'each other's family'; and (d) shared their own limitations, mistakes, and errors. Some teachers also consciously explored and participated in students' areas of interest (songs, cartoons, games). Students saw Kamala[MBK] to be much like themselves. Many of her observations, comments, and suggestions were phrased like the children themselves would have phrased them. On her part, she consciously used different language when interacting with students of different ages and was mindful of their sensitivities, for example, specific children or specific topics that children were sensitive to. Similarly, other teachers (Jayanthy[MBK], Baren[MBK], and non-participant teacher[MBK]) also noted that she became like a child when with children and that "Kamala[MBK] didi has a very motherly figure; she can scold and laugh, she has that in her" (Baren[MBK]). A few teachers also pointed to 'a line' of closeness that should not be crossed. This stemmed from the view that students should not be overpampered, become too attached to the extent that it harmed the child or their peers, take teachers for granted, interfere too much in children's personal lives, and impose one's own aspirations and beliefs on the child. Several teachers (due to personality types) were not as close to students as some of their peers and they questioned whether close relations were necessary. However, they had all established mutual care and respect-based relations, which became central to LTLTH.

Care, Love, and Respect-Based Relations

Trust, care, love, and respect formed the basis of most of the relations. Teachers cared deeply about students. They were aware of their emotional states and catered to their needs when students felt 'low', 'left out', angry, not heard, had lost confidence, struggled with project completion, or sought attention. Bharat[Shreyas] suggested that *laagani*-based relations helped establish and maintain a deep sense of care. All teachers suggested that such relations underpinned all the teaching-learning processes. They had a sense of unconditional love, which they asserted as being linked to (a) the teacher-student relation being like a parent-child relation; (b) one must do what is right for a child; or (c) 'children are children'. Notably during a secondary data collection visits a school leader suggested that when making educational decisions (be it classroom-based or school-wide) one must let the love for the child guide the processes. While teachers at another secondary data collection school suggested that if one loves the child then it will ensure that all other educational principles and philosophies will be followed; it will ensure that the children are kept at the centre rather than visions, principles, and curriculum that the teachers, philosophers, or the state/nation call for.

Teachers respected children as individuals, frequently empathising with them and avoiding treating them as objects, judging, or ordering them to do something. Hema[MGIS] stated, "[R]emember that thing [is] so much [ingrained] in my mind that right from birth how children are treated like objects and that kind of callousness with which we treat the younger people". Teachers suggested that respect is integrated and manifested through small things, including listening and valuing children, looking into their eyes while speaking to them, wishing good-morning, and not comparing children. This led to a school-wide ethos of collaboration, mutual respect, and student autonomy. Teachers treated students as adults: they stated facts rather than giving judgemental responses, consciously avoided embarrassing students, preferred one-on-one discussions after class, were inclusive, and respected diversity. They were mindful of children's backgrounds, individuality, individual differences, the child's right to not engage, and possible mood changes. Many teachers let students be, if they did not want to participate, were disengaged, or disruptive, later helping them to catch up when they reengaged. For example, Baren's[MBK] students joined the prayers, disengaged, and reengaged, much like the natural ebb and flow of a river and he did not force them one way or the other (he later explained that in the previous year certain children were continually active in the classroom prayers and this year others were more active). Additionally, they perceived students as equals and aimed to learn how to live harmoniously from students (to be more accepting, loving, and forgiving). This prevented "saviourism" and hierarchies and ensured that both teachers and students remained co-learners.

Teachers drew a distinction with having a love/care-based relation with children and doing things to expect love/respect from them. Teachers were careful to not appease students. As Tanuj[RVS] explained:

> Love from children and the respect from them are by-products. ... This is not something you have to work [towards] or I do not look at it that sense and that's a wrong way. ... Otherwise you just end up doing things to appease. That's indulgence and I would say that's not the right approach.

Teachers differentiated between a good teacher and an appeasing one. Senior teacher[RVS] commented:

> This kid asked me 'do not you want to be popular, like so and so teacher'. I said 'listen, if by doing what is right by you, it gives me popularity fine, if by doing something right by you and I become unpopular that is also fine. So, if my doing right to you is going to bring anger into [you] I am fine by it. Later, you will realise I am not going to overindulge you. I am not going to say nice things to you all the time.'

Teachers did not mind being firm or putting 'their foot down', but they remained mindful of children's needs as well as being respectful and tried being strict without being angry. Students frequently commented that the teachers were fair and even asked them to be stricter. For example, Anita[MGIS] contended:

> Children are mature even at this age, knowing that: father gets angry, mother gets angry, and teacher would also gets angry. I feel included in that you can also get angry; that's it. They are not asking you to get angry, they are giving me permission. 'I understand, if it needs to be done, then we are okay, because we accept that you are teaching us, that's all.' [But] They expect me to be fair.

Anita[MGIS] further explained how the depth of the bond and the fact that the children and teacher had gone through a lot allowed her to *'hak thi bolvu'* (speak with the right to) and that it was taken in the spirit of the relation (much like that with a friend/parent) as opposed to being seen as authoritative.

Warm and Safe Classroom Environment

Teachers created a safe, warm environment through their relations, non-judgemental acceptance, and the ethos of autonomy and collaboration. They believed that safety ensued due to acceptance of a person for who-ever they were. There was a belief in intrinsic motivation and student autonomy, where students did something, not because a teacher told them to (or because of rewards/punishments), but rather because they were intrinsically motivated to do so. Students were comfortable speaking with teachers about personal lives and problems. They generally did not feel the need to hide or lie; they recognised that there might be 'fair consequences', but these were seen as just and never harsh. Additionally, students were uninhibited in voicing their opinions to the teachers when they were bored, disengaged, or if they thought the teacher had erred. Teachers believed that all students needed to be actively included and cared for. Surojit[PB] suggested:

> School is a place where they socialise. If you reject them, they have a kind of emotional storm, kind of emotional shock, because they feel that they have been rejected by the society and social institutions.

Teachers frequently motivated and appreciated students across various non-academic purposes, especially attitudes, participation, and internalisa-tion of LTLTH, which led to a warm environment. Teachers focused on building students' self-esteem ('feeling good about oneself/the subject') and frequently motivated them. However, they remained careful with praising students (if and when they praised someone, they also praised other children; either as a group or individually). For example, in instances when teachers praised students' work, they appreciated one skill or another including drawing, observation, academic writing, academic understand-ing, and so on. They also sought to ensure that students did not do some-thing for the sake of being praised, but rather for the intrinsic satisfaction from the process. Teachers strongly emphasised that rewards can be a false yardstick and instead they hoped for their students to do what they did because of the internal satisfaction. Jyothi[RVS] (like Tanuj[RVS]) nuanced the discussion and questioned the role of praise and rewards:

When I worked in England, there was this constant demand on me to praise children. I had teacher observations, and they would say I have to encourage the students, and their way of encouraging is 'well done' and 'good job'. I think you can appreciate without all that. … [Why do we say] even very inane comments like 'have you been a good boy?' I do not know why you would put that moral construct on them at a very young age. It is tremendous moral pressure on them.

All teachers were generally very wary of rewards (and even more so for a carrot and stick approach), holding the view that these generally harm both those rewarded and those who are not. Rewards can lead to false comparisons and competitions, harming everyone involved in the process. Teachers believed rewards to be very arbitrary: in terms of who set the criteria for them, what the rewards are, and who receives them and who does not. Furthermore, they emphasised that each child was on a different educational trajectory and rewarding some of them based on arbitrary criteria (or those set by others) was unjust.

Autonomous Behaviour Management

Freedom and Autonomy as the Basis of Intrinsic Behaviour Regulation

The schools embodied an ethos of freedom and autonomy, which was a powerful behaviour management strategy that led to higher student intrinsic motivation, responsibility, and onus taking. The levels of freedom extended to and beyond "[students'] right not to participate" (Surojit[PB]) and "the freedom to be [who you are] and to choose what you want to learn" (Anita[MGIS]). Teachers saw externally imposed rules as meaningless and unsustainable, preferring students to become more responsible and find an inner discipline for themselves. Kamala[MBK] proposed that this kind of freedom leads to a sustainable impact and underpins LTLTH:

So, building oneness is looked upon as something that will be imposed from top and that is done in school's uniform, assembly, bells. We all do the same homework; we all have to get the same marks. It is kind of a numbing equality. It's not diversity, it irons everybody's differences out and that is very comfortable. In that we are one, but the minute such people are given freedom, then all the convolutions start to form and there are fights and opinions there is ignorance there is intolerance. So, I feel that oneness is not something that will be built by imposition. It has to come by building each individuals faith and trust in being themselves and adjusting to the others … building genuine mutual respect in each person.

The more restrictions you place, the more people want to break them. … I do not want to go about in that way, because we can always place restrictions, which will be more like, you know, somebody dictating things from the top, but rather, it should come from within. Maybe I can tell them that hereafter do not eat certain things or do not bring certain things, but unless they realise the importance of it, they will do it just for me, but they won't do it for the sake of [itself]. They won't understand why, they may not feel part of the movement. So, I think they need to realise it fully for themselves to do it. I do tell them something, but then I do not insist that it should be done.

All the schools are built around philosophies of freedom, independence, and self-governance. In the mid-twentieth century, at RVS, teachers and students were free to pick the subjects and teachers/students who they wanted to work with (Thapan, 2018). Whilst that level of freedom does not exist anymore, there was still a substantial amount of it. Students had the freedom to decide whether to attend class (all schools); what to wear (all schools except PB); the curricula (MGIS and MBK); which parts of a project to contribute to (MGIS, MBK, and RVS); project timelines and deadlines (all schools); which skills, character, and physical qualities to develop (MBK); and multiple ways to approach a question. Some examples of student freedom are demonstrated by classroom incidents of students being free to sing as they worked in Shreya's[PB] classes, different groups following different plans to complete a project in MGIS, students going for a walk in Joona's[MGIS] class, when they did not feel engaged, and MGIS and RVS students deciding classroom norms and routines. Students frequently reported that there was a lot of freedom at the various schools, and it was one of the reasons that they attended. At RVS, unlike the other three schools, students had a highly structured day (although there was freedom within each timeslot), but the degree of structure was an ongoing dialogue within the teaching body.

Teachers' beliefs and values underpinned their commitment to student freedom; for example, Surojit[PB] commented, "At all times teachers have to keep in mind that each child is an individual, they need to be respected, and there needs to be freedom". There was a commonly held belief across all teachers that they developed students' interests and then allowed freedom and flexibility to explore or not explore a given area. The teachers focused on building student onus and the processes as opposed to the final target. Baren[MBK] said:

> 'You do it now or do not do it now', whatever, the child should take the responsibility. Give them the sense of responsibility and at the target time, if they have not done it, then you can see it in their face, they are not feeling good. If they are interested, then they will do it simply because of their interest.

However, there were times when students lost intrinsic motivation midway and at these points teachers engaged in dialogue to reassess the purpose, current interests, and new directions.

There was a strong understanding that freedom must coexist with responsibility and inner discipline (self-governance or '*atma shakti*'). Bodhirupa[PB] commented that seeing discipline as confinement of the soul is a limited perspective and that she perceived no contradiction between freedom and inner discipline. She suggested that they were integrally linked, like two sides of a coin and that freedom was incomplete (and not possible) without inner discipline. Freedom was not seen as just an external freedom, for teachers perceived freedom as also from oneself, one's emotions, and unchecked reactions. Teachers consciously worked towards building student responsibility, which was seen through a community-based lens, where an individual was responsible for their self, others around, and the physical surroundings. They extended students' responsibility from regulating their own behaviour to helping regulate that of their peers. This, at times, took the form of elected (on a rotation basis) monitors or supervisors; however, more frequently teachers placed emphasis on **everyone,** taking the responsibility for the physical environment, the classroom ethos, and classroom behaviours. Similarly, Krishnamurti (2000, 2004) described freedom as not plainly doing what one wants, but rather being informed by the interconnected world around oneself and then making decisions that do right by everyone. For example, at RVS while individual freedom would have meant students could eat leisurely over multiple hours, however, they recognised that if they did so, various support staff members would have to wait for longer. Therefore, children often didn't linger in the dining hall once they completed their meals; in some instances, teachers or peers would remind others and students did not feel as if their freedom was being curtailed and/or they were being

imposed upon. Across the fieldwork I observed a range of student attitudes to responsibility taking, linked to individual differences in students,
ranging from completing a role because they had been assigned/elected
to students going out of their way to help the school environment/peers
or doing something because they perceived it to be the "right thing to do"
(this understanding of right thing to do was based on a broad interconnected awareness of the people and surroundings around them). Teachers
usually got involved through dialogue if and when students became hierarchical or didn't demonstrate a sense of community onus and responsibility to explore the underlying reasons and introduce new perspectives.

"Student-Centred" Behaviour Management Strategies

Many behaviour management strategies involved autonomy, with students
developing their own set of rules and regulating each other's behaviours.
The teachers reminded students of the rules or drew their attention to
their behaviours and then let them self-regulate. All schools had school-
wide student committees, which informed decisions ranging from menus/
movies to watch to adapting school policies (boarding schools had a wider
range of committees). Some students democratically set up classroom
rules, discussed their logical consequences, and helped implement these.
Students commonly developed new behaviour management strategies and
suggested these to the teachers. These rules at MGIS took the form of a
classroom poster, whilst at RVS they led to a discussion. This contrasts
with practices used by half of the teachers, who claimed that rules did not
have to be explicitly written down, but rather must be embedded in the
way of life. Regarding which, Bharat[Shreyas] said:

> Everyone says Namaste to each other when they meet in the morning.
> No-one has told anyone to do so; there are no written rules for it. … They
> say Namaste to others, throw waste in the waste bin, but it's never been
> written anywhere. Everyone does it, the rule is established by every-
> one doing it.

Shreya[PB] expanded on this, asking:

> Can students take self-responsibility, or do we need rules? Do we need to
> run after them, or can they run after each other, or no-one runs after anyone
> as they all see the importance of what they do?

This difference in the use of explicit rules is highly contextualised; however, there are very different approaches that can bring about education for harmony.

Students frequently regulated their own and their peers' behaviours. Teachers built a forum for peer regulation through previously described routines, like dialogic reflections, democratic rule-setting, council meetings, and introducing new perspectives. Students frequently developed new routines to manage their peers' behaviours, including counting down, use of actions and sounds to ask everyone to settle down, as well as electing monitors and supervisors. There were several notable incidents: supervisors frequently wrote and reported themselves when they could not self-regulate, students changed their seats by themselves when they felt they were becoming disruptive, and two students in one of Srila's[MBK] classes expressed that they had discussed whether their behaviour was 'really disruptive', concluding that they had disrupted the teachers and other students, and therefore, they had resolved to try and change. At times there were generally logical and fair consequences of students' behaviours, many of these pre-decided by the students themselves. Students came up with logical, 'meaningful'/'thoughtful' consequences; however, at times, they went 'overboard' (especially younger children), and teachers stepped in to provide a perspective on the harshness of their position. Teachers were generally against various forms of punishment due to their strong belief in student freedom as well as intrinsic discipline and motivation. There were instances where teachers implemented the pre-determined consequences, but they remained respectful and mindful of a child's perspective. A noted example was from the pilot study, where Bharat[Shreyas] asked children to give him a chit that they were passing between themselves and at the end of the class returned it to the child who had passed it, without opening it. He later explained that students play a game where they pass chits, and he just wanted them to discontinue it during the class.

At times, there were tensions about certain school-wide rules. This led to multiple discussions, where teachers explained the rules and students discussed them where they apparently made no sense to them. However, most of these tensions came from national or societal contexts. For example, RVS was forced to put limits on areas students could visit (it is a large open campus in a valley) due to the increasing presence of relatively unknown people (many colleges and construction sites had come up); RVS had installed fences around the school, because of a national order for children's safety; and at MBK, students were told not to visit an old building that was under a legal dispute. These discussions, while dialogic in nature, ended with some degree of imposition; however, some teachers themselves were wary of some of the rules.

The subsection title suggests a dichotomy between teacher and student-centred learning: terminology that was used by the teachers. However, the use of this terminology is a remnant of various teacher training discourses or as Alexander (2008) suggested, they are an imposition of western 'child-centred' pedagogy on non-western contexts. In practice, they transcended this dichotomy, with the classroom behaviour management involving a constant interplay and interaction between the teacher and the students.

Balancing Teachers' Freedom and Needs

Cultures of freedom must run through the whole school; they cannot just be limited for students and not apply to teachers. While systems of autonomy for teachers are discussed later in the next chapter, it is important to note that, within classrooms, both teachers and students had their individual freedoms. Teachers frequently stated their own needs and when these were not met, they would discontinue teaching and let the class settle down or wait until the students regulated theirs and their peers' behaviours. One of these needs was their own wellbeing and most of the teachers refused to raise their voices. There were several instances when teachers' needs were not met, and they would just sit down or go for a short walk. Notably, Srila's[MBK] students were not able to cooperate, and she decided to head out of the class and into the ashram for her own meditative practices. She returned after 1.5 days when the students had reflected on the classroom incident, resolved an internal conflict, and had figured out a plan on how to work together. Once this was done, the students went and spoke to her about the same and the classes resumed as normal, with neither the students nor Srila[MBK] holding onto the incident. Teachers at MGIS and MBK frequently stepped out of the class when students were too hard to handle. They did so to either (a) regain control of their emotions, for example, "that's okay I am get upset and that's allowed; it's okay … [but] first that you control yourself. I do not care how much [upset or angry you maybe], you go for a walk, and I often do that. I take a round and come back" (Anita[MGIS]); or (b) allow time for the students to calm down, reflect, and settle down.

Teachers believed that within the freedom, at times, they had to put their 'foot down'. They did not shy away from 'putting their foot down' when they perceived harm to other students, when a student 'speaks down' to another, or when a child was being excluded. Additionally, at times there were certain non-negotiables based on the teachers' own well-being or philosophy, such as not raising their voice or requiring a certain level of engagement. They frequently commented, "[D]o I want to be a nice teacher, or do I want to be a good teacher?". Teachers generally were quite moderate and calm when responding to students. Examples of such included stating something was not okay (especially in cases of potential harm to peers), insisting on something, stepping out of the classroom, or having students reflect on an incident. A senior teacher[RVS] explained:

> I believe in taking the middle path, I believe in being the best of their friends and when it comes to, I can also be quite a task master. ... There is a fine balancing between discussing and explaining vs saying something that is unacceptable as being unacceptable (children 'walking over others'). ... So, sometimes you have to be that straight, with compassion.

Children also appreciated teachers for their fairness and ability to be strict when needed. They realised that sometimes they were driven by emotions, and it might require a little firmness. For example:

> The children want her to be firm, but still loving (much like with Anita[MGIS] they wanted her to be strict and fair). Children respect her even when she raises her voice; they say 'it makes sense to us; we understand her and why she raises her voice. She does not go beyond.' (Field notes from discussions with Srila's[MBK] students)

Conflict Resolution

Conflicts in any community are inevitable and the same is the case with any school. These conflicts can arise between students, teachers and students, as well as the management and students. It is essential that the conflicts are resolved through empathetic dialogue and mutual understanding (Herzberger, 2018; Krishnamurti, 2000). While it is easy to sweep issues under the carpet or to exert power to get back to work, unresolved conflicts frequently lead to many other issues. Herzberger (2018) emphasises that conflict resolution processes should be underpinned by a sense of commitment to each other, each other's wellbeing, and the community.

Teachers across the schools actively sought conflict resolution interventions, including one-on-one conversations, small group discussions, theatre-based resolution (Anita[MGIS] only), council meeting practices (MGIS only), and/or reflective practices. Reflective practices, as discussed in the previous chapter (and council meetings at MGIS), were regarded as central or as 'the nucleus' of LTLTH. Council meetings usually involved every child getting an opportunity to appreciate another child or raise a concern and the opportunity for other child(ren) to respond. The rest of the class actively listened, weighed-in, and helped decide next steps (students had official roles of moderating, chairing, and note-taking). The teacher remained present but did not get involved unless required. These conflict resolution practices allowed students to become aware, get a different perspective on their behaviours ('others act like mirrors'), and outline actionable next steps for the whole class (as opposed to just the individual). For example, in Hema's[MGIS] class, students complained about a child who constantly 'irritated' others; this led to a council meeting wherein the students decided to not react and help the child become aware and self-regulate whenever he 'irritated others'. During these practices, teachers focused on deep understanding of an issue and not laying the blame on each other. In order to do so, Baren[MBK] carried out reflections only after a couple of days, once students had stopped blaming and started actively listening to each other.

Teachers proactively engaged during the classes; they constantly observed students, remained aware of arising conflicts, looked for behavioural trends and any unexamined comments, stepped in to help students regulate their behaviours, and looked for teachable moments for LTLTH. They were extremely observant, aware, and mindful, frequently picking up the minutest of student responses and reactions. For example, Tanuj[RVS] narrated:

> Responding makes a good teacher. One of the things of a good teacher is that they are actually very alert in the classroom as to what is happening. They're seeing things rather than assuming. They are not caught up with creating order or discipline, and so on. So, you watch, and you see where you need to intervene and think how you do it?

For many teachers, their proactive behaviour and awareness of students' behaviours and activities extended beyond the classrooms; they had a strong sense of onus and saw themselves as responsible for the whole school, remaining aware of things happening outside the class.

Conflicts between teachers and students were rare as teachers were mindful of their own behaviours and remained sensitive to students' needs. Any arising conflicts were resolved through previously described practices; however, at times, other teachers would come in to help moderate. This allowed both teachers and students to openly share and express their experiences and needs. There were issues that led to conflicts between students and the school management (described previously, e.g., fencing at RVS and installation of cameras at MBK) and these resulted in extensive and repeated dialogic discussions. Many a time the issues were such that there was limited flexibility in what could or could not be done but the sessions allowed for a space to voice (shared) disagreement and understand reasons and context underpinning decisions.

Conclusion

Both curricula and pedagogical practices can contribute to education for harmony, but education for harmony needs to transcend beyond a given subject or activities across multiple subjects to a continuum of lived experiences across the day and time at the school (and hopefully beyond). This form of a lived experience of harmony has to be underpinned by the school culture and ethos. These are actively built and rebuilt by everyone in the school and the culture informs and is informed by relations and structures of power. This chapter has presented case studies of how a few alternative schools co-construct the continuum of lived experiences of education for harmony through caring, loving, freedom-centric, inclusive, collaborative, and dialogic school ethos, TSR, as well as effective governance/regulation (school, classroom, and student) processes. I invite you to explore and share, in your given contexts, what can be done to co-create a continuum of lived experiences of (active) harmony? What kind of school cultures, ethos, and within school relations can bring about education for harmony? How can these be developed? How can we build a sense of intrinsic responsibility and inner discipline for all children? What are the potential limitations of autonomous behavioural regulation and how can these be overcome?

CHAPTER 9

Teachers' Ways of Living and Being: Teachers as Reflective Lifelong Learners of Harmonious Living

Indian thinkers have frequently emphasised LTLTH and its various equivalents as being caught rather than taught. They believed that teachers' ways of living and being impact on those of their students. Therefore, education for harmony cannot be taught through lectures, but is rather caught through shared lived experiences. Baren[MBK] suggested that pursuing LTLTH as a set of pre-set processes is superficial and that it must be a deeper pursuit that stems from a teacher's way of life (and a different philosophy of education and LTLTH).

> Other schools and institutions aspire to become like Mirambika, and they come to us and say we will do this and that, but they lack the core. What we do does not matter, but how it is done and where it comes from is important. For them it comes from the mind; for us it comes from the soul.

Gandhi noted, "Education of the heart can only be done through the living touch of the teacher". This resonates with my own experiences as well, where Brahmavedantji's ways of living and being touched me and became seeds of transformation. I hardly attended any of his talks or read his books, but his behaviour, approach to life, and loving and compassionate relations not only showed me a different way of living and being, but also inspired me to find ways to transform myself.

© The Author(s), under exclusive license to Springer Nature Switzerland AG 2023
J. Patel, *Learning to Live Together Harmoniously*, Spirituality, Religion, and Education,
https://doi.org/10.1007/978-3-031-23539-9_9

Furthermore, several scholars (including Noddings 2002; National Council of Education and Research Training 2012) have called for teachers modelling behaviours. However, teachers in the study suggested a more nuanced understanding of the word 'modelling'. They noted that students easily see through masks, if and when teachers are superficially trying to behave differently in front of the students. Instead, the teachers called for teachers to actively **try** to live differently and harmoniously, not just model behaviours. They needed to make a genuine effort to embed behaviours that they hoped to model in their ways of living and being. Teachers trying to live together was understood to be much deeper than modelling; for example, a senior teacher[PB] suggested that "it has to be a way of life. Teachers need a sense of vision and need to believe in it." They believed that they could 'carry' peace or emotions into class. A senior teacher[RVS] reflected:

> Maybe a teacher carries silence into the room, yeah, teachers can carry quietness into the room and that's something that they bring with themselves. And students feel that, and it becomes a live experience.

In this chapter, I discuss the importance of teachers' philosophy for education, teachers' commitment to LTLTH for both themselves and their students, and ways to support teachers in their journeys of education for harmony. Finally, I propose extending our understanding of schools as spaces for transferring academic knowledge to those of ashrams/centres of lifelong learning for all.

TEACHERS' PHILOSOPHY OF EDUCATION

Teachers commonly discussed the importance of their philosophical stances to education. Surojit[PB] suggested, "Perhaps the ideologies need to be at the back of teachers' minds [constantly]". These philosophies (including their perceptions of the purposes of education, their teaching process beliefs, and their understanding of how children learn to live harmoniously) directly or indirectly influenced their teaching. Surojit[PB] further explained that, whilst pedagogies are skills that one can be trained for, it is more important to build the 'outlook' of a teacher. Many of the philosophies have been discussed in Part I of the book; here, I focus on teachers' sense of commitment to LTLTH. Many teachers strongly emphasised that education for LTLTH was their primary goal of education and were strongly driven by their vision for the purpose, and a desire to live differently (more harmoniously), to work with children and shape a more compassionate society. However, a few teachers questioned if there should be a purpose of education (especially one defined by teachers, parents, or the nation). Such teachers were notably put off when I first asked them about their vision for education. Instead advocated for a bottom-up approach where students lead (resonating with previously discussed ideas of Educere-ing) and educators practice 'mindful purposelessness', where one consciously attempts to not be driven by their own visions (and rather by those of the child).

In either case, both sets of teachers were strongly committed to their visions and approaches to education. Anju[MGIS] suggested:

It is a commitment when they come here. They are following a passion, because they say that they want to teach, and they want to be in a different school, and they are excited about this kind of the thing.

While Tanuj[RVS] commented:

Passion comes from a different source. [In] more standard kind of school, some may love teaching and they just love being with children. In a school [like RVS] the source [of passion] is life itself; wanting to understand life and wanting to understand basic questions of life, which have been put over the years.

This resonates with Sen (2005) and Frelin and Fransson's (2017) ideas of commitment and responsibility, where teachers pour all their time, energies, and effort into supporting students and working towards their wellbeing and best interests (Hansen, 1998; MacBeath et al., 2020). This commitment aligns with Noddings (1986, 2013a) and Valli's (1990) relational ethics of care, where care is privileged over rationality. Teachers, at times, described teaching as their *Dharma* (duty). This notion of commitment was also described by Krishnamurti, who frequently discussed the need for "educating the educator" (Krishnamurti, 2013), where he described a true teacher as being rooted in self-knowledge and committed to transforming **him/herself** as a human being and practising 'critical looking'/'choiceless awareness' as a form of self-discovery (Krishnamurti & Martin, 1997), with this commitment being underpinned by a strong moral passion and responsibility to establishing a 'good society' (Krishnamurti, 1993, 2013).

The teachers were committed to LTLTH not just for their students, but also for themselves. Most of the teachers commented on joining the respective schools to explore a different way of living and being for themselves: one without negative emotions, like fear, ego, and jealousy. The teachers' willingness to be learners makes them 'take the journey with the child' and helps build more equal relations. This learning ability also requires teachers to be open-minded, understanding, exploratory, and engaged in experiential learning. While opportunities and systems for teachers to question, discuss, and share their visions and purposes of education are critical to the development of the sense of commitment, the space for reflection, introspection, meditation, and social action is critical for teachers engaging in learning to live harmoniously for themselves.

TEACHERS LIVING HARMONIOUSLY AND LTLTH

(Learning to) Living Together Harmoniously as a Way of Life

Building on the idea that LTLTH is primarily caught, teachers' own ways of living and being become quite important. For example, Bharat[Shreyas] believed:

> It is through our *vaani* (speech), *vartan* (conduct) and *vyavhar* (behaviour) that we are able to teach. *Vaani, vartan* and *vyavhar*, these three have a direct effect. If I am teaching a wonderful lesson and a child raises his hand and I say [acts as if telling the child to put his hand down], all three are gone. *Vaani, vartan* and *vyavhar* have a major effect.

Similarly, teachers living harmoniously was seen as essential to students' LTLTH, with Anita[MGIS] asserting:

> Our duty is to touch the life of the child in some way and that comes through learning to live together. That I am taking the onus to live together with them for this year. If I am able to live with even the naughtiest, most mischievous, or most problematic child then they will also learn.

Teachers commonly lived harmoniously as a way of life for themselves. They frequently embodied various components from the LTLTH framework (Chap. 5) and this underpinned the various teaching-learning processes as well as all the various interactions (inside and outside the classroom). They were committed to LTLTH for themselves as much as they were for their students. There were innumerable references (>400) coded for teachers living harmoniously as a way of life (Table 9.1 summarises some of these).

Teachers strongly believed that, first, they must try to live harmoniously as a way of pursuing their own lives not just instrumentally (so students would learn to do so), but also intrinsically (because of the value they themselves placed on the way of living). Krishnamurti (2013) emphasised teachers' need to have a fiery desire to understand themselves and should pursue learning to live harmoniously as 'live enquiry' for themselves. He suggested that sustained aspiration and effort would transform teachers' lives, making them lifelong learners and forging equal relations with students (Thapan, 2001). Resonating with this, Baren[MBK] suggested, "[O]ur aspiration is to have psychic education or living from the soul and that is lifelong goal. We are not here to achieve it, but we are just here to walk on that path."

Conscious Effort to Learn to Live Together Harmoniously

While teachers embodied various aspects of LTLTH, they believed that it was more important for them to consciously try to (learn to) live harmoniously (rather than actually living harmoniously 24×7, which was seen as a near impossible task). For example, Srila[MBK] noted: "The day I stop learning and growing inwards I will stop coming to the school". There was a constant sentiment that LTLTH requires one to work consciously on oneself and all teachers shared an inner conviction to changing themselves. In order to do so, they were frequently engaged in dialogues, sessions where they read spiritual texts, meditation, as well as regular and constant introspection/reflection.

Teachers **consciously trying** to live harmoniously was seen as the key driving force for students' LTLTH. They worked towards consciously living harmoniously, being non-judgemental, and respecting every child as an equal; these led to harmonious lived experiences for students and, in turn, LTLTH. As Anju[MGIS] suggested:

Table 9.1 Summary data of teachers living harmoniously

Dimensions		*Discovery of the Self*	*Discovery of Other*	*Discovery of the World*
			Domains	
	Awareness and understanding	"What I have come to accept about myself is that I am not that fast" (Hema[MGIS]). "We will have to negotiate amongst ourselves, if we cannot handle it, we will be honest" (Jayanthy[MBK]).	"Even if you are never going to acknowledge that I did it, I know you know that I am wrong, but you just do not want somebody to shout at you" (Anita[MGIS]). "Sometimes it gets emotionally challenging, frustrating, but one has to remember that children are people too and if one remembers one's own childhood, then you realise that there is no point in getting frustrated" (senior teacher[secondary school]).	"I am not Congress; I am not BJP; I have my own ideology. And that ideology stems from a sense of equality" (Kamala[MBK]).
	Empathetic and caring relations	"At times I do not mind going down ... because I cannot always remain joyful and happy. At times we will definitely fall down" (Baren[MBK]).	All teachers demonstrated patience, care, sensitivity, and love for students (these have been previously discussed); however, they did not shy away from 'putting their foot down' when needs be. "I want to be like a nice teacher, or do I want to be a good teacher?" (Anita[MGIS] and Senior teacher[RVS]).	"Do things for the sake of that thing rather than for yourself, for presenting yourself in a way, for how it might appear to others, for the outcome, but for the beauty in the process" (teacher[RVS]). "[there are no constraints or enablers]. They are [situations/factors] I have available. They do not enable, they do not in any way discourage me, but they exist, and I try to work around them the best I can" (Kamala[MBK] and Srila[MBK]).
	Sense of purpose	Teachers aspired to live harmoniously as a way of life. "At some point, you know you reach a stage in your life, where you do what you think is right or what is required without letting all these other things influence you" (Hema[MGIS]).	Teachers were driven by their philosophy of education and a sense of responsibility (stemming from notions of commitment).	"I am blessed that I am not poor, hungry or ill-clothed, but there are so many around me who are, and as long as they are I am also poor; I am also ill clothed and I'm also hungry, so I have to feel that pain and I cannot wish it away" (Kamala[MBK]).

		Domains		
		Discovery of the Self	*Discovery of Other*	*Discovery of the World*
Dimensions	Change in perspective	"See, I am not going to learn in one day. We do not learn in one go" (Anita[MBK])	Teachers were very mindful of the child's perspective. "Arun might change, [he] might have a complete turnover a few years from now, you never know, because I have seen the most difficult children change into beautiful human beings by the time, they go to class 9 and there are very, very sober and nice children that turn into monsters" (Senior teacher[RVS]).	"There is nothing like a good teacher, because the moment you say there is a good teacher, then it also means that there is a bad teacher" (Srila[MBK]). "In everyone's personal lives I find difficulties and challenges and life is tough. It's just being human and understanding that he also has, the parent will be having ... everyone has some difficulty" (Anita[MBK]).
	Compassion (-ate action)	The teachers demonstrated and discussed the importance of patience, non-reaction, and non-judgement with themselves, students, parents, and peers, to the extent that this level of self-governance is also expressed as kindness. "You should be yourself; you shouldn't become someone else" (Aaditya[PB]).	Teachers had a keen sense of justice that drove their actions within and beyond classroom. "Peace is not the absence of war, but presence of justice" (Anita[MGIS]).	Several teachers (Kamala[MBK], Santharam[RVS], Tanuj[RVS], Shreya[PB], and Baren[MBK]) were involved in various social action projects outside the school, while Baren[MBK], Anita[MGIS], Joona[MGIS], Hema[MGIS], and Surojit[PB] were active in school-based community activities. These are further discussed below.
	Meaningful engagement	"The day I am close to my inner being there comes a different tone in the class. Finding and connecting with your own psychic being is the most important thing you can do as a class teacher" (Expert teacher[MBK]). "In this whole six months maybe once or twice it has happened to me ... during these 20–25 minutes I try to bring, as I said, contagious vibration, I try to remain connected" (Baren[MBK]).	"The overall goal is to be kind. It's my prayer that I will be kind in class, just help me to be kind" (Anita[MGIS]).	Most of the teachers naturally took community and school based responsibility as a form of commitment and deep engagement. "The whole thing is to move towards bringing this greater goodness into the world to counter the sorrow, and unhappiness" (Kamala[MBK]).

A compassion part comes in looking at a human being as a human being, as somebody worthwhile, somebody worthy, somebody who has some contribution to give to the world and when we bring that non-judgmental eye on the child, then all those pressures that the child must be feeling, whether coming from parents or peers or anybody begin to fall away. So then, that's the way to discover your true self; that I have something to give, and I have something to contribute. [1]

Teachers engaging in a constant, conscious process to learn to live differently allows for shared lived experiences between them and students of learning to live harmoniously. These shared conscious attempts, experiences, and processes of harmonious living bring about LTLTH.

There is a resonance with Aristotelian ideas of lived experiences and this opens the findings to the paradox of moral development. The paradox states that given that a child in the formative years has limited rationality, intelligence, virtues, and experiences of harmonious living, they would struggle to live harmoniously as children and would probably also have limited development over time (Haydon, 2009; James, 1986; Peters, 2015). Aristotle's solution to the paradox was based on teachers being moral exemplars (Curren, 2007), which has its own limitations, especially if teachers are expected to be their best selves all the time. However, the teachers extended this and their solution to the paradox was based on not seeing harmonious living as a binary; they understood that everyone's lives have instances of harmonious living and at some or other times one of the students, teachers, or community members would live harmoniously offering others a shared lived experience. Additionally, teachers believed that LTLTH does not require their living harmoniously, but rather it requires them to have a fiery desire to do so, pursuing LTLTH as a living enquiry (to keep learning) and making conscious efforts to do so. The imperative word in the discussions was try: "[T]eachers have to try to live together harmoniously".

---

[1] Please note that the teacher used the phrase something to give/contribute; resonating with non-modernist ideas of education, where education isn't extractive but rather facilitates/helps one to bring about a social change.

SUPPORTING TEACHERS' JOURNEYS OF LTLTH

An Ethos of Harmonious Living, Autonomy, and Reflection for and by Administrators, Teachers, and Students

The school systems helped build an ethos of freedom, collaboration, dialogue, experiential learning, and collective responsibility of the school for both teachers and students. These strongly aligned with schools' vision for education and over the years had created a school-wide ethos for these aspects. For example, the schools held an ethos of oneness, where teachers perceived each other as a part of a community/family engaged in similar pursuits and focussed on a common vision, with Shreya[PB] commenting:

> PB is a community; it's not become secluded. It has a very inclusive character and an informal sense of being together.

Ethos of Harmony

School administrators and teachers commonly believed that any vision for children must be 'through and through', embedded and embodied by the school and held for all its members. This aligns strongly with Noddings' (1992) recommendation that "school administrators cannot be sarcastic and dictatorial with teachers in the hope that coercion will make them care for students ... the likely outcome is that teachers will then turn attention protectively to themselves rather than lovingly to their students". The school environments embodied Southworth's (2000) call for conditions that empower teachers: autonomy, being valued, trusted, listened to, belonging to a collegial environment, with space for creativity, initiative taking, innovation, and pursuing what one values (LTLTH). The ethos can be seen as an extension of school connectedness (McNeely et al., 2002), where, like students, even teachers feel cared, valued, and included in the school community. School leaders were compassionate towards their teachers and held a strong belief that the teachers were also on their own journeys of finding themselves. Their teaching styles and philosophies of teaching/learning were constantly evolving, and the evident systems of dialogue, reflection, and freedom allowed for continued exploration. Bodhirupa[PB] said that she had faith in her colleagues and that, even if they were not convinced by the foundational philosophy today, in time, through experience, experimentation, and dialogue, they would become so. Whilst this shared ethos of harmonious living was built by all the members of the schools, a core group of teachers believed in an alternative vision for education and LTLTH as being central to the process. Furthermore, there was a strong sentiment that a school is created by the individuals within it and that the role of the management and leaders is to build a system that helps tap into the potential of all its individuals by building a supportive system around them. Herzberger (2018) calls for and attempted to develop cultures of transrationality within RVS through non-hierarchical and non-authoritarian systems allowing for the possibility of individuals and the school being informed by the sacred.

Ethos of Autonomy and Freedom

Teachers frequently commented that if there was one tenet that the schools held, then it would be freedom: freedom for teachers to explore what and how they wanted to teach and for students to explore what and how they wanted to learn. The schools had systemically weaved in freedom, in terms of freeing teachers from external pressures of the state and the parents (e.g., teaching certification requirements, curricula, parental pressure), challenging and freeing teachers from their past experiences of mass education, and freeing them from the schools' own structures. This freedom allowed teachers to explore their own styles, experiment, try out different projects, and completely 'come into their own'. Teachers weighed in on school-wide policy discussions and usually these entailed lengthy discussions. Jyothi[RVS] suggested that discussions often involved '10 teachers having 10 different views'.

There are many nuances to the teachers' freedom that need to be considered. For example, their freedom also necessitated regular teacher dialogue and decision-making processes for common community-wide decisions. This highlighted the importance of basic structures and support within the freedom, such as timetabling, school philosophy, vision, and a diverse list of skills that students needed to develop within a given time span. This was also supported by schools actively building and promoting a strong sense of responsibility and trusteeship. Additionally, Aaditya[PB] suggested that the freedom must come along with capability development, for if one does not know what to do and does not have the capacity/desire to experiment, then that person would revert to following predefined materials with only tokenistic changes.

The following extract from an interview with Anju[MGIS] demonstrates multiple aspects of a freedom-filled school ethos:

> Freedom, that's given, not given [but] it's there and it's equally there for teachers too and it's the whole ensemble. I think you cannot have controlled teachers and expect freedom for the kids, it's a culture that you create, so the

teachers have freedom in terms of which projects they want to do, when they want to do it, sometimes also what classes they want ....

Sometimes you need a teacher with particular competences in a particular group. Then, we discuss with the teacher saying, 'listen, we know you want to be in this group, but that group might need you more'. [If] somebody says, 'no I want to be with this group, because last year I started this project and I know where it's going and I was not able to complete it', then we will negotiate, 'alright let's do one thing you go into this class by rotation. ... They are happy, we work out there is a lot of dialogue, so that freedom I feel is something which is a culture otherwise, I do not think it will percolate ....'

By and large they have a great deal of autonomy; there are many things I do not come to know at all. Like, you are going to France next month? All right you decided the dates, oh great! There are things that I do not know, and they do everything.

Supporting Dialogue, Experimentation, Collaboration, Reflection, Introspection, Meditation, and Social Action: Integral Support for Learning to Live Together Harmoniously

The schools' ethos was developed and maintained by non-hierarchical structures, supporting systems and processes that foreground autonomy, dialogue, experimentation, reflection, and social action. These led to teachers being driven by an internal commitment, sense of onus and responsibility (further described in next subsection), and they "put all their heart and love into their children" (Jayanthy[MGK]).

Dialogue, Collaboration, and Experimentation
All teachers frequently collaborated with each other to resolve issues they faced, to discuss students and their behaviours on projects, and to run cross-curricular modules for students. Teachers frequently learned from each other, describing the best practices of their peers that they were trying to emulate (especially teachers at PB and MBK and Anita[MGIS] and Hema[MGIS]), guiding each other, and seeking each other's guidance. Anju[MGIS] pointed out:

See, when you are talking about collaborative work, the teachers have to do collaborative work for the projects. The one teacher cannot teach everything in that project, because you are not an expert in every part. ... I mean, you have to create the culture [of collaboration], if the teachers do not experience it, it will not percolate to the kids. We have created the structures for it also, because we said that it's project work and the teachers have to teach in teams.

There was more collaboration at MGIS and MBK compared to RVS and PB due to the complete reliance on project-based pedagogies at the former two schools. Albeit, at RVS and PB there were other opportunities for collaboration due to the residential aspect of those schools.

Teachers frequently commented on the need for coherence of vision on the purposes of education. They appreciated that people could be vastly different from each other, have different opinions and perspectives, but still be like-minded in their aspirations to live harmoniously for themselves and bring about education for a different way of living and being. Further building on this a senior teacher[RVS] commented:

> Teachers need not just coherence, coherence is an ideological level, but cohesion where everyone are not just thinking ideologically but are also cohesively working towards it.

At times, teachers in RVS and PB commented on the lack of coherence, suggesting that many a time the efforts were reduced to individual efforts, rather than concerted ones by all working with a given child (within a given school year or later through the rest of the child's schooling years). Teachers explained that this had to come to be the case owing to their size; however, there was a core group of teachers who held the school's vision and that this slowly spread to others. At MBK, there was a strong coherence in the vision for education (regular teacher dialogue, introspection, and extremely selective recruitment), whilst at MGIS the regular teacher workshops brought a sense of coherence of vision, which allowed for systems of organised chaos to bring about LTLTH.

Teachers Involved in Reflection, Introspection, and Meditation

Many teachers engaged in regular reflection through diaries, introspection, reflections with peers or family members, discussion meetings, and/or school-based systems of reports. Reflections spanned from how a given class went to the teachers' own spiritual, emotional, and mental states of being. All teachers were engaged in active reflection to improve their practice (critically reflecting through various perspectives, planning the immediate next steps, and exploring what they could do differently). Shreya[PB] stressed that:

> You have to be self-critical; you just cannot say I am right. … There is nothing called the right process; it changes depending upon the child's psychol-

ogy. The entire things change so fast that you just sit there and say what I did was wrong.

Additionally, reflection as form of improvement was also seen as something that happens constantly as a way of being and living. For example, "[W]hatever you do you have to be mindful—what message you give—what do they take up", Srila[MBK] or as Tanuj[RVS] explained:

And that continually watching [of] how you are in that space, you know, with the children and your behaviour. So, being very much aware of that helps you to move. Yeah, and it's a journey, it's not that you reach your destination, it's a journey. So that makes this whole thing light, otherwise this can become heavy also.

Several teachers pointedly used reflection to challenge and question the purpose of education and its practices, for example, "No-one knows why they are teaching maths—they are because that is how it is". Atul[RVS] and Kamala[MBK] questioned, "[I]s there a certain quantum of humanism in what I am trying to teach?", whilst Surojit[PB] said:

Teacher training programmes need to focus on the purpose of education; questioning what is happening, the relevance or meaningfulness of it ... we haven't really got to think about a lot of this and questioning. There are so many other things that we blindly follow, like the syllabus, exams, and it's nice to question them, but teachers that are supposed to be the most rational beings do the most irrational things by just following many irrational things.

Many teachers constantly reflected on whether they were able to bring about meaningful education and how they could do this better. For example, teachers at RVS commonly questioned their own practices inspired by Krishnamurti's prompt for teachers to shape fundamentally different students and not just 'mice' or 'faster mice'.

They [students] remain mice—tame, domestic mice ... here we are, nearly a thousand students in our schools and we do not seem to be able to produce one gazelle or one lion or even a big elephant. Why is this? (Krishnamurti, 1985)

This reflexivity along with intrinsic commitment to a holistic education fuelled regular and constant discussions (both on classroom and on school-wide practices and policies) and experimentation, keeping the pursuit of education for harmony a live enquiry (and not something that had a fixed blueprint).

Teachers' Social Work and Spiritual Journeys

Teachers were strongly driven by and engaged in either social or spiritual/ inner transformation. The freedom to do so was essential for the teachers; these were the major reasons for them joining the school (either to experiment with education as a form of transforming society or to experiment with a different way of living and being). I frequently saw teachers as either *sadhaks* (spiritual practitioners) engaged in their spiritual journeys or social changemakers engaged in other social action projects within and beyond the school; they were committed to and actively pursued what mattered to them. Those driven by a desire to contribute to/serve/uplift society suggested that other pursuits of life are not as meaningful as helping to make the world a more beautiful place. Kamala[MBK] explained:

> And highest in priority is the desire to [help the] society, to work with children, to change the world we live in. I feel that it's important for me to put education of the heart as the core for whatever I am doing.

They hoped to contribute to the society through education as a form of social change, indirectly through the children one taught and through various social action projects (within and beyond the school; further described below). These resonate with Giroux and McLaren (1986) and Giroux's (2010) ideas of teachers primarily being responsible for engaging students in transformative work and that this, in turn, helps students to understand social ideologies, find a voice, and act to bring about social justice. Teachers were involved in several social change initiatives within and outside the schools (summarised in Table 9.2). Some believed that systemic changes were required, while others hoped to bring about a change through small changes or 'doing one's bit'. They also engaged with and inspired students to partake in similar initiatives within the schools.

Table 9.2   Teachers and their social action engagements

Teacher	Social action project(s)'s description
Bharat[SF]	His wife and he coordinate an on-campus orphanage.
Anju[MGIS]	Coordinating and implementing large-scale teacher training programme for other schools affiliated with Central Board of Secondary Education (including tribal schools); the school is engaging its teachers in training other teachers around the country in pedagogies like generated resource learning, toy-based education, and activity-based learning.

(continued)

Table 9.2 (continued)

Teacher	Social action project(s)'s description
Anita[MGIS]	Actively integrated social action initiatives into the school projects, volunteered at the centre for environment education, and was involved in one-off teacher training for external teachers. Additionally, she is currently involved in other large-scale teacher training efforts.
Hema[MGIS]	Actively integrated social action initiatives into the school projects. Used to run a school and a reading library before joining the school. Additionally, she is currently involved in other large-scale teacher training efforts.
Joona[MGIS]	Actively integrated social action initiatives into the school projects and was involved in a teacher training initiative before joining the school.
Baren[MBK]	Contributed to the ashram and coordinated and conducted multiple 1–2 weeklong residential teacher training workshops for science, sports, English, and mathematics for teachers from villages and NGOs.
Srila[MBK]	Contributed to the ashram and conducted vocational training.
Kamala[MBK]	Coordinated the Delhi Science Forum to promote public engagement in scientific advancements, conducted teacher training in a village in Ramgarh, actively engaged in composting at schools, was exploring several village-based cooperatives that aimed to conduct rural development through community-based interventions, and conducted vocational training at the ashram. In the past, she had helped with the National Curricular Framework (NCF) 2005 and ran an eco-club for multiple Delhi-based schools to promote students' appreciation of nature.
Santharam[RVS]	Involved in ornithology, was helping to set up and run the Rishi Valley Ornithology Institute, and was actively involved in various school-based and region-based birdwatching trips and research.
Tanuj[RVS]	Actively involved in a Gujarat-based orphanage school and was actively involved in developing mathematics learning materials and kits for NGOs and the Rishi Valley Rural Education Centre.
Surojit[PB]	Involved in directing plays written by Rabindranath Tagore.

All teachers commonly read, reflected, and were inspired by spiritual leaders' books, talks, or lectures; however, one set of teachers was deeply invested in their respective spiritual journeys. They did not perceive that they were there to 'serve the society' (while a few hoped that the children would go on to change society), but rather they believed that 'working with children' and working on one's own self was far more meaningful. They used the spiritual leaders' ideologies to push and challenge themselves and their practices. They had weekly reading circles, where they explored works from the spiritual leaders, and held reflection meetings, where they reflected on their own spiritual journeys. Their own spiritual practices commonly contributed to teaching practices influencing planning and pedagogy, TSR, and helping them LTLTH. For example, Baren[MBK] commented:

> *Vipassana* has also helped me (become more flexible), because it gives me time to relax. Once I am at peace and relaxed when I sit for meditation, then the thoughts come flowing like a film; what is to be done and what is not to be done, clearly.

Flat Hierarchies: Equitable and Humane Leadership

The school leaders actively experimented in developing school-wide systems to empower teachers. They helped them explore different perspectives, built their confidence in themselves, supported them in learning and experimentation, as well as creating systems for reflection and dialogue. School leaders generally knew all the teachers very well in relation to their personalities, behaviours, eccentricities, and backgrounds. Many of the school leaders were actively engaged in the school, including regularly teaching classes. They were frequently inspirational and models for teachers, who frequently commented that they felt heard, valued, and respected. For example, Anita[MGIS] shared:

> Compassion expected first from the teachers has been at first given by [the school leaders]; it starts from the top. We can go and tell them anything that we are going through. I am not a blind follower; I am still saying it, that he has these saintly qualities through which he feels the sadness you can feel, that he feels your pain. … He will sit with you, if you are facing problems. … 'What's missing here, have you taken them out, given them a break, have you integrated?'. So, there is a lot of handholding and freedom to meet and discuss.

School leaders aimed to build a flat hierarchy and were very easily accessible. All teachers had a powerful sense of onus (next subsection) and drove changes within the wider schooling system. Leaders consciously broke down definitions of power structures and if labels were needed, then they were just to distinguish roles, though everyone was equally responsible for the school. Many a time, teachers and coordinators delegated work to school leaders, and school leaders were accountable to them as well. For example, Anju[MGIS] (the school leader) narrated:

I am going to her (another teacher) as a teacher. [She would say] 'Anju you need to give me the dates for this and this, when are you taking this aspect'. [I would say] 'okay when do we do this, to whom is it going to go and what's my deadline? Can you help me with this and how do I fill up these forms and things like that?'. Anytime she would call the meeting we would all be there. I would attend it as teacher and I would respect her, because she knows things about the whole programme.

One senior school leader[RVS] contended that there is always going to be a power dynamic, because one can hire/fire a teacher. However, other principals suggested that there are different kinds of power and that they did not work from a place of power, because of their position, but rather aimed to build 'soft power' through the teachers' trust and respect in them.

All schools had an ongoing dialogue about the level of structuring and support. Schools as a space were not seen as structured and crystallised, but rather as continuously evolving and in flux, depending on the context, people, and the ongoing experimentation. Teachers were against "mechanical systems" that have no "organicity", "spontaneity", or "space for intimate human relation and connections" (Aronson, 1961). Those at PB described the school as an organism and not an organisation, holding that any attempt to turn it into an educational factory was bound to fail. MBK, a much smaller school, embodied ideas, systems, and processes based on constant dialogue, reflection, and collaborative decision-making, where all teachers came together to adapt structures on a regular basis (daily, if necessary). MGIS believed in an unstructured, and dynamic chaotic system; they believed that the process was more important and did not want teachers to follow predefined procedures; however, a few teachers found it to be overwhelming at times. While other schools, albeit larger, had more structures (RVS and PB needed a hierarchy given their organisational size and their residential school natures). RVS had a lot more structured systems relative to MBK or MGIS: freedom was woven into what and how things took place within the broader structure (despite Krishnamurti being opposed to any kind of structuring and institutionalisation). PB had developed informal structures (not put in place by the management, but that had evolved over time). Teachers at both these schools expressed the view that the system might have become crystallised, mechanical, and needed reviewing. However, RVS teachers also appreciated structures of reflection, dialogue, and behavioural reporting. To summarise, it is important to strike a balance between having certain supportive structures and allowing significant teacher autonomy; a few systems for dialogue, reflection, communication of core philosophies, support (when challenges were encountered), and documentation of the outcomes of dialogues can be beneficial. I posit that, while smaller school sizes are ideal (both for teachers and for students), bigger schools also have a potential for LTLTH, albeit of a different kind, with separate set of systems and processes.

A Powerful Sense of Onus and Responsibility

The ethos, along with the schools' supporting systems, helped teachers develop a strong sense of onus. The school administrations trusted, respected, and appreciated teachers' sense of it. They saw themselves and the teachers as being engaged in a project as peers. Teachers in all schools joined the schools as a partner, with the aim of experimenting with diverse ways of teaching/learning and being. At all schools, teachers were actively involved in school policy decision-making and initiated independent projects. There was a keen sense of collective responsibility, with all teachers being aware of things outside their classrooms and stepping in as and when required (from leaking taps, aligning students' shoes so others do not trip over them to helping students regulate their behaviours). Teachers felt responsible for the whole school and stepped in whenever anything was amiss (rather than passing it off to a designated person). They believed that it was their responsibility to do so, while others explained that the school was like one's home and if something were amiss, one would instantly act.

Teachers had a strong sense of onus and collective responsibility. These stemmed from a Gandhian sense of trusteeship as a non-violent form of ownership. They frequently commented, acted, and believed that they were responsible for the school, children, and the school's vision. This has widely been suggested as being important for educational processes, leading to intrinsic motivation and commitment (Pierce et al., 2001; Struckman & Yammarino, 2003). In many instances, school leaders did not need to delegate responsibilities, for teachers took these up themselves and at times also delegated responsibilities to school leaders (MGIS and MBK). This resonates with Frost's (2017) recommendation of non-positional leadership as a form of teacher empowerment.

Teachers who developed a sense of ownership commonly expressed and communicated what they found meaningful (Pierce et al., 2001, 2003) and also had a strong sense of agency (Ketelaar et al., 2012). In accordance with Metcalfe and Greene (2007) and Vähäsantanen et al.'s (2008) description of agency as control over one's actions and being able to be true to oneself, teachers had developed a sense of agency, challenged precepts, actively experimented, and attributed results to themselves as opposed to external factors (Marshall & Jane Drummond, 2006), which, in turn, led to the development of a strong professional identity (Beijaard et al., 2004). Schools commonly asked teachers to challenge, 'think for themselves', and experiment. The sense of agency extended to a collective form, where teachers as a group felt responsible for the school, its members, and, accordingly, supported each other. M. W. Apple and Beane (1999) suggested that such collective agency is possible due to an environment that promotes 'open flow of ideas', faith in each other, and collective capacity. Additionally, the systems of dialogue and collaboration were paramount for mutual inspiration, improved practice, and collective agency (Frost, 2017; MacBeath et al., 2020).

Schools as Lifelong Learning Centres, Ashrams, and Communities for Harmonious Living

The schools understood and appreciated that education for LTLTH should be a lifelong pursuit (for themselves and students), with education (for both teachers and students) and living/being seen as inseparable. Similarly, Cajete (1999) contended that indigenous education should be a lifelong process bringing about harmonious living through reflection and introspection of experiences and participation in the community. The schools were designed as learning spaces for everyone, rather than just as a school. RVS is housed on a larger campus named the Rishi Valley Education Centre, MGIS was designed as a centre for learning, MBK (and MGIS) runs various teacher training courses and workshops, and PB has an integrated university and school. Srila[MBK] commented, "The purpose of the school is to begin teachers' journeys … this place is a Utopia for learning [for everyone]". The centres were places of learning through experimentation and experience (rather than teaching), and in some cases, teachers and administrators commented that they actively 'chased out teaching' so both teachers and students could learn together. The spaces are free and collaborative learning ones, where teachers are frequently engaged in their own experiential learning: experimenting, maintaining notes, reflecting, theorising, and dialoguing with each other (Kolb, 1984).

All schools engaged teachers in experiential learning, (peer) observation, dialogue, reflection, and reading groups. There were several learning opportunities, ranging from workshops, inviting visitors, continuous professional development, dialogic meetings, and collaborative projects that involved learning from students as well. At MBK, all teachers were required to learn and develop a new skill (music, dance, sport, weaving, wood/bamboo work, further education courses and degrees, etc.) over a couple of years and then pick up another one once they relatively mastered the previous one. This learning process helped teachers build confidence, self-esteem, as well as understanding students' perspectives and struggles. Teachers at MBK and RVS consciously and constantly worked on themselves and tried to live harmoniously.

The schools were commonly referred to as home, safe space, communities, collective living experiments, *ashrams*, or sacred spaces of transformation. Teachers at PB and MBK referred to the schools as an *ashram* (a space for spiritual learning/exploration or 'ground of self-realisation'). The schools were more than just learning centres, for they were spaces for learning ways of being/living life differently, 'fully, and wholly'. Regarding which, Tanuj[RVS] suggested, "In a school source (of passion) is life itself, wanting to understand life and wanting to understand basic questions of life, which have been put over the years". Kamala[MBK] commented on the school being an experiment in collective living: "To me school is a place where a collective is being built, and to me that is important. Learning together. … Because so many children come together and so many adults come together, it is a collective space for sharing and exploring, experimenting." MGIS teachers also commented on the schools becoming comfort zones or home-like, where they stopped being work places, but instead were spaces where one was safe, comfortable, and had a sense of ownership. MBK, RVS, and PB teachers commented on there being a strong sense of community or 'one family', where teachers, students, administrators, and non-teaching staff were connected, sharing relations of equality and mutual respect.

Krishnamurti (1981) suggested:

> Surely, [schools] must be centres of learning a way of life, which is not based on pleasure, on self-centred activities, but on understanding of correct action, the depth and beauty of relationships and the sacredness of life. … These places exist for the enlightenment.

Teachers had joined the schools looking for different ways of living and being for themselves and different ways of education. Schools aimed to maintain and promote this lived enquiry of the teachers.

Conclusion

Education for harmony is fundamentally dependent on the educators and their own ways of living and being. This chapter has highlighted that the teachers were deeply committed to education for harmony as an aim for both their students' and their ownselves. They were engaged in conscious meaningful journeys of transforming their own ways of living and being, both within and beyond the school. I would like to invite you to explore: what does education for harmony mean to you? What would a school of the future emphasising education for harmony look like? How would you go about transforming your own ways of living and being? How do you develop a fiery desire to keep the enquiry a live one? For me, writing this book has been a process of transformation and I am hopeful that it helps do the same for you. Furthermore, the chapter took a deep dive into the ethos and systems of dialogue, collaboration, reflection, introspection, meditation, and autonomy that can help shape and support teachers along this journey of education for harmony. I would finally like to invite you to explore: if and how we can go beyond seeing schools as spaces for educating young people to a space where a community of people are engaged in a joint exploration of education for harmony? And what are the ways to proceed such that the processes include everyone in the school communities, including students, teachers, parents, administrators, non-teaching/support staff, and the nature around the school?

CHAPTER 10

Provocations, Reflections, and Call to Action

How do we build lived environments for peace education?
Where life is lived in the spirit of collective onus;
Where teachers and students are coparticipants in a shared learning journey
Where the inner child survives in every teacher and every student-teacher

Perhaps it is through infusing daily process with harmony;
Teachers with a fiery desire for a different way of life;
Classrooms with the fragrance of laughter, free spiritedness, and compassion;
And with schools that embody the *ethos* of experiential learning.

Perhaps these are not schools but are ashrams;
Where everyone partakes in learning to live differently;
Where relations are forged through shared experiences and exploration of new interests;
Where the spirit of exploration, creativity and *freedom* becomes the soul of the place.

~Jwalin Patel 2020

This chapter concludes the book by summarising the key contributions. Primarily, the chapter is a call to action, where I call upon the reader to take onus and to reflect for themselves, contextualise the various frameworks and to **adapt**, rather than **adopt**, the ideologies and pedagogies in the book, explore other alternative educational visions from their

J. Patel, *Learning to Live Together Harmoniously*, Spirituality, Religion, and Education,
https://doi.org/10.1007/978-3-031-23539-9_10

contexts, build their own visions for education, and act upon these visions. The chapter also includes a few epistemological considerations that have underpinned the book and that I hope the reader will hold onto as they engage in developing their own visions and practices. Finally, I also recognise that schools and teachers trying to adopt LTLTH can find it an all too radical shift; to aid the process I also highlight a few kernels of practices that can help them experiment and get started on their own journeys.

The educational research subfields of LTLT, GCE, peace education, SEL, and EI would benefit from these empirical findings on ideologies and practices for LTLTH. I believe that the book's propositions and frameworks are extremely relevant to academics, masters, and undergraduate students from both education and development studies, as well as to PGCE (teacher training) students. Furthermore, the findings could also guide teachers, school leaders, teacher trainers, and policymakers in bringing about education for LTLTH.

Concluding Notes

In this book, I question the vision, philosophy, approaches, practices, systems, and impact of the modern, mass education system and instead call for a very different education: one for togetherness and harmony. Throughout the book, I have drawn upon various Indian and international thinkers, experienced educators, and school leaders for a sacred form of integral education of the whole person (for both teachers and students).

Notably, I have brought together various voices, experiences, and practices from the Indian context to build an interconnected 2D framework for LTLTH. The framework is a call for engaging in processes of discovery of the self, others, and the world, each of which has six dimensions of awareness, empathetic and caring relations, sense of purpose, change in perspective, compassion(ate action), and meaningful engagement. The proposed framework is neither an exhaustive nor a complete exposition of all possible means of understanding LTLTH and should not be utilised as an evaluative framework, but rather as a way of helping practitioners and researchers in exploring and better understanding education for harmony. Furthermore, all models are a simplification; they break a continuous whole into components (albeit interacting) and reduce lived experiences into a few words. I hope that the reader takes the onus of contextualising the model to their own setting, exploring various indigenous and precolonial visions of education, and recreating the whole by seeing the interconnectedness between components within simplified frameworks.

In practice, whilst Delors et al. (1996) suggested that education for LTLT happens through the inclusion of certain subjects (history, geography and philosophy, history of religions), the findings have provided evidence that education for harmony is brought about through a continuum of (shared) lived experiences (of harmony). Therefore, the pedagogy goes beyond bringing about a content- or skills-based education to lived experience-based (project-based, dialogic, embodied, and experiential) teaching-learning practices, equal and caring TSR, autonomous behavioural regulation, harmonious classroom and school-wide ethos, and teachers consciously (trying to) learning to live together harmoniously. It is important to note that education for harmony is a holistic vision for education for everyone, including students, teachers, school administrators, and potentially parents. Therefore, the schools were referred to and structured as communities or learning centres that promoted life-long learning (about a different way of living and being) for everyone.

While this book focused on classroom settings, I must emphasise the importance of school-wide ethos, home environments, and the wider community in bringing about an education for togetherness and harmony. These are beyond the scope of the current book though I hope to continue exploring these in my other work.

A Few Epistemological Considerations

In hindsight, as I reflect upon the book, I find that it both embodies and advocates post-critical, transrational, holistic, and non-anthropocentric ways of knowing, being, and living as opposed to many of the current anthropocentric, modernist, consumerist, and reductionists ways. I recommend that the reader keeps these in mind as they rethink their own philosophy and approach to education.

While I have highlighted the many limitations of the current education systems, I must note that there are many positives as well. Similarly, while I have drawn upon visions of education proposed by thinkers from the last century, we must remain acutely aware of the limitations of education during that time. Education for harmony neither calls for one to completely discard all the present practices, nor is it being romantic about the past. Instead, it is inspired by visions and calls for an alternative that has been proposed by thinkers throughout time (including in the present and in the last century) to propose an integrated and more holistic vision and practices. In the book, I have adopted a post-critical and transrational approach that, while valuing the rational, also integrates the emotional, embodied, and spiritual aspects (Cremin et al., 2018; Echavarría Alvarez & Koppensteiner, 2018). It is not a rejection of rationality (Cremin, 2018; Cremin & Archer, 2018; Dietrich, 2012, 2013, 2018) and instead aims to bring the various aspects together into an integrated whole. The book is a post-critical and holistic inquiry into alternative approaches that are currently being used in various schools.

It is important to note that much of the modern education has developed interesting ways to develop the mind and these are all relevant and important. I do not advocate against the development of the mind, but instead call for it to be based on a non-anthropocentric epistemology allowing for a deep critical understanding of interconnectedness, innovative, and creative thinking, as well as problem-solving to tackle the many twenty-first-century issues that have been created by modernised way of thinking, living, and being. I do, however, caution against the (narrow focus on the) development of a fragmented, violent, and a colonising and a colonised mind and instead call for transrational and holistic approach for the development of the whole person who is situated within the larger whole.

Through the book I also incorporate a 'holistic epistemology', one that actively aims to understand the interconnectedness, interdependence, and the whole. I advocate holism across approaches to life (understanding of the links between the harmony within and harmony in the larger society), epistemologies (non-anthropocentric), educational philosophy (emphasising the importance of educating the whole person), educational systems (calling for systems to run throughout the school for every stakeholder), educational approaches (understanding education as a continuum of lived experiences rather than a single subject), and educational practices (promoting embodied and experiential learning). Furthermore, education for harmony is embedded in a strong non-anthropocentric approach. It fundamentally calls for the awareness and understanding interconnectedness and interdependence across the world (human, non-human, living, and non-living).

A CALL FOR REFLECT(ACT)ION

How Can One Bring About Education of the Harmony: It Seems like a Complete Reform?

I realise that while education for harmony might appear as nothing short of a radical whole school-wide reform, a comprehensive shift can be time-intensive, overwhelming, and sudden. Instead, I advocate a multi-stepped and multi-tiered approach (Lane et al., 2010, 2012) to building holistic, school-wide LTLTH interventions. One could begin with simple strategies, followed by stand-alone kernels of practices to be transferred across contexts (Embry & Biglan, 2008; Jones & Bouffard, 2012); the use of integrative practices that bridge divides like those between subjects, student ages, spaces, and so on; the pursuit of individual developmental trajectories for different students; and, finally, building a continuity of experiences for all students through the ethos.

I believe that in reality we cannot take a one-size-fits-all approach. Instead, every teacher and school (community of teachers) would need to (collaboratively) reflect on their vision for education, understanding of education for harmony, as well as systems, processes and practices to bring about education for harmony (for both teachers and students).

'Kernels' of Best Practices

Whilst I propose a systemic and holistic school-wide approach, I also highlight potentially scalable 'kernels' (Embry & Biglan, 2008; Jones & Bouffard, 2012) of teaching-learning processes that can be transferred across contexts and have a potential impact as stand-alone practice, albeit limited. These could serve as a starting step to a multi-tiered approach to adoption of a school-wide approach (some of these are described below). However, I would caution the reader while using these scalable kernels; that they should not be perceived as ad hoc or the only practices for the following reasons: (a) education for harmony is based on a continuum of lived experiences; (b) there are innumerable differences in the micro-contexts (different children, environments, and teacher backgrounds), which necessitate different practices; (c) doing so can lead to consequentialist and utilitarian approaches to the kernels, whereas education for harmony follows a nonlinear trajectory; and (d) prevent the possibility of perceiving the kernels as a prescriptive framework.

The classroom-based kernels of practice could include the following: (a) student (interest)-driven learning processes; (b) student autonomy and self-regulation; (c) dialogic discussions; (d) project-based learning; (e) collaborative team-based exploration (including peer learning); (f) opportunities for social action; (g) meditation/prayer, reflection, and introspection; (h) extended time in nature through nature walks; (i) embodied pedagogies; (j) spaces and time for (school-wide) shared activities (meals, prayer, sports, projects); (k) spaces and opportunities for informal teacher-student interactions; (l) warm and safe classroom environments; (m) democratic peer-based behaviour regulation (e.g., rule-making, council sessions to resolve conflicts); and (n) the use of behavioural reports over assessments as a means of deeply understanding a child.

An Invitation to Walk Your Own Path

Recently, in order to build an agroforest, I was visiting a plant nursery. I have been visiting this nursery for several years, but for the first time I ran into one of the co-owners. He shared that he hadn't completed his schooling but was very well educated in all senses of the word. As the conversation evolved, he shared that he didn't agree with the modern education system and its practices and had decided to deschool his children. Subsequently, he had joined a community of parents who had set up an alternative education system for their children. He touched upon many different key themes from the book, and it appeared that the community that he was a part of embodied many of these ideas. For a moment, I was stunned; I found that I didn't have too much to add to what he was sharing, and that his experiences and reflections were spot on. I remember thinking to myself perhaps the only way to truly understand education for harmony is for each of us to walk our own paths.

I believe that there can be no-one-size-fits-all solution or a blueprint for education for harmony and instead it is up to each one of us to question, reflect, and explore what we understand by education, how we envision its purpose, and how we practise the same. It is up to each of us to build our own understanding, contextualise suggestions, and flexibly adapt to any given child that one works with. This can also be seen in the recommendations from Krishnamurti who strongly advocated against a blueprint and refrained from suggesting any given practices. Instead, he called upon teachers constantly to question and reflect for themselves. Furthermore, I believe that while this book can be an interesting read, education for harmony cannot be understood through the transfer of content-based knowledge/understanding. Instead, it has to be experienced and lived. Resonating with the reflection in the boxed text above, I believe that one can develop a unique, original, and genuinely deeper understanding of education for harmony through engaging in a journey of (self/community-based) discovery.

I call upon you to explore, reflect, and develop your own visions, philosophies, process-oriented approaches, and holistic educational practices. How can we go beyond instrumental education for academic knowledge or development of narrow set of skills, to an education for thriving and flourishing of the child, and even better still to an education that foregrounds and supports the flourishing of all beings on the planet? I recommend starting with questioning and reflecting for yourself and thereafter engaging in dialogue with others who may help provide a different perspective, question your stance, and help build a more nuanced understanding. And finally incorporating the ideas into your own practices. You might find reading books like this, watching short documentaries, or visiting alternative schools interesting and helpful, but I would caution against trying to replicate/duplicate anything that you see. For practitioners, I believe that some extended deep immersive stays in alternative learning spaces can lead to a shift in epistemology and way of living and being, which can be extremely valuable. However, once you develop a different epistemological approach, I doubt if long visits to schools with a similar epistemological stance would help and at that point it would be important to implement your practices, experiments, and develop your own pedagogy. For policymakers and school leaders, I believe that the challenge lies in shaping an alternative epistemology, empowering, and supporting teachers, and not imposing a one-size-fits-all solution.

Finally, I would like to invite you to share your own journeys and practices. I would love to hear your thoughts and experiences. I invite

you to share your insights, stories, and practices on www.empowereduca-
tors.in, a website that I hope will engage various readers and promote
sharing, networking, and hopefully future collaboration. The website will
also act as a resource for public good compiling resources, providing
examples, and proposing recommendations from people around
the globe.

AFTERWORD

Om Shanti and Greetings of Peace.

Congratulations to Dr Jwalin Patel for bringing out this book on *Education for Harmony*. Laying the foundation of a harmonious world is both the biggest need and the biggest challenge of the present times. Exploring visions, approaches, and practices to take it into the classrooms is a worthy endeavour that merits kudos.

Education has the potential to become the lens which shows diversity as strength at a time when mutual differences are perceived as a weakness. In that direction, sensitising the young and impressionable minds of students to imbibe the values like understanding, acceptance, empathy, and co-operation is the key to create and sustain harmony. This book looks well set to achieve the objective of driving unity and mutual respect as individuals and as communities. So, I am certain it will not just be considered as another source for learning, but its readers will be inspired to embrace the wealth of knowledge and information to manifest harmony.

The well-researched content, as well as the sequential, structured, and focused approach, will prompt the reader to explore ways to make learning an interesting and valuable experience. The broad spectrum of classroom

---

Brahma Kumari Shivani practitioner and teacher of Rajyoga Meditation at Brahma Kumaris

J. Patel, *Learning to Live Together Harmoniously*, Spirituality, Religion, and Education,
https://doi.org/10.1007/978-3-031-23539-9

examples makes it easier to understand and relate to the concepts, terms, and contexts of harmony and peaceful co-existence in real-life situations.

Thank you for bringing your experience and expertise in creating this book. It should be a rewarding experience for readers to maintain a personal sense of harmony and to be in sync with others, along their journey with the book and live a more meaningful life.

REFERENCES

Alexander, H. A. (2016). Assessing virtue: Measurement in moral education at home and abroad. *Ethics and Education, 11*(3), 310–325. https://doi.org/10.1080/17449642.2016.1240385

Alexander, R. J. (2001). *Culture and pedagogy: International comparisons in primary education*. Wiley-Blackwell Publishing Ltd.

Alexander, R. J. (2003). *Culture and pedagogy: International comparisons in primary education*. Blackwell Publishing.

Alexander, R. J. (2004). Still no pedagogy? principle, pragmatism and compliance in primary education. *Cambridge Journal of Education, 34*(1), 7–33. https://doi.org/10.1080/0305764042000183106

Alexander, R. J. (2008). *Education for all, the quality imperative and the problem of pedagogy* (Institute of Education & Consortium for Research on Educational Access Transitions and Equity, Eds.). CREATE. https://doi.org/10.1353/bcs.2007.0002

Apple, M. W., & Beane, J. A. (1999). *Democratic schools: Lessons from the chalk face*. Open University Press.

Aristotle. (2000). *Aristotle: Nicomachean ethics* (R. Crisp, Ed.). Cambridge University Press. https://doi.org/10.1017/CBO9780511802058

Aronson, A. (1947). Rabindranath's educational ideals and the west. *Visva Bharati Quarterly, 13*(3), 30–37.

Aronson, A. (1961). Tagore's educational ideals. *International Review of Education, 7*(4), 385–393.

Badheka, G. (1962). *Divaswapna*. Sanskar Sahitya.

Baker, J. A. (2006). Contributions of teacher-child relationships to positive school adjustment during elementary school. *Journal of School Psychology, 44*(3), 211–229. https://doi.org/10.1016/j.jsp.2006.02.002

Bandura, A. (1986). *Social foundations of thought and action: Social cognitive theory*. Prentice Hall.

Bandura, A. (2012). On the functional properties of perceived self-efficacy revisited. *Journal of Management, 38*(1), 9–44. https://doi.org/10.1177/0149 206311410606

Bangs, J., & Frost, D. (2015). Non-positional teacher leadership: Distributed leadership and self-efficacy. In *Flip the system* (pp. 91–107). Routledge. https://doi.org/10.4324/9781315678573-12

Barb, T., & Howard, Z. (2012). Ways of knowing for a restorative worldview. In *Restorative justice in context: International practice and directions* (pp. 257–271). Willan. https://doi.org/10.4324/9781843924821

Bar-On, R. (2011). *The handbook of emotional intelligence: Theory, development, assessment, and application at home, school, and in the workplace*. Jossey-Bass.

Barsalou, L. W. (2007). Grounded cognition. *Annual Review of Psychology, 59*, 617–645. https://doi.org/10.1146/ANNUREV.PSYCH.59.103006.093639

Battistich, V., Solomon, D., Watson, M., & Schaps, E. (1997). Caring school communities. *Educational Psychologist, 32*(3), 137–151. https://doi.org/10.1207/s15326985ep3203_1

Battistoni, R. M., Longo, N., & v, & Jayanandhan, S. R. (2009). Acting locally in a flat world: Global citizenship and the democratic practice of service-learning. *Journal of Higher Education Outreach and Engagement, 13*(2), 89–108. https://doi.org/10.1177/105382591103400205

Beijaard, D., Meijer, P. C., & Verloop, N. (2004). Reconsidering research on teachers' professional identity. *Teaching and Teacher Education, 20*, 107–128. https://doi.org/10.1016/j.tate.2003.07.001

Berry, D. R., Cairo, A. H., Goodman, R. J., Quaglia, J. T., Green, J. D., & Brown, K. W. (2018). Mindfulness increases prosocial responses toward ostracized strangers through empathic concern. *Journal of Experimental Psychology: General, 147*(1), 93–112. https://doi.org/10.1037/xge0000392

Bhola, H. S. (1997). Adult education policy projections in the Delors report. *Prospects, 27*(2), 207–222. https://doi.org/10.1007/bf02737166

Black, C. (2010). *Schooling the world*. Schooling the world. www.schoolingtheworld.org/

Blyth, D. A., Jones, S., & Borowski, T. (2018). *SEL frameworks—What are they and why are they important?* CASEL. www.measuringsel.casel.org/frameworks/

Bonnett, M. (2009). Education and selfhood: A phenomenological investigation. *Journal of Philosophy of Education, 43*(3), 357–370. https://doi.org/10.1111/J.1467-9752.2009.00698.X

Bourn, D. (2022). *Education for social change: Perspectives on global learning* (1st ed.). Bloomsbury Academic. https://doi.org/10.5040/9781350192874

Bowles, S., & Gintis, H. (2011). *Schooling in capitalist America: Educational reform and the contradictions of economic life*. Haymarket Books.

Brackett, M. A., Bailey, C. S., Hoffmann, J. D., & Simmons, D. N. (2019). RULER: A theory-driven, systemic approach to social, emotional, and academic learning. *Educational Psychologist, 54*(3), 144–161. https://doi.org/10.1080/00461520.2019.1614447

Brighouse, H., & Unterhalter, E. (2010). Education for primary goods or for capabilities? In *Measuring justice: Primary goods and capabilities* (pp. 193–214). Cambridge University Press. https://doi.org/10.1017/CBO9780511810916.009

Cajete, G. (1994). *Look to the mountain: An ecology of indigenous education*. Kivakí Press.

Cajete, G. (1999). The making of an indigenous teacher: Insights into the ecology of teaching. In J. Kane (Ed.), *Education, information, and transformation essays on learning and thinking*. Prentice Hall.

Campbell, R. J. (2004). *Assessing teacher effectiveness: Developing a differentiated model*. Routledge Falmer.

Capra, F. (2007). *The science of Leonardo: Inside the mind of the great genius of the Renaissance*. Doubleday.

Cardona, M. (2017). *The very process of living together educates learning in, from and for co-operative life in rural Malta*. Scholars' Press.

Carneiro, R., & Draxler, A. (2008). Education for the 21st century: Lessons and challenges. *European Journal of Education, 43*(2), 149–160. https://doi.org/10.1111/j.1465-3435.2008.00348.x

CASEL. (2003). *An educational leader's guide to evidence-based Social and Emotional Learning (SEL) programs*. CASEL. www.communityschools.org/assets/1/AssetManager/1A_Safe_&_Sound.pdf

Caspi, A., McClay, J., Moffitt, T. E., Mill, J., Martin, J., Craig, I. W., Taylor, A., & Poulton, R. (2002). Role of genotype in the cycle of violence in maltreated children. *Science, 297*, 851–854. https://doi.org/10.1126/science.1072290

Celio, C. I. (2011). Helping others and helping oneself: A meta-analysis of service-learning programs. *Journal of Experiential Learning, 3*, 164–181.

Central Board of Secondary Education. (2012). *Values education a handbook for teacher*. Central Board of Secondary Education India.

Charney, R. (2002). *Teaching children to care: Classroom management for ethical and academic growth, K-8*. Northeast Foundation for Children.

Chaube, S. P. (2005). *Recent philosophies of education in India*. Concept Publishing Company.

Chaube, S. P., & Chaube, A. (2016). *Educational ideals of the great in India*. Neelkamal Publications Pvt Ltd.

Chavan, S. B. (1999). *Chavan Committee Report; report on value based education.*

Chazot, P. (2006). *Co-naissance de la connaissance: Un voyage au sein des processus d'apprentissage à l'école internationale Mahatma Gandhi, en Inde.* Universite de Paris.

Chernyshenko, O., Kankaraš, M., & Drasgow, F. (2018). *Social and emotional skills for student success and well-being: Conceptual framework for the OECD study on social and emotional skills* (No. 173; OECD Education Working Papers). https://doi.org/10.1787/db1d8e59-en

Chödrön, P. (2012). *Living beautifully with uncertainty and change.* Shambhala Publications.

Clotfelter, C. T., Ladd, H. F., Vigdor, J., Clotfelter, C. T., Ladd, H., & Vigdor, J. (2006). Teacher-student matching and the assessment of teacher effectiveness. *Journal of Human Resources, 41*(4), 778–820. https://doi.org/10.3386/w11936

Committee on Religious and Moral Instruction. (1959). *Sri Prakasa Committee Report; Report of The Committee on Religious and Moral Instruction.* www.14.139.60.153/handle/123456789/2287

Conrad, D., & Hedin, D. (1982). The impact of experimental education on adolescent development. *Child & Youth Services, 4*(3–4), 57–76. https://doi.org/10.1300/j024v04n03_08

Cougoureux, M., & Tawil, S. (2013). Revisiting learning: The treasure within; assessing the impact of the 1996 'Delors Report.' *UNESCO Education Research and Foresight Occasional Papers*, 10. www.unesdoc.unesco.org/ark:/48223/pf0000220050

Council of Europe. (2017). *Learning to live together: Report on the state of citizenship and human rights education in Europe.* Council of Europe.

Creemers, B., Kyriakidēs, L., & Antoniou, P. (2013). *Teacher professional development for improving quality of teaching.* Springer.

Cremin, H. (2016). Peace education research in the twenty-first century: Three concepts facing crisis or opportunity? *Journal of Peace Education, 13*(1), 1–17. https://doi.org/10.1080/17400201.2015.1069736

Cremin, H. (2018). What comes after post/modern peace education? *Education Philosophy and Theory, 50*(14), 1564–1565. https://doi.org/10.1080/00131857.2018.1461384

Cremin, H. (2022). *Rewilding education (book proposal).*

Cremin, H., & Archer, T. (2018). Transrational education: Exploring possibilities for learning about peace, harmony, justice and truth in the twenty first century. In J. E. Alvarez, D. Ingruber, & N. Koppensteiner (Eds.), *Transrational resonances* (pp. 287–302). Springer.

Cremin, H., Echavarría, J., & Kester, K. (2018). Transrational peacebuilding education to reduce epistemic violence. *Peace Review, 30*(3), 295–302. https://doi.org/10.1080/10402659.2018.1495808

Csikszentmihalyi, M. (1990). *Flow: The psychology of optimal experience.* Harper & Row.

Culham, T., Oxford, R., & Lin, J. (2018). Cultivating the abilities of the heart; educating through a pedagogy of love. In J. P. Miller, K. Nigh, M. J. Binder, & B. Novak (Eds.), *International handbook of holistic education* (pp. 170–177). Routledge. https://doi.org/10.4324/9781315112398-21

Curren, R. R. (2007). *Philosophy of education: An anthology.* Blackwell Publisher.

Dalai Lama. (2014). *Wisdom of compassion: Stories of remarkable encounters and timeless insights.* Riverhead Books.

Dalai Lama. (2015). *Beyond religion: Ethics for a whole world.* Harper Element.

Dalai Lama, Tutu, D., Tolle, E., Robinson, K., Ricard, M., & Omidyar, P. (2009). *Peace summit—educating the heart and mind.* www.youtube.com/watch?v=suojNzKZ8ew

Dalai Lama XIV, & Hougaard, R. (2019). The Dalai Lama on why leaders should be mindful, selfless, and compassionate. *Harvard Business Review.* www.hbr.org/2019/02/the-dalai-lama-on-why-leaders-should-be-mindful-selfless-and-compassionate

Dale, R. (1982). Education and the capitalist state: Contributions and contradictions. In M. Apple (Ed.), *Cultural and economic reproduction in education.* Routledge and Kegan Paul.

Darroch-Lozowski, V. (2018). Experiencing nets of holism through the threshold body. In J. P. Miller, K. Nigh, M. J. Binder, & B. Novak (Eds.), *International handbook of holistic education* (pp. 17–24). Routledge. https://doi.org/10.4324/9781315112398-3

Das, A., Teotia, A., Ravindranath, S., Talreja, V., & Bhat, S. (2022). Building social and emotional skills of children in Delhi: Insights from the happiness curriculum. In A. Smart & M. Sinclair (Eds.), *NISSEM global briefs volume III: Educating the social, the emotional and the sustainable* (pp. 184–205). NISSEM.

Davies, L. (2006). Global citizenship: Abstraction or framework for action? In *Educational review* (Vol. 58, pp. 5–25). Routledge. https://doi.org/10.1080/00131910500352523

de Oliveira Andreotti, V. (2011). (Towards) decoloniality and diversality in global citizenship education. *Globalisation, Societies and Education, 9*(3–4), 381–397. https://doi.org/10.1080/14767724.2011.605323

de Souza, M. (2018). Belonging, identity, and meaning making—the essence of spirituality. In J. P. Miller, K. Nigh, M. J. Binder, & B. Novak (Eds.), *International handbook of holistic education* (pp. 304–312). Routledge. https://doi.org/10.4324/9781315112398-38

de Souza, M., Bone, J., & Watson, J. (2016). *Spirituality across disciplines: Research and practice* (pp. 1–352). Springer. https://doi.org/10.1007/978-3-319-31380-1

Decety, J., & Jackson, P. L. (2004). The functional architecture of human empathy. *Behavioral and Cognitive Neuroscience Reviews, 3*(2), 71–100. https://doi.org/10.1177/1534582304267187

Delhi State Council of Educational Research and Training. (2019). *Happiness curriculum.* SCERT. www.edudel.nic.in/welcome_folder/happiness/Happiness CurriculumFramework_2019.pdf

Delors, J., Mufti, I., Amagi, I., Roberto, C., Chung, F., Geremek, B., Gorham, W., Kornhauser, A., Manley, M., Quero, M. P., Savane, M.-A., Singh, K., Stavenhagen, R., Suhr, M. W., & Nanzhao, Z. (1996). *Learning: The treasure within.* UNESCO.

Dewey, J. (1916). *Democracy and education: An introduction to the philosophy of education.* Macmillan.

Dewey, J. (1938). *Experience and education.* Kappa Delta Pi.

Dewey, J. (1944). Between two worlds. *Printed in Dewey's Collection of Later Works, 1981, 451*–465.

DfID & DfEE. (2000). *Developing a global dimension in the school curriculum.* Department for International Development & Department for Education and Employment.

Diamond, A., & Lee, K. (2011). Interventions shown to aid executive function development in children 4–12 years old. *Science (New York, N.Y.), 333*(6045), 959–964. https://doi.org/10.1126/science.1204529

Dietrich, W. (2012). *Interpretations of peace in history and culture.* Palgrave Macmillan. https://doi.org/10.1057/9780230367715

Dietrich, W. (2013). *Elicitive conflict transformation and the transrational shift in peace politics.* Palgrave Macmillan. https://doi.org/10.1057/9781137035066

Dietrich, W. (2018). Imperfect and transrational interpretations of peace(s). *PROSPECTIVA. Revista de Trabajo Social e Intervención Social, 26,* 195–210. https://doi.org/10.25100/prts.v0i26.6623

Duckworth, A. (2016). *Grit: The power of passion and perseverance.* Vermilion.

Duckworth, C. (2006). Teaching peace: A dialogue on the Montessori method. *Journal of Peace Education, 3*(1), 39–53. https://doi.org/10.1080/17400 200500532128

Durkheim, E. (2013). Emile Durkheim: Selected writings on education. In *Emile Durkheim: Selected writings on education.* Routledge. https://doi.org/10.4324/9781315020860

Durlak, J. A., Domitrovich, C. E., Weissberg, R. P., & Gullotta, T. P. (2015). *Handbook of social and emotional learning: Research and practice.* The Guilford Press.

Durlak, J. A., Weissberg, R., & Pachan, M. (2010). A meta-analysis of after-school programs that seek to promote personal and social skills in children and adolescents. *American Journal of Community Psychology, 45*(3–4), 294–309. https://doi.org/10.1007/s10464-010-9300-6

Durlak, J. A., Weissberg, R. P., Dymnicki, A. B., Taylor, R. D., & Schellinger, K. B. (2011). The impact of enhancing students' social and emotional learning: A meta-analysis of School-Based Universal Interventions. *Child Development, 82*(1), 405–432. https://doi.org/10.1111/j.1467-8624.2010.01564.x

Echavarría Alvarez, J., Ingruber, D., & Koppensteiner, N. (2018). *Transrational resonances: Echoes to the many peaces.* Springer International Publishing AG.

Eisenberg, N., Eggum, N. D., & di Giunta, L. (2010). Empathy-related responding: Associations with prosocial behavior, aggression, and intergroup relations. *Social Issues and Policy Review, 4*(1), 143–180. https://doi.org/10.1111/j.1751-2409.2010.01020.x

Eisenberg, N., Valiente, C., & Eggum, N. D. (2010). Self-regulation and school readiness. *Early Education and Development, 21*(5), 681–698. https://doi.org/10.1080/10409289.2010.497451

Embry, D. D., & Biglan, A. (2008). Evidence-based kernels: Fundamental units of behavioral influence. *Clinical Child and Family Psychology Review, 11*(3), 75–113. https://doi.org/10.1007/s10567-008-0036-x

Emory University, & SEE Learning. (2019). *SEE learning; social, emotional & ethical learning. Educating the heart and mind.* Center for Contemplative Science and Compassion-Based Ethics, Emory University. www.seelearning.emory.edu/

Escobar, A. (1995). *Encountering development: The making and unmaking of the Third World.* Princeton University Press. https://doi.org/10.2307/j.ctt7rtgw

Fennell, S., Duraiswamy, M., & Shanmugam, S. (2016). *Activity based learning (ABL); Report 4 on dissemination and scaling up of the activity based learning programme.* www.assets.publishing.service.gov.uk/media/58db967940f0b606e7000057/Report_4.pdf

Feshbach, N. D. (1975). Empathy in children: Some theoretical and empirical considerations. *The Counseling Psychologist, 5*(2), 25–30. https://doi.org/10.1177/001100007500500207

Forbes, S. (2000). Jiddu Krishnamurti and his insights into education. In *The encyclopaedia of informal education.* www.infed.org/mobi/jiddu-krishnamurti-and-his-insights-into-education/

Foucault, M. (1977). *Discipline and punish: The birth of the prison.* Pantheon Books.

Four Arrows, a. D. T. J. (2018). From a deeper place: Indigenous worlding as the next step in holistic education. In J. P. Miller, K. Nigh, M. J. Binder, & B. Novak (Eds.), *International handbook of holistic education* (pp. 33–41). Routledge. https://doi.org/10.4324/9781315112398-5

Freire, P. (1970). *Pedagogy of the oppressed: 30th anniversary edition.* The Continuum International Publishing Group Inc.

Freire, P. (2005). *Pedagogy of the oppressed: 30th anniversary edition* (30th Anniv). Bloomsbury Academic. https://doi.org/10.1016/B978-1-4160-4389-8.50161-8

Freire, P., Macedo, D. P., Oliveira, A. K., Carnoy, M., Dowbor, L., & Freire, A. M. A. (2016). *Pedagogy of the heart*. Bloomsbury Academic.

Frelin, A., & Fransson, G. (2017). Four components that sustain teachers' commitment to students—a relational and temporal model. *Reflective Practice, 18*(5), 641–654. https://doi.org/10.1080/14623943.2017.1307722

Frost, D. (2017). *Empowering teachers as agents of change: A non-positional approach to teacher leadership*. Cambridge University Press.

Gallese, V. (2001). The '"shared manifold"' hypothesis: From mirror neurons to empathy. *Journal of Consciousness Studies, 8*, 33–50. www.ingentaconnect.com/content/imp/jcs/2001/00000008/f0030005/1208

Galtung, J. (1964). An editorial. *Journal of Peace Research, 1*(1), 1–4. https://doi.org/10.1177/002234336400100101

Galtung, J. (1969). Violence, peace, and peace research. *Journal of Peace Research, 6*(3), 167–191. https://doi.org/10.1177/002234336900600301

Gandhi, M. K. (1968a). *The selected works of Mahatma Gandhi; selected letters. Volume 5*. Navjivan Publication.

Gandhi, M. K. (1968b). *The selected works of Mahatma Gandhi; voice of truth. Volume 6*. Navjivan Publication.

Gandhi, M. K. (1983). *Autobiography: The story of my experiments with truth*. Navjivan Publishing House.

Gandhi, M. K., & Kumarappa, B. (1953). *Towards new education*. Navjivan Press.

Gharse, P., & Sharma, S. (n.d.). *Youth as an agent for social transformation: Mahatma Gandhi's view on education*. Retrieved November 22, 2019, from www.gandhiashramsevagram.org/on-education/youth-as-agent-for-social-transformation.php

Ghosh, R. (2019). Juxtaposing the educational ideas of Gandhi and Freire. In *The Wiley handbook of Paulo Freire* (pp. 275–290). Wiley. https://doi.org/10.1002/9781119236788.ch14

Gillies, V. (2011). Social and emotional pedagogies: Critiquing the new orthodoxy of emotion in classroom behaviour management. *British Journal of Sociology of Education, 32*(2), 185–202. https://doi.org/10.1080/01425692.2011.547305

Giroux, H. A. (1983). Theories of reproduction and resistance in the new sociology of education: A critical analysis. *Harvard Educational Review, 53*(3), 257–293. https://doi.org/10.17763/haer.53.3.a67x4u33g7682734

Giroux, H. A. (1992). Educational leadership and the crisis of democratic government. *Educational Researcher, 21*(4), 4–11. https://doi.org/10.3102/0013189X021004004

Giroux, H. A. (2010). Rethinking education as the practice of freedom: Paulo Freire and the promise of critical pedagogy. *Policy Futures in Education, 8*(6), 715–721. https://doi.org/10.2304/pfie.2010.8.6.715

Giroux, H. A., & McLaren, P. (1986). Teacher education and the politics of engagement: The case for democratic schooling. *Harvard Educational Review, 56*(3), 213–239.

Global Education Monitoring Report. (2012). *Youth and skills: Putting education to work*. UNESCO. www.unesdoc.unesco.org/ark:/48223/pf0000218003

Global Education Monitoring Report. (2016). *Education for people and planet: Creating sustainable futures for all*. UNESCO. www.unesdoc.unesco.org/ark:/48223/pf0000245752

Goleman, D. (1995). *Emotional intelligence*. Bantam Books.

Goleman, D. (1998). *Working with emotional intelligence*. Bantam Books.

Goodenow, C. (1993). The psychological sense of school membership among adolescents: Scale development and educational correlates. *Psychology in the Schools, 30*(1), 79–90. https://doi.org/10.1002/1520-6807(199301)30:1<79::AID-PITS2310300113>3.0.CO;2-X

Greenberg, M. T., Domitrovich, C. E., Weissberg, R. P., & Durlak, J. A. (2017). *Social and emotional learning as a public health approach to education* (Vol. 27, Issue 1). www.futureofchildren.org

Greene, M. (2005). Teaching in a moment of crisis: The spaces of imagination. *New Educator, 1*(2), 77–80. https://doi.org/10.1080/15476880590934326

Greene, M. (1995). *Releasing the imagination: Essays on education, the arts, and social change*. Jossey-Bass Publishers.

Guha, R. (2016). *Democrats and dissenters*. Penguin Random House.

Gurze'ev, I. (2010). The nomadic existence of the eternal improviser and diasporic co-poiesis in the era of mega-speed. *Policy Futures in Education, 8*, 271–287. https://doi.org/10.2304/pfie.2010.8.3.271

Hadot, P. (2002). *Philosophy as a way of life: Spiritual exercises from Socrates to Foucault*. Blackwell.

Hamre, B. K., & Pianta, R. C. (2001). Early teacher-child relationships and the trajectory of children's school outcomes through eighth grade. *Child Development, 72*(2), 625–638. https://doi.org/10.1111/1467-8624.00301

Hansen, D. T. (1998). The moral is in the practice. *Teaching and Teacher Education, 14*(6), 643–655. https://doi.org/10.1016/S0742-051X(98)00014-6

Hanushek, E. A., Welch, F., Machin, S., & Woessmann, L. (2011). *Handbook of the economics of education, volume 4*. Elsevier.

Hardman, F. (2015). *Making pedagogical practices visible in discussions of educational quality*. www.unesdoc.unesco.org/ark:/48223/pf0000232449

Hargreaves, A., Earl, L. M., & Ryan, J. (1996). *Schooling for change: Reinventing education for early adolescents*. Falmer Press.

Hart, T. (2018a). Beauty and learning. In J. P. Miller, K. Nigh, M. J. Binder, & B. Novak (Eds.), *International handbook of holistic education* (pp. 25–32). Routledge. https://doi.org/10.4324/9781315112398-4

Hart, T. (2018b). Toward an integrative mind. In J. P. Miller, K. Nigh, M. J. Binder, & B. Novak (Eds.), *International handbook of holistic education* (pp. 336–343). Routledge. https://doi.org/10.4324/9781315112398-42

Hattie, J. (2009). *Visible learning: A synthesis of over 800 meta-analyses relating to achievement.* Routledge.

Haydon, G. (2009). Reason and virtues: The paradox of R. S. Peters on moral education. *Journal of Philosophy of Education, 43*(SUPPL. 1), 173–188. https://doi.org/10.1111/j.1467-9752.2009.00717.x

Hayes, D., Moore, A., Stapley, E., Humphrey, N., Mansfield, R., Santos, J., Ashworth, E., Patalay, P., Bonin, E.-M., Moltrecht, B., Boehnke, J. R., & Deighton, J. (2019). Promoting mental health and wellbeing in schools: Examining mindfulness, relaxation and strategies for safety and wellbeing in English primary and secondary schools: Study protocol for a multi-school, cluster randomised controlled trial (INSPIRE). *Trials, 20*(1), 640. https://doi.org/10.1186/s13063-019-3762-0

Hein, V., Ries, F., Pires, F., Caune, A., Heszteráné Ekler, J., Emeljanovas, A., & Valantiniene, I. (2012). The relationship between teaching styles and motivation to teach among physical education teachers. *Journal of Sports Science & Medicine, 11*(1), 123–130.

Herzberger, R. (2018). Values and the culture of schools. *J. Krishnamurti and educational practice,* 68–97. Oxford University Press. https://doi.org/10.1093/OSO/9780199487806.003.0003

Hooks, B. (1994). *Teaching to transgress: Education as the practice of freedom.* Routledge.

Hunt, F. (2017). *Global citizenship education framework.* Schools for Future Youth. www.sfyouth.eu

Illich, I. (1971a). *Deschooling society.* Harrow Books.

Illich, I. (1971b). The breakdown of schools: A problem or a symptom? *Interchange, 2*(4), 1–10. https://doi.org/10.1007/BF02287078

Istance, D., & Paniagua, A. (2019). *Learning to leapfrog: Innovative pedagogies to transform education.* Brookings Institute.

Jaeger, W. (1944). *PAIDEIA; The ideals of Greek culture; three volumes.* Oxford University Press.

Jaffe, P., Wolfe, D., Crooks, C., Hughes, R., & Baker, L. (2004). The fourth R: Developing healthy relationships through school-based interventions. In P. G. Jaffe, L. L. Baker, & A. J. Cunningham (Eds.), *Protecting children from domestic violence: Strategies for community intervention* (pp. 200–218). The Guilford Press.

James, D. N. (1986). The acquisition of virtue. *The Personalist Forum, 2*(2), 101–121.

Jinan, K. (2021). *Initiating enquiry: Reclaiming ourselves, saving our children.* Existential Knowledge Foundation.

Jinan, K. (2022). *Awakening aesthetic awareness. Revisiting the aesthetic education.* www.jinankb.medium.com/awakening-aesthetic-awareness-93a77201027f

Jones, D. E., Greenberg, M., & Crowley, M. (2015). Early social-emotional functioning and public health: The relationship between kindergarten social competence and future wellness. *American Journal of Public Health, 105*(11), 2283–2290. https://doi.org/10.2105/AJPH.2015.302630

Jones, S. M., & Bouffard, S. M. (2012). Social and emotion learning in schools: From programs to strategies. *Social Policy Report, Society for Research in Child Development, 26*(4), 20. www.srcd.org/spr.html

Jones, S. M., Brush, K., Bailey, R., Brion-Meisels, G., Mcintyre, J., Kahn, J., Nelson, B., & Stickle, L. (2017). *Navigating social and emotional learning from the inside out: Looking inside & across 25 leading SEL programs: A practical resource for schools and OST providers.* The Wallace Foundation.

Jones, S. M., & Doolittle, E. J. (2017). Social and emotional learning: Introducing the issue. *The Future of Children, 27*(1), 3–11.

Kessler, R. (2000). *The soul of education: Helping students find connection, compassion and character at school.* The Association for Supervision and Curriculum Development.

Kester, K. (2007). Peace education: Experience and storytelling as living education. *Peace and Conflict Review, 2*(37), 1–14.

Ketelaar, E., Beijaard, D., Boshuizen, H. P. A., & den Brok, P. J. (2012). Teachers' positioning towards an educational innovation in the light of ownership, sensemaking and agency. *Teaching and Teacher Education, 28*(2), 273–282. https://doi.org/10.1016/j.tate.2011.10.004

Khoo, S., & Jørgensen, N. J. (2021). Intersections and collaborative potentials between global citizenship education and education for sustainable development. *Globalisation Societies and Education, 19*(4), 470–481. https://doi.org/10.1080/14767724.2021.1889361

Kolb, D. A. (1984). *Experiential learning: Experience as the source of learning and development.* Prentice-Hall International.

Krathwohl, D. R., & Bloom, B. S. (1964). *Taxonomy of educational objectives: The classification of educational goals.* McKay.

Kraut, R. (2008). *The Blackwell guide to Aristotle's Nicomachean ethics.* Blackwell Publishing Ltd. https://doi.org/10.1002/9780470776513

Krishnamurti, J. (1977). *Teachers discussion.* J. Krishnamurti - Official Channel. www.youtube.com/watch?v=FRMNiIlkXVo

Krishnamurti, J. (1981). *Letters to the schools.* Krishnamurti Foundation India.

Krishnamurti, J. (1982). Malibu 39th entry 4th April 1975. In *Krishnamurti's Journal* (p. 100). Harper Collins.

Krishnamurti, J. (1985). *Third discussion with teachers at the Rishi Valley School.* J. Krishnamurti - Official Channel. www.jkrishnamurti.org/content/if-you-stand-alone-you-are-related

Krishnamurti, J. (1993). *A timeless spring: Krishnamurti at Rajghat* (2nd ed.). Krishnamurti Foundation India.

Krishnamurti, J. (2000). *Krishnamurti on education.* Krishnamurti Foundation India.

Krishnamurti, J. (2004). *What does freedom mean?.* Krishnamurti Foundation India.

Krishnamurti, J. (2013). *Educating the educator.* Krishnamurti Foundation India.

Krishnamurti, J., & Martin, R. (1997). *Krishnamurti: Reflections on the self.* Open Court.

Kumar, A. (2008). Development education and dialogical learning in the 21st century. *International Journal of Development Education and Global Learning, 1*(1), 37–48. https://doi.org/10.18546/IJDEGL.01.1.04

Kumar, K. (2010a). Quality in education. In *National council of educational research and training.* National Council of Educational Research and Training. https://doi.org/10.1177/0973184913411197

Kumar, K. (2010b). The context. In *Ways to peace; a resource book for teachers.* National Council of Educational Research and Training.

Kumar, K. (2017). *Routledge handbook of education in India: Debates, practices, and policies.* Routledge.

Lane, K. L., Oakes, W., & Menzies, H. (2010). Systematic screenings to prevent the development of learning and behavior problems: Considerations for practitioners, researchers, and policy makers. *Journal of Disability Policy Studies, 21*(3), 160–172. https://doi.org/10.1177/1044207310379123

Lane, K. L., Oakes, W., Menzies, H., & Kalberg, J. (2012). A comprehensive, integrated three-tier model to meet students' academic, behavioral, and social needs. In *American psychological association educational psychology handbook* (3rd ed., pp. 551–581). American Psychological Association.

Lange, E. A. (2004). Transformative and restorative learning: A vital dialectic for sustainable societies. *Adult Education Quarterly, 54*(2), 121–139. https://doi.org/10.1177/0741713603260276

Leary, M. R. (2010). Affiliation, acceptance, and belonging: The pursuit of interpersonal connection. In *Handbook of social psychology.* John Wiley & Sons, Inc. https://doi.org/10.1002/9780470561119.SOCPSY002024

Lees, H. E. (2012). *Silence in schools.* Trentham Books.

Lees, H. E. (2017). Hanging around, pottering about, chilling out: Lessons on silence and wellbeing from Summerhill School. *Revista Hipotese, 3*(2), 192–210. www.revistahipotese.emnuvens.com.br/revista

Lin, J. (2006). *Love, peace, and wisdom in education: A vision for education in the 21st century.* Rowman & Littlefield Education.

Lin, J., Culham, T., & Edwards, S. (2019). *Contemplative pedagogies for transformative teaching, learning, and being.* Information Age Publishing. www.infoagepub.com/products/Contemplative-Pedagogies-for-Transformative-Teaching-Learning-and-Being

Luberto, C. M., Shinday, N., Song, R., Philpotts, L. L., Park, E. R., Fricchione, G. L., & Yeh, G. Y. (2018). A systematic review and meta-analysis of the effects of meditation on empathy, compassion, and prosocial behaviors. *Mindfulness,* *9*(3), 708–724. https://doi.org/10.1007/s12671-017-0841-8

Lynch, J. (1992). *Education for citizenship in a multicultural society.* Cassell.

MacBeath, J. E. C., Galton, M., & Bangs, J. (2020). *Reforming or re-inventing schools?: Key issues in school and system reform.* Routledge.

Macedonia, M. (2019). Embodied learning: Why at school the mind needs the body. *Frontiers in Psychology,* *10*, 2098. https://doi.org/10.3389/FPSYG.2019.02098/BIBTEX

Macy, J., & Brown, M. Y. (n.d.). *Coming back to life: The updated guide to the work that reconnects.* New Society Publishers.

Magra, I. (2019, February 4). Schools in England introduce a new subject: Mindfulness. *The New York Times.* www.nytimes.com/2019/02/04/world/europe/uk-mindfulness-children-school.html

Mani, L. (2009). *Sacred secular: Contemplative cultural critique.* Routledge.

Mani, L. (2013). *Integral Nature of Things: Critical reflections on the present.* Routledge.

Marshall, B., & Jane Drummond, M. (2006). How teachers engage with assessment for learning: Lessons from the classroom. *Research Papers in Education,* *21*(2), 133–149. https://doi.org/10.1080/02671520600615638

Mayer, J. D., & Salovey, P. (1997). What is emotional intelligence? In *Emotional development and emotional intelligence: Implications for educators* (pp. 3–31). Basic Book. https://doi.org/10.1177/1066480710387486

Mayer, J. D., Salovey, P., & Caruso, D. (2000). Models of emotional intelligence. In R. J. Sternberg (Ed.), *Handbook of intelligence* (pp. 396–420). Cambridge University Press. https://doi.org/10.1017/cbo9780511807947.019

McDonald, F. J., & Elias, P. (1976). A report on the results of phase I I of the beginning teacher evaluation study: An overview. *Journal of Teacher Education,* *27*(4), 315–316. https://doi.org/10.1177/002248717602700418

McKown, C. (2017). Social and emotional learning: A policy vision for the future. *The Future of Children, Policy Brief, Spring, 2017*, 5.

McNeely, C. A., Nonnemaker, J. M., & Blum, R. W. (2002). Promoting school connectedness: Evidence from the national longitudinal study of adolescent health. *Journal of School Health,* *72*(4), 138–146. https://doi.org/10.1111/j.1746-1561.2002.tb06533.x

Mehra, B. (2011). Aims of true education: Sri Aurobindo and Mahatma Gandhi. *New Race: A Journal of Integral Studies, XII*(2), 3–17.

Metcalfe, J., & Greene, M. J. (2007). Metacognition of agency. *Journal of Experimental Psychology: General, 136*(2), 184–199. https://doi.org/10.1037/0096-3445.136.2.184

Mignolo, W., & Walsh, C. E. (2018). *On decoloniality: Concepts, analytics, praxis.* Duke University Press.

Miller, J. P. (2000). *Education and the soul: Toward a spiritual curriculum.* SUNY Press.

Miller, J. P. (2007). *The holistic curriculum* (2nd ed.). University of Toronto Press.

Miller, J. P. (2010). *Whole child education.* University of Toronto Press. www.jstor.org/stable/10.3138/j.ctt2tttcq

Miller, J. P. (2014). *The contemplative practitioner: Meditation in education and the workplace.* University of Toronto Press.

Miller, J. P. (2016). Equinox: Portrait of a holistic school. *International Journal of Children's Spirituality, 21*(3–4), 283–301. https://doi.org/10.108 0/1364436X.2016.1232243

Miller, J. P. (2018a). *Love and compassion: Exploring their role in education.* University of Toronto Press. https://doi.org/10.1080/1364436x.2018.1490058

Miller, J. P. (2018b). Holistic education. In J. P. Miller, K. Nigh, M. J. Binder, & B. Novak (Eds.), *International handbook of holistic education* (pp. 5–16). Routledge. https://doi.org/10.4324/9781315112398-2

Miller, J. P., Karsten, S., Denton, D., Orr, D., & Kates, I. C. (2005). *Holistic learning and spirituality in education: Breaking new ground.* State University of New York Press.

Miller, J. P., Nigh, K., Binder, M. J., Novak, B., & Crowell, S. (2018). *International handbook of holistic education.* Routledge. https://doi.org/10.4324/978 1315112398

Miller, R. (1991). Educating the true self: Spiritual roots of the holistic worldview. *The Journal of Humanistic Psychology, 31*(4), 53–67. https://doi.org/10.1177/0022167891314004

Mondal, A., & Mete, J. (2014). Education for peace; in the light of national curriculum framework 2005. *EDUCARE: International Journal for Educational Studies, 6*(2), 129–136.

Montessori, M. (1949). *Education and peace.* Henry Regnery.

Moore, T. (2018). Care of the soul in education. In J. P. Miller, K. Nigh, M. J. Binder, & B. Novak (Eds.), *International handbook of holistic education* (pp. 51–56). Routledge. https://doi.org/10.4324/9781315112398-7

Morling, B., & Fiske, S. T. (1999). Defining and measuring harmony control. *Journal of Research in Personality, 33*(4), 379–414. https://doi.org/10.1006/jrpe.1999.2254

Moulin, D. (2011). *Leo Tolstoy.* Continuum.

Musafir-Chazot, A. (2019). *Learning (how not) to teach: A study of the impact of generated resources learning (GRL) pedagogy as in-service teacher training in some schools across India.* Kings College London.

National Council of Education Research and Training. (2003). *Monitoring formats for quality dimensions under SSA: Tools for monitoring.* National Council of Educational Research and Training.

National Council of Educational Research and Training. (2005). *National curricular framework*. National Council of Educational Research and Training.

National Council of Educational Research and Training. (2006). *Position paper national focus group on education for peace 3.4*. National Council of Educational Research and Training.

National council of educational research and training. (2010). *Ways to peace; a resource book for teachers*. National Council of Educational Research and Training.

National Council Of Educational Research And Training. (2012). *Education for values in schools—A framework*. National Council of Educational Research and Training.

Neill, A. (1960). *Summerhill: A radical approach to child rearing*. Hart Publishing Company.

NEP. (2020). *National education policy*. Ministry of Human Resource Development.

Niemiec, C. P. (2014). *Eudaimonic well-being BT—encyclopedia of quality of life and well-being research* (A. C. Michalos, Ed., pp. 2004–2005). Springer Netherlands. https://doi.org/10.1007/978-94-007-0753-5_929

Noddings, N. (1988). An ethic of caring and its implications for instructional arrangements. *American Journal of Education, 96*(2), 215–230. https://doi.org/10.1086/443894

Noddings, N. (2003). *Happiness and education*. Cambridge University Press.

Noddings, N. (2013a). *Caring: A relational approach to ethics and moral education*. University of California Press.

Noddings, N. (2013b). *Education and democracy in the 21st century*. Teachers College Press.

Noddings, N. (1986). *Caring, a feminine approach to ethics & moral education*. University of California Press.

Noddings, N. (1992). *The challenge to care in schools: An alternative approach to education*. Teachers College Press.

Noddings, N. (2002). *Educating moral people: A caring alternative to character education*. Teachers College Press.

Nussbaum, M. C. (1997). *Cultivating humanity: A classical defense of reform in liberal education*. Harvard University Press.

Nussbaum, M. C. (2010). Tagore, Dewey, and the imminent demise of liberal education. In *The oxford handbook of philosophy of education*. Oxford University Press. https://doi.org/10.1093/oxfordhb/9780195312881.003.0004

O'Connell, K. M. (2003). *Rabindranath Tagore on education*. The Encyclopaedia of Informal Education. www.infed.org/mobi/rabindranath-tagore-on-education/

Oberle, E., Domitrovich, C. E., Meyers, D. C., & Weissberg, R. P. (2016). Establishing systemic social and emotional learning approaches in schools: A framework for schoolwide implementation. *Cambridge Journal of Education,* *46*(3), 277–297. https://doi.org/10.1080/0305764X.2015.1125450

OECD. (2015). *Skills for social progress; The power of social and emotional skills* (Issue January). OECD. https://doi.org/10.1787/9789264226159-en

OECD. (2018). *The future of education and skills: Education 2030* (OECD Future of Education and Skills 2030). OECD.

Osterman, K. F. (2000). Students' need for belonging in the school community. *Review of Educational Research, 70*(3), 323. https://doi.org/10.2307/1170786

Oxfam. (1997). A curriculum for global citizenship. In *Oxfam's development education programme.* Oxfam.

Oxley, L., & Morris, P. (2013). Global citizenship: A typology for distinguishing its multiple conceptions. *British Journal of Educational Studies, 61*(3), 301–325. https://doi.org/10.1080/00071005.2013.798393

Page, J. (2008). *Peace education: Exploring ethical and philosophical foundations.* Information Age Publishing.

Pais, A., & Costa, M. (2017). An ideology critique of global citizenship education. *Critical Studies in Education, 61*(1), 1–16. https://doi.org/10.108 0/17508487.2017.1318772

Parekh, B. C. (1989). *Gandhi's political philosophy: A critical examination.* Macmillan.

Patel, J. (2020). *Education for togetherness and harmony; Learning and teaching through lived experiences.* University of Cambridge. https://doi.org/10. 17863/CAM.64123

Patel, J. (2021a). The role of dissent, conflict, and open dialogue in learning to live together harmoniously. *Educational Philosophy and Theory,* Ahead of print, 1–12. https://doi.org/10.1080/00131857.2021.2006057

Patel, J. (2021b). Learning to live together harmoniously: A conceptual framework. *Cambridge Journal of Education, 52,* 327–347. https://doi.org/10.108 0/0305764X.2021.1993791

Patel, J. (under review). *Education of heart; a central purpose of education in teachers in alternative schools in India.*

Patel, J., & Ehrenzeller, C. (under review). *Nature as a peace educator: Towards social justice and inner peace through learning and being in natural environments.*

Peters, R. S. (2015). *Moral development and moral education.* Routledge. https://doi.org/10.4324/9781315710167

Petrides, K., & v, & Furnham, A. (2001). Trait emotional intelligence: Psychometric investigation with reference to established trait taxonomies. *European Journal of Personality, 15*(6), 425–448. https://doi.org/10.1002/per.416

Pianta, R. C. (1999). *Enhancing relationships between children and teachers.* American Psychological Association. https://doi.org/10.1037/10314-000

Pianta, R. C., & Stuhlman, M. W. (2004). Teacher-child relationships and children's success in the first years of school. *School Psychology Review, 33*(3), 444–458. https://doi.org/10.1037/10314-000

Pierce, J. L., Kostova, T., & Dirks, K. T. (2001). Toward a theory of psychological ownership in organizations. *Academy of Management Review, 26*(2), 298–310. https://doi.org/10.5465/AMR.2001.4378028

Pierce, J. L., Kostova, T., & Dirks, K. T. (2003). The state of psychological ownership: Integrating and extending a century of research. *Review of General Psychology, 7*(1), 84–107. https://doi.org/10.1037/1089-2680.7.1.84

Pinar, W. F. (2015). *Curriculum studies in India: Intellectual histories, present circumstances* (1st ed.). Palgrave Macmillan.

Power, C. N. (1997). Learning: A means or an end? A look at the Delors Report and its implications for educational renewal. *Prospects: Quarterly Review of Comparative Education, XXVII*(2), 187–199.

Prasad, D., & Bilgrami, A. (2020). *Gandhi and revolution.* Taylor & Francis. https://doi.org/10.4324/9781003157946

Prophet, R. B. (1994). Educational research in Botswana 1986–1991: Recent trends and future directions. In S. Burchfield (Ed.), *Research for educational policy and planning* (pp. 97–108). Macmillan.

Radhakrishnan, S. (1956). *My search for truth.* Shiva Lal Agarwala & Co.

Radhakrishnan, S. (1959). *Sarvepalli Radhakrishnan (combined edition Oct. 1952 to Feb. 1959). Occasional speeches and writings.* Government of India Press.

Radhakrishnan, S. (1964). *President Sarvepalli Radhakrishnan's speeches and writings (May 1962 to May 1964).* Government of India Press.

Radhakrishnan, S. (2005). *Foundation of civilization. ideals and ideas.* Oriental Paperback.

Rajesh, R. (2002). National curriculum framework and its values: A parent's perspective. *Economic and Political Weekly, 37*(42), 4273–4277.

Ramachandran, V. S. (2011). The tell-tale brain: A neuroscientist's quest for what makes us human. In *The tell-tale brain: A neuroscientist's quest for what makes us human.* W W Norton & Co.

Ramana, M. (1985). *Be as you are: The teachings of Sri Ramana Maharshi.* Penguin Random House.

Reardon, B. A., & Cabezudo, A. (2002). *Learning to abolish war teaching toward a culture of peace: Rationale for and approaches to peace education.* Hague Appeal for Peace.

Regnier, R. (1995). Bridging western and first nations thought: Balanced education in whitehead's philosophy of organism and the sacred circle. *Interchange, 26*(4), 383–415. https://doi.org/10.1007/BF01434743

Reimers, F. M., Chopra, V., Chung, C. K., Higdon, J., & O'Donnell, E. B. (2016). *Empowering global citizens: A world course.* CreateSpace Independent Publishing Platform. www.tinyurl.com/y286hz3j

Robinson, K., & Aronica, L. (2015). *Creative schools: The grassroots revolution that's transforming education*. Viking Penguin.

Rogers, C. (1961). *On becoming a person*. Houghton Mifflin.

Rogers, C. (1979). *Freedom to learn*. Charles E. Merrill Publishing Co.

Rosenberg, E. L., & Cullen, M. C. (2013). Working with emotions in the cultivation of compassion. In T. Singer & M. Bolz (Eds.), *Compassion: Bridging practice and science (a multimedia book)*. Max Planck Society. www.compassion-training.org/

Rosenberg, E. L., & Rutsch, E. (2012). *Dialogs on how to build a culture of empathy with education—YouTube*. Center for Building a Culture of Empathy. www.cultureofempathy.com/References/Experts/Erika-Rosenberg.htm

Rosenberg, E. L., Zanesco, A. P., King, B. G., Aichele, S. R., Jacobs, T. L., Bridwell, D. A., MacLean, K. A., Shaver, P. R., Ferrer, E., Sahdra, B. K., Lavy, S., Wallace, B. A., & Saron, C. D. (2015). Intensive meditation training influences emotional responses to suffering. *Emotion, 15*(6), 775–790. https://doi.org/10.1037/emo0000080

RTE Forum. (2021). *Status of implementation of the Right of Children to Free and Compulsory Education Act 2009: A report card of the last decade*. RTE Forum.

Ryan, R. M. (1995). Psychological needs and the facilitation of integrative processes. *Journal of Personality, 63*(3), 397–427. https://doi.org/10.1111/J.1467-6494.1995.TB00501.X

Ryan, R. M., & Deci, E. L. (2000). Self-determination theory and the facilitation of intrinsic motivation, social development, and well-being. *American Psychologist, 55*, 68–78. https://doi.org/10.1037/0003-066X.55.1.68

Salovey, P., & Mayer, J. D. (1990). Emotional intelligence. *Imagination, Cognition and Personality, 9*(3), 185–211. https://doi.org/10.2190/DUGG-P24E-52WK-6CDG

Sankar, D., & Linden, T. (2014). *How much and what kind of teaching is there in elementary education in India? Evidence from three states* (Issue 67). www.openknowledge.worldbank.org/

Santos, B. de S. (2014). Epistemologies of the south justice against Epistemicide. In *Études Rurales* (p. 187). Routledge.

Santos, B. d. S. (2018). *The end of the cognitive empire: The coming of age of epistemologies of the South*. Duke University Press.

Schonert-Reichl, K. A., & Hymel, S. (2007). Educating the heart as well as the mind. Social and emotional learning for school and life success. *Education Canada, 47*(2), 20–25.

Schonert-Reichl, K. A., & Roeser, R. W. (2016). *Handbook of mindfulness in education: Integrating theory and research into practice*. Springer. https://doi.org/10.1007/978-1-4939-3506-2

Schwartz, S. (2007). Educating the heart. *Educational Leadership, 64*(7), 76–78. https://doi.org/10.2307/40220291

Seider, S. (2012). *Character compass: How powerful school culture can point students towards success.* Harvard Education Press.

Sen, A. (1985). Well-being, agency and freedom: The Dewey lectures 1984. *The Journal of Philosophy, 82*(4), 169. https://doi.org/10.2307/2026184

Sen, A. (1999). *Development as freedom.* Oxford University Press.

Sen, A. (2003). Equality of what? In *Inequality reexamined.* Harvard University Press.

Sen, A. (2005). Why exactly is commitment important for rationality? *Economics and Philosophy, 21*(1), 5–14. https://doi.org/10.1017/S0266267104000355

Sharma, N. (2018). Value-creating global citizenship education. In *Value-creating global citizenship education.* Palgrave Macmillan. https://doi.org/10.1007/978-3-319-78244-7

Sheldrake, R. (2018). *Science and spiritual practices: Transformative experiences and their effects on our bodies, brains, and health.* Counterpoint.

Shor, I. (1992). *Empowering education: Critical teaching for social change.* University of Chicago Press.

Sibia, A., Raina, M. K., & National Council of Educational Research and Training. (2006). *Life at Mirambika: A free progress school.* National Council of Educational Research and Training.

Siegel, R. D., & Germer, C. K. (2012). Wisdom and compassion: Two wings of a bird. In *Wisdom and compassion in psychotherapy: Deepening mindfulness in clinical practice* (pp. 7–34). The Guilford Press.

Sinclair, M. (2013). *Learning to live together: Education for conflict resolution, responsible citizenship, human rights and humanitarian norms.* UNESCO. www.unesdoc.unesco.org/

Sinclair, M. (2017). *The challenge of Target 4.7 in fragile and low-resource contexts.* GEM Report; World Education Blog. www.gemreportunesco.wordpress.com/2017/02/28/the-challenge-of-target-4-7-in-fragile-and-low-resource-contexts/

Skinner, A., Blum, N., & Bourn, D. (2013). Development education and education in international development policy: Raising quality through critical pedagogy and global skills. *International Development Policy, 4*(3). https://doi.org/10.4000/poldev.1654

Sklad, M., Diekstra, R., de Ritter, M., Ben, J., & Gravesteijn, C. (2012). Effectiveness of school-based universal social, emotional, and behavioral programs: Do they enhance students' development in the area of skill, behavior, and adjustment? *Psychology in the Schools, 49*(9), 892–909. https://doi.org/10.1002/pits.21641

Southworth, G. (2000). Leading and developing pedagogies; keynote address at professional development network for school leaders. In T. O'Donoghue & S. Clarke (Eds.), *Leading learning: Process, themes and issues in international contexts.* Routledge. https://doi.org/10.4324/9780203876961

Stecher, B., & Hamilton, L. (2017). Measuring hard-to-measure student competencies: A research and development plan. In *Measuring hard-to-measure student competencies: A research and development plan*. RAND Corporation. https://doi.org/10.7249/rr863

Struckman, C. K., & Yammarino, F. J. (2003). Organizational change: A categorization scheme and response model with readiness factors. *Research in Organizational Change and Development, 14,* 1–50. https://doi.org/10.1016/s0897-3016(03)14079-7

Tagore, R. (1917). *Personality.* Macmillan & Co.

Tagore, R. (1929). Ideals of education. *The VisvaBharati Quarterly, 73*(4), 72–76.

Tagore, R. (1962). *Towards universal man.* Asia Publishing House.

Taneja, A. (2021). *World Bank funded project stars: A critique.* Oxfam. www.oxfamindia.org

Thapan, M. (2001). J. Krishnamurti (1895–1986). *Prospects: The Quarterly Review of Comparative Education, 31*(2), 253–265. www.ibe.unesco.org/sites/default/files/krishnamurtie.pdf

Thapan, M. (2018). *J. Krishnamurti and educational practice: Social and moral vision for inclusive education.* Oxford University Press. https://doi.org/10.1093/oso/9780199487806.001.0001

Thapan, M. (2006). *Life at school: An ethnographic study.* Oxford University Press.

Thapar, R. (2021). *Voices of dissent; an essay.* Seagull Books.

The Mother. (1977a). *Collected works of the mother; on education.* Sri Aurobindo Ashram Press.

The Mother. (1977b). *Collected works of the mother; question and answers* (2nd ed.). Sri Aurobindo Ashram Press.

Tirath, R. (2017). Role and impact of Rabindernath Tagore education philosophy in contemporary Indian education. *International Journal of Business Administration and Management, 7*(1), 2278–3660.

Torres, C. A., & Bosio, E. (2020). Global citizenship education at the crossroads: Globalization, global commons, common good, and critical consciousness. *Prospects, 48,* 99–113. https://doi.org/10.1007/s11125-019-09458-w

Trier, U. P. (2002). Key competencies in OECD countries—similarities and differences. In *Contributions to the second DeSeCo symposium.* OECD, DeSeCo. www.oecd.org/edu/skills-beyond-school/41529505.pdf

UN General Assembly Resolution. (2015). *Transforming our world: The 2030 agenda for sustainable development.* www.un.org/

UNESCO. (2014a). *Global citizenship education: Preparing learners for the challenges of the 21st century.* UNESCO. www.unesdoc.unesco.org/

UNESCO. (2014b). *Learning to live together: Education policies and realities in the Asia-Pacific.* UNESCO. www.unesdoc.unesco.org/

UNESCO. (2018). *Learning to live together sustainably (SDG4.7): Trends and progress.* UNESCO. www.en.unesco.org/themes/gced/sdg47progress/

United Nations. (2013). *Making education for all a reality—Beyond 2015* (Beyond 2015 Position Paper). UN. www.right-to-education.org

Unterhalter, E. (2017). Negative capability? Measuring the unmeasurable in education. *Comparative Education, 53*(1), 1–16. https://doi.org/10.1108/03050068.2017.1254945

Vähäsantanen, K., Hökkä, P., Eteläpelto, A., Rasku-Puttonen, H., & Littleton, K. (2008). Teachers' professional identity negotiations in two different work organisations. *Vocations and Learning, 1*(2), 131–148. https://doi.org/10.1007/s12186-008-9008-z

Valli, L. (1990). Moral approaches to reflective practice. In *Encouraging reflective practice in education: An analysis of issues and programs* (pp. 39–56). Teachers College Press.

Vishnu Purana. (n.d.).

Vittachi, S., Raghavan, N. N., Raj, K., & Raj, K. (2007). *Alternative schooling in India.* Sage Publications.

Vivekananda, S. (1947). *The complete works of Swami Vivekananda. Volume II.* Advaita Ashram.

Vygotsky, L. (1986). *Thought and language.* MIT Press Books.

Wade, R. C. (1997). *Community service-learning: A guide to including service in the public school curriculum.* State University of New York Press.

Watt, H. M. G., & Richardson, P. W. (2008). Motivation for teaching. *Learning and Instruction, 18*(5), 405–407. https://doi.org/10.1016/j.learninstruc.2008.06.009

Weissberg, R. P., Durlak, J. A., Domitrovich, C. E., & Gullotta, T. P. (2015). Social and emotional learning: Past, present, and future. In R. P. Weissberg, J. A. Durlak, C. E. Domitrovich, & T. P. Gullotta (Eds.), *Handbook of social and emotional learning: Research and practice* (pp. 3–19). The Guilford Press.

Yoder, N. (2014). *Teaching the whole child.* Center on Great Teachers and Leaders. www.gtlcenter.org/sites/default/files/TeachingtheWholeChild.pdf

Zimmerman, B. J., & Bandura, A. (1994). Impact of self-regulatory influences on writing course attainment. *American Educational Research Journal, 31*(4), 845–862. https://doi.org/10.3102/00028312031004845

Zins, J. E. (2004). *Building academic success on social and emotional learning: What does the research say?* Teachers College Press.

Zovko, M. É. (2018). Worldly and otherworldly virtue: Likeness to God as educational ideal in Plato, Plotinus, and today*. *Educational Philosophy and Theory, 50*(6–7), 586–596. https://doi.org/10.1080/00131857.2017.1373340

Index[1]

A

Acceptance, vi, 70, 71, 73, 86, 94, 116, 168
Active communities, 57
Active democracies, 57, 75–77
Active harmony, 57, 74, 75, 177
Active peace, 57, 74
Advaita, 105, 110, 143
Aesthetic peace, 62, 63
Affective empathy, 86
Anityata, 152
Anthropocentric, 12, 13, 17, 32, 88, 113, 114, 145, 147, 203
Appease, 167
Appreciate and celebrate diversity, 23, 24, 96
Arbitrary separation, 7, 15, 17, 106
Aristotle, 29, 109, 112, 156, 186
Ashramites, 23, 24, 54
Ashram(s), 3, 14, 23, 25, 54, 112, 122, 150, 155, 159, 174, 180, 197–199

Attitudes, 15, 65, 66, 70, 75, 76, 95, 108–110, 123, 125, 158, 162, 168, 172
Aurobindo Ghose, v, 1, 19, 26, 30, 35–37, 39, 44, 45, 47n5, 58, 87
Autonomous decision-making, 32, 52, 70, 119, 127, 155
Autonomous behaviour regulation, 2, 9
Autonomous decision-making, 32, 70, 119, 155
Autonomy, 2, 9, 18, 31, 39, 52, 54, 70, 86, 119, 127, 137, 139, 155, 166, 168–172, 174, 187–189, 196, 199, 206
Awareness, vi, 2, 8, 28, 37, 38, 41, 42, 64, 84, 86, 87, 89, 92, 99, 105, 108, 140–142, 147, 172, 176, 202, 204

---

[1] Note: Page numbers followed by 'n' refer to notes.

J. Patel, *Learning to Live Together Harmoniously*, Spirituality, Religion, and Education, https://doi.org/10.1007/978-3-031-23539-9

Printed in the United States
by Baker & Taylor Publisher Services